Courting
Failure

Courting Failure

How Competition
for Big Cases
Is Corrupting the
Bankruptcy Courts

Lynn M. LoPucki

THE UNIVERSITY OF MICHIGAN PRESS
Ann Arbor

2008   2007   2006   2005   4   3   2   1

A CIP catalog record for this book is available from the British Library.

Library of Congress Cataloging-in-Publication Data

LoPucki, Lynn M.
Courting failure : how competition for big cases is
corrupting the bankruptcy courts / Lynn M. LoPucki.
      p.   cm.
Includes index.
ISBN 0-472-11486-7 (cloth : alk. paper)
1. Bankruptcy—United States.   2. Forum shopping—
United States.   3. Judicial corruption—United States.
I. Title.

KF1526.L67   2005
346.7307'8—dc22   2004021715

To Frances, who made it happen

Acknowledgments

M_y work on this book was supported by grants from the National Conference of Bankruptcy Judges Endowment for Education and the American Bankruptcy Institute Endowment for Education. The content of the book is based in part on work supported by the National Science Foundation under grant SES-8618353 and also in part on findings from a series of research projects conducted and reported with coresearchers and coauthors. These colleagues are Professor William C. Whitford of the University of Wisconsin Law School; Professor Theodore Eisenberg of the Cornell Law School; Joseph W. Doherty, associate director of the Empirical Research Group at the UCLA Law School; and Sara Kalin, a graduate of the UCLA Law School who currently practices with the Securities and Exchange Commission.

I thank Mike Campion, Christian Dodd, Scott Halvorsen, L. Nicolle Hollingsworth, Michael Kovaleski, Drew LoPucki, and Richard Scheelings for assistance with research and Frances H. Foster, Jim Reische, Gary D. Rowe, Lynn A. Stout, Elizabeth Warren, and Jay L. Westbrook for comments on the manuscript or portions of it, and Susan Rabiner for guidance. Jim Reische, my editor at the University of Michigan Press, did a marvelous job of rescuing this project from obscurity and guiding me through the publication process.

I am also deeply indebted to the dozens of bankruptcy lawyers and judges who furnished leads for my investigations. Their only reward will be the contribution they made to the integrity of the bankruptcy system; nearly all of them requested anonymity. Without their help, I would not have found the facts and documents that make the case presented in this book.

Contents

A Note on the Statistics in This Book

Most of the statistics that appear in this book are based on data contained in the author's Bankruptcy Research Database (BRD). The BRD includes data on all bankruptcy cases filed by or against large public companies in the U.S. bankruptcy courts since October 1, 1979—presently a total of 683 cases. Cases are considered "large" if the debtor's assets exceeded $220 million, measured in current dollars as of the time of filing ($100 million in 1980 dollars). They are "public" if the company was required to file annual reports with the Securities and Exchange Commission in any of the three years before bankruptcy. (About 80–90 percent of the companies large enough for their cases to be included in the BRD are public companies.) Unless otherwise specified, the numbers of "big" or "large" cases reported in this book are the numbers of such cases in the BRD.

The cases included in the BRD are not a sample. They are all cases filed by or against large public companies. For that reason, it was neither necessary nor possible to calculate the likelihood that the BRD cases are representative of some larger group. They are the larger group.

An abbreviated version of the BRD is available without charge at http://lopucki.law.ucla.edu. Using that version, readers can examine the data behind most of the statistics reported in this book, calculate statistics not reported in this book, and see how the pattern of big bankruptcy reorganizations has changed since the publication of this book.

A Judge Shall Avoid Impropriety and the Appearance of
Impropriety in All of the Judge's Activities.
—Canon 2, American Bar Association
Model Code of Judicial Conduct (1990)

Any . . . judge . . . of the United States shall
disqualify himself in any proceeding in which his
impartiality might reasonably be questioned.
—Title 28, United States Code, § 455(a)

Prologue

In 1884, James B. Dill was a young lawyer with a small New York City practice and a big idea. He had already pitched the idea to the New York political bosses, and they had turned him down. Now he had a second chance—with Leon Abbett, the Democratic governor of New Jersey. The muckraking journalist Lincoln Steffens later described the meeting.

> [Dill] was . . . taken aback to be directed from the capitol at Trenton to the governor's law office in New York, but he went there; and there, to the governor "in his shirt sleeves," he showed how Jersey, by granting license to business to do what other states were trying to forbid, might become the Mecca of corporations and make an enormous revenue.[1]

In essence, Dill proposed that the state of New Jersey enter the already competitive business of selling corporate charters.[2]

A corporate charter is the document that brings a corporation into existence. Once the corporation is in existence, its affairs are governed by the law of the charter-issuing state. If New Jersey issued a corporation's charter, the corporation was a "New Jersey corporation." That corporation could operate anywhere in the United States, subject only to New Jersey law.[3] Under today's law and practice, the chartering state's exclusive control extends only to the "internal affairs" of its corporations. But in the late nineteenth century, that control extended more broadly, covering much of what is known today as the law of antitrust, fair trade, price fixing, and securities. The sum total of it was that in 1884 New Jersey had the power to authorize New Jersey corporations to do things in other states that violated the laws of those other states—and there was nothing the other states could do about it.

That part of the idea was not entirely new. Other states had already hit on the idea of "liberalizing" their corporation laws in order to sell corporate charters. Dill had heard "how the secretary of state of the state of West Virginia was in [New York City], at the Fifth Avenue Hotel, where, with the great seal of his state by his side, he was displaying the liberality of his laws and selling charters—for fees."[4]

Dill's idea went further. Dill realized it was not enough to create, offer, and explain the New Jersey charter; New Jersey would have to package its charters and market them so the great corporations buying them would never miss a stride. The New Jersey charter was to cease to be a regulation and instead become a convenience. To accomplish that, Dill, along with the governor, the New Jersey secretary of state, the clerk of New Jersey's Court of Chancery, and an assortment of the most powerful business leaders in New Jersey founded the Corporation Trust Company of New Jersey.[5] The Corporation Trust Company was a privately owned corporation that would provide full services to those who wished to incorporate in New Jersey, supplying everything from the official forms to the required New Jersey–resident member of the corporation's board of directors. As it did so, the new company would make Dill, and the political and business leaders of New Jersey who invested in it, rich.

New Jersey Takes the Lead

New Jersey enacted its first Dill-proposed corporation law in 1888. That law allowed New Jersey corporations to buy and sell the stock of other corporations. The intent was to allow New Jersey corporations to eliminate their competition by buying their competitors.[6] To make the state's stance perfectly clear, in 1892 New Jersey repealed its own antitrust law.[7]

In 1894, New Jersey elected a Republican "reform" governor.[8] There was concern that the new administration might abandon Dill's plan. But in the prior year, New Jersey had collected $434,000—a considerable amount of money at the time—from its corporate customers, and that money had been integrated into the state's finances. Abandoning Dill's plan would have required that the new administration raise an equivalent amount elsewhere.

Instead, the new administration kept the plan and systematized it. The new governor appointed Dill to chair a committee that completely revised New Jersey's corporation law. New Jersey enacted the revision in 1896. The new law removed all limits on corporation size, market concentration, and corporate life. It eased the financing of mergers and acquisitions by authorizing New Jersey corporations to conceal the target company's actual worth when seeking financing from public investors and instead reveal only the prices the New Jersey corporations had agreed to pay. The new corporation law also made it easier for corporate promoters to retain control of a corporation while supplying only a small portion of the capital investment in the corporation.[9]

Oddly, in addition to drafting the New Jersey corporation law, James B. Dill also became the law's principal whistle-blower. Shortly after the law took effect, Dill visited muckraking journalists, including Lincoln Steffens, and explained to them the mischief that the captains of industry could do with New Jersey charters. The journalists wrote the story, sparking outrage in the rest of the country. But because the foundations of charter competition seemed to be in the United States Constitution, as interpreted by the Supreme Court of the United States, the public had no power to end the competition.[10]

Steffens and Dill became friends. Much later, Steffens asked Dill "why he, of all men, had led and inspired and provided the ammunition for the exposure of the James B. Dill laws of New Jersey." Dill replied:

Why, Dr. Innocent, I was advertising my wares and the business of my State. When you and the other reporters and critics wrote as charges against us what financiers could and did actually do in Jersey, when you listed, with examples, what the trust-makers were doing under our laws, you were advertising our business—free.[11]

After enactment of the New Jersey corporation law of 1896, big corporations—including John D. Rockefeller's Standard Oil (1899) and Andrew Carnegie's United States Steel (1901)—flocked to New Jersey. By 1900, an estimated 95 percent of the nation's "major" corporations were chartered there.[12]

The state flourished. By 1902, New Jersey was able to abolish property taxes and pay off its entire state debt.[13] By 1904, the state's governor could boast that nearly 78 percent of the revenues of the state of New Jersey came from the railroads and business companies domiciled there and that "of the entire income of the government, not a penny was contributed directly by the people."[14]

New Jersey's corporation law triggered what Professor Joel Seligman in 1976 called "the greatest merger movement in American history."[15] Combinations effected from 1888 to 1905 controlled roughly two-fifths of the manufacturing capital of the United States. Seventy-eight major trusts controlled 50 percent or more of the sales in their respective fields.[16] New Jersey's victory in the charter competition had put the country's industrial power in the control of monopolists.

Delaware Plays Catch-Up

In 1899, Delaware revised its corporation law in the hope of competing with New Jersey. In the words of a contemporary report:

[T]he little community of truck-farmers and clam-diggers have had their cupidity excited by the spectacle of their northern neighbor, New Jersey, becoming rich and bloated through the granting of franchises to trusts which are to do business everywhere except New Jersey. . . . [L]ittle Delaware, gangrened with envy . . . is determined to get her little tiny, sweet, round, baby hand into the grab-bag of sweet things before it is too late.[17]

Delaware copied not only much of New Jersey's law but also Dill's methods. Delaware established the Corporation Trust Company of Delaware with capital of $100,000 to operate in New York organizing Delaware corporations.[18] The company issued a circular that explained the advantages of a Delaware charter over one from New Jersey.[19] The principal advantage was that Delaware's fees and taxes were set at 50–60 percent of those of New Jersey.[20] In essence, Delaware was a copycat discounter. In the 13 years that followed, the numbers of Delaware charters sold increased steadily. Then, in 1913, New Jersey self-destructed, leaving the field to Delaware.

New Jersey Self-Destructs

Even as New Jersey became rich, the people of the state remained concerned about the effects of its charter mongering on the nation's economy. In 1905, Lincoln Steffens branded New Jersey a "traitor" to the United States.[21] A nationwide movement for corporate reform arose and attained full recognition with the election of Woodrow Wilson as governor of New Jersey in 1910.[22] In his campaign for governor, Wilson had declared "the control of corporations [by government]" to be one of "the three great questions before us" and pledged action to bring the corporations under public control.[23] In 1912, Wilson was elected president of the United States. Stung in the presidential campaign by the criticism that he had done nothing in his two years as governor to reform New Jersey's notorious corporation laws, Wilson determined to fulfill his campaign promise in New Jersey before assuming the presidency in March 1913.[24]

To do that, Wilson proposed seven bills—which became known as the Seven Sisters. The bills outlawed

any corporation or combination of corporations from acquiring a monopoly, conspiring to limit production or increase prices; preventing competition; fixing prices; buying stock in competing corporations with a view towards controlling them; discriminating in price save on the basis of quantity, quality, transportation, or other "valid" charges; or issuing stock for property unless the property was the full equivalent of the money value of the stock.[25]

In an article titled "Drastic Nature of Wilson Bills Not Realized by Corporations"[26] the *Wall Street Journal* expressed its opposition to the bill, leading with this hypothetical.

> If you happened to have a retail business of your own, what would you think if you were told you couldn't legally agree with your competitor across the street to close Saturday afternoons? Well, the language of the Wilson anti-trust bills is broad enough to prohibit even such a harmless agreement as that.[27]

New Jersey enacted the Seven Sisters within days of Wilson's final message as governor. That same year, Delaware took the lead in the competition, chartering 1,613 new corporations in comparison with New Jersey's 1,445.

Support for the Seven Sisters in New Jersey may have rested on a failure to appreciate the magnitude of the effects that their passage would have on the financing of the state. Under the constitutional doctrine of the time, a charter, once issued, was a contract between the state and the corporation. The state could change it only by mutual agreement. That meant that the provisions of the Seven Sisters would not apply to the corporations already chartered in New Jersey. Observers assumed most of them would retain their New Jersey charters, even after the reform.

After enactment of the Seven Sisters, the *Wall Street Journal* opined that "Whether the movement [out of New Jersey] will amount to anything is questionable. It involves heavy expense, and the companies have no guarantee that Delaware or other states to which they may move, will afford them, permanently, a safer haven than New Jersey."[28] By the end of 1914, the question had been answered. That year, for the first time in the history of New Jersey, the number of corporations assessed for taxation in the state declined. The big corporations were abandoning New Jersey for Delaware (see table 1).[29]

Finally realizing the drastic effects that the Seven Sisters would

TABLE 1.   New Corporate Charters Issued

Year	New Jersey	Delaware
1884	232	—
1899	2,186	421
1903	2,035	746
1907	1,840	671
1911	1,856	1,342
1913	1,445	1,613
1915	1,428	1,916
1918	1,272	2,460

Source: George Heberton Evans, Jr., *Business Incorporations in the United States 1800–1943* (New York: National Bureau of Economic Research, 1948), 101, 126–27. Copyright 1948 by National Bureau of Economic Research.

have on the state's finances, New Jersey began the repeal process in 1915. By 1917, most of the provisions of the Seven Sisters had been excised from New Jersey law.[30] It was, however, already too late. By enacting the Seven Sisters, New Jersey had breached the great corporations' trust. New Jersey corporate business dwindled to insignificance.

James B. Dill had prospered along with the New Jersey corporation law he authored. He published a treatise, *Dill on Corporations,* and developed a thriving Wall Street legal practice. He negotiated, among other deals, the merger that created United States Steel.[31] In 1902, while New Jersey remained at the peak of its success, Dill gave a speech at the Harvard Law School in which he advocated putting an end to the state charter competition by enacting a law requiring that corporations operating in multiple states be nationally chartered. As Dill put it: "*We can look for no effective publicity—no effective restrictions or regulation of corporate power under a system of diverse state legislation.*"[32] Whether this was his sincere opinion, part of his surreptitious promotion of New Jersey incorporation—or both—is anyone's guess. In 1907, Dill left a law practice in which he earned an estimated $250,000 to $500,000 a year to accept a seat on a New Jersey appellate court that paid $3,000 a year.[33] He died in 1910.[34]

By 1918, Delaware held a commanding lead in the corporate

charter competition. Since then, other states have mounted campaigns in the hopes of becoming the new Delaware, but none has even come close. A substantial majority of large public companies operating in the United States today are chartered in Delaware. Their fees and franchise taxes cover about 27 percent of Delaware's budget, enabling the state to operate with no sales tax and to have only a moderate personal income tax.[35]

Introduction

In late 2001, the Enron Corporation was preparing to file what remains to this day the biggest bankruptcy case in history.[1] At the time, a half dozen or more U.S. bankruptcy courts were competing to attract big cases. For those courts, Enron was the ultimate prize. The court that got Enron would be the focus of the bankruptcy world's attention for years and distribute a billion dollars in professional fees.

The stakes were especially high because big-case bankruptcy was booming. The number of large public companies[2] filing bankruptcy in the United States had increased steadily from 15 in 1996 to 97 in 2001—a sixfold increase in just five years. The court that got Enron—and handled it to the satisfaction of the Enron lawyers and executives who chose the court—would get many more. The judge who presided would win national attention for him- or herself and, possibly, a billion-dollar-a-year or more bankruptcy reorganization industry for his or her city. It would be like winning the competition to host the Olympic Games—not just for a year but every year—for as long as the court continued to please the lawyers and executives who could supply the cases.

The United States Bankruptcy Court for the District of Delaware was a major contender for the Enron case. Delaware had 41 new big-case filings in 2001, compared with runner-up New York's 15. But Delaware lacked the judges it needed to process the cases it had attracted already, and the bankruptcy legislation that would have provided them was stalled in Congress. Delaware's lead in the competition for big cases remained vulnerable. Other courts, including Chicago, Houston, and Dallas, had—like New York—copied Delaware's practices and procedures and publicly declared themselves in competition with Delaware. But at the end of 2001, they remained minor players. Only Delaware and New York had more than five big cases that year.

This competition among the bankruptcy courts for big cases put Kenneth Lay, the founder and chairman of the board of the Enron Corporation, in the catbird seat. Lay would have his choice of courts for the Enron bankruptcy. If he chose wisely, the grateful court would protect him from cresting public outrage and, by so doing, make itself attractive to the corrupt or incompetent executives of future bankrupt firms.

Ken Lay was not a man who deserved protection. In 1999 and 2000, he had approved the Rhythms and Raptor transactions that resulted in gross misstatements of Enron's financial position.[3] From 1998 to the day Enron filed bankruptcy in December 2001, Lay sold over $200 million of his Enron stock.[4] In the final year before bankruptcy, Lay was selling the stock to Enron itself, even though Enron's board of directors had not given the approval required by law for the corporation to make such purchases.[5] As the evidence of Enron's impending failure mounted in the spring and early summer of 2001, Lay accelerated his stock "sales," taking $24 million from the company for worthless stock in June and another $16 million in August. In mid-August 2001, as the end neared and he dumped his own stock at the rate of $4 million a week, Lay issued his famous memo to Enron employees assuring them that "I have never felt better about the prospects for the company. . . . Our performance has never been stronger; our business model has never been more robust; our growth has never been more certain."[6] On October 17, 2001, the day after the Securities and Exchange Commission began the investigation that put the final nail in Enron's coffin, Enron "locked down" its retirement plan.[7] The effect was to prevent the company's employees from selling the Enron stock in their 401(k) pension accounts.[8] The stock was trading at $32 when Enron imposed the lockdown; it was trading at $9 when the lockdown ended 30 days later.[9] During the lockdown, Lay sold an additional $6 million of his own stock to Enron.[10] Lay continued dumping the worthless stock on Enron to the very end, grabbing his last $1 million on November 27, 2001[11]—five days before Enron filed bankruptcy. Shareholders who kept their shares until the bankruptcy filing got nothing for them. Conveniently, Enron's auditors, Arthur Andersen, shredded many of the records that prosecutors would need to investigate Lay and Enron.[12] Lay refused to testify about any of what he had done, invoking his Fifth Amendment privilege against self-incrimination.[13]

Ken Lay was a personal friend of the president of the United States and the president's largest campaign contributor. Until recently, the president had called him Kenny-Boy and sought his advice on energy policy. But as Kenny-Boy prepared to choose a bankruptcy court, the president was pretending not to know him. Employees who had lost their pensions were crowding the evening news, and Congress was gearing up to do something about the abuses in corporate America. In December 2001, the shareholders, the creditors, and the press were all at Enron's door. The investigators would be there soon. Kenny-Boy needed protection. He would find it in a bankruptcy court.

From Lay's perspective, the key was to retain control of Enron, if not personally, then through others who owed their jobs—and thus their allegiance—to him. As long as Lay, or others beholden to him, retained control of the company the investigators would deal with Enron from across the table.

What Lay probably feared more than anything else was that the bankruptcy court would appoint a trustee. A Chapter 11 trustee is a genuinely independent individual chosen by a division of the United States Department of Justice to take complete, direct control over the bankrupt company. If that happened, the trustee would employ the investigators, and the investigators would be inside. They would not be demanding documents in discovery and fighting about their right to access in court.[14] They would control

Enron's employees, attorneys, and accountants and have the full, free run of the files. Enron's lawyers would be required to divulge to the trustee everything Lay had told them—before and after the bankruptcy filing. The attorney-client privilege would no longer apply.[15] Everything would come out.

Absent the bankruptcy court competition, a trustee probably would have been appointed in the opening days of the Enron bankruptcy. Bankruptcy law required the court to appoint a trustee "for cause, including fraud, dishonesty, incompetence, or gross mismanagement . . . by current management, either before or after the commencement of the case."[16] If Enron didn't fit that bill, it was hard to imagine a company that would. Nor does a bankruptcy judge have to wait for someone to request the appointment of a trustee; the only federal appeals court to address the question ruled that if a case warranted appointment of a trustee, the court could order that appointment even if no creditor requested it.[17] Once Enron filed, all that would stand between Ken Lay and justice would be a judge of the bankruptcy court Lay had chosen.

Enron was a Houston, Texas, company. The company's headquarters were a gleaming 50-story glass tower in downtown Houston known simply as the "Enron Building." That building was the center of the company's national and international operations, the office space for thousands of the company's employees, and the most widely recognized symbol of the company. The offices of Enron's top managers were on the fiftieth floor. Ken Lay's was among them.

The United States Bankruptcy Court for the Southern District of Texas, Houston, Texas, Division was just seven blocks away. In an earlier time—before the rampant forum shopping of the 1980s— the Houston bankruptcy court would have owned the Enron case by virtue of geography. But in 2001, the Houston bankruptcy court was merely the most conveniently located of a half dozen competitors for Enron's business.

The Houston bankruptcy court had joined the competition for big bankruptcy cases just two years earlier. It did so by copying the rules and procedures of the Delaware bankruptcy court and publicly announcing the judges' willingness to approve higher fees for bankruptcy lawyers who brought cases to the court.[18] The Houston court's move had been only a modest success. The court had attracted no bankrupt companies from other cities in 2000 or 2001, but it had hung on to the bankruptcies of eight of the ten big Houston companies that filed bankruptcy during that period. Considering that Delaware got almost half the big cases filed in the United States during those two years, Houston's 80 percent retention rate was not bad.

Enron spoiled the Houston court's record by choosing the United States Bankruptcy Court for the Southern District of New York, Manhattan Division. The New York court was more than 1,600 miles from Enron's headquarters, in a city where the company had almost no physical presence (57 employees worked for an Enron subsidiary in New York).[19] But New York had other advantages.

One was that the New York bankruptcy court had more to gain—or lose—from Enron than did other courts. New York was home to many, if not most, of the country's leading bankruptcy professionals, which gave it an edge in attracting cases. Despite that natural advantage, the New York court had stumbled in the mid-1990s, allowing Delaware to take center stage. Only in 2000, after several years with almost no big cases, had the New York bankruptcy court's effort to attract cases begun to pay off. Although New York joined the competition at about the same time as Houston, New York had greater success. Enron was the fifteenth big case the New York court had attracted from other cities in 2000 and 2001. With Delaware short of judges and unable to manage its caseload, New York was positioned to once again become the bankruptcy capital of the United States.

Another reason Delaware was not a good choice for Enron was that one of the district judges there had recently appointed a trustee in a big case merely because the relationships among the parties had been acrimonious. The Third Circuit Court of Appeals had

upheld the appointment, thus imposing on the Delaware bankruptcy court perhaps the most liberal standard for appointment of
a trustee applicable anywhere in the United States.[20]

New York bankruptcy judge Arthur J. Gonzalez drew the Enron
case. From Ken Lay's perspective, Gonzalez performed splendidly.
The creditors moved to transfer the case to Houston. Judge Gonzalez denied the motion.[21] Several major creditors requested the
appointment of a trustee.[22] Gonzalez delayed a hearing until he
brokered a deal that left most of Enron's management in place.[23]
During the delay Ken Lay was able to choose Stephen Cooper as
Enron's new CEO.[24] Because Cooper was a respected turnaround
manager, the prospects for appointment of a trustee dimmed. The
creditors soon gave up the fight. That meant that directors chosen
by Ken Lay and in office long before the scandal broke remained in
control of the company through the crucial stages of the bankruptcy case. They resigned only after they too had chosen their
own successors.

As a result, the investigators remained on the outside for the
duration of the Enron case. For a management engaged in massive
fraud, it was the best bankruptcy result for which one could hope.
The government took almost three years putting together a case
sufficient to indict Lay. Lay has still not been sued for his mismanagement of Enron, and it seems likely he never will be. The New
York bankruptcy court had proven itself a trustworthy protector
of managements accused of fraud.

The market reacted swiftly. By mid-2002 managements accused
of fraud delivered three more corporate giants—Global Crossing, a
supposedly Bermudan company actually run from Los Angeles;
Adelphia Communications, a Coudersport, Pennsylvania, company; and Worldcom, a Clinton, Mississippi, company—to the
New York bankruptcy court. The managers of all three were able
to remain in control through the crucial stages of the cases and
choose their own successors. By its deft handling of the four cases,
the New York bankruptcy court surpassed Delaware in 2002 to
become the nation's most attractive bankruptcy court.

The Structure of Bankruptcy Court Competition

The competition that broke out among the U.S. bankruptcy courts in the 1990s was the product of a complex set of laws, practices, and institutions. One must understand those laws, practices, and institutions to understand the competition, and so it is with them we begin.

The U.S. government operates bankruptcy courts at about 200 locations throughout the United States. Each court consists of a "panel" of one or more bankruptcy judges and serves a specifically designated geographical area called a "district" or "division." Generally speaking, when a bankruptcy case is filed by or against a debtor located in the court's district or division, a judge from the panel hears the case.

Determining where a debtor is located can sometimes be difficult. This is particularly true for large public companies that have operations throughout the United States. Such companies can be incorporated in one state, have their headquarters in another, and conduct the bulk of their operations in a third. A truly national company can be everywhere and thus nowhere in particular. To address the problem, Congress enacted a "venue" statute that specifies the appropriate court or courts based on characteristics of the debtor. ("Venue" is legal jargon for "place." A venue statute prescribes the places where cases should be heard.)

The venue statute that allowed the bankruptcy court competition to develop was initially written and adopted as a bankruptcy rule by the recently formed Bankruptcy Rules Committee in 1974. From 1974 to 1978, Congress comprehensively revised and codified the bankruptcy laws of the United States. In so doing, Congress incorporated the bankruptcy venue rule into the statute. The provisions so adopted would have surprising, unintended consequences in the 1980s and 1990s, as large public companies began filing bankruptcy cases in significant numbers and bankruptcy judgeships gained stature and became viable career paths. The bottom line, however, was that by the 1980s, large public companies were free to file their bankruptcies pretty much anywhere they chose.

For the law to offer a litigant a choice among courts is not particularly unusual. For many kinds of cases, the law gives the person filing the case a choice between filing in a state or a federal court or a choice between filing in the court where the defendant resides or the court where the events in litigation occurred. The exercise of such choices is referred to as "forum shopping." The choices offered large companies under the 1974 rule and 1978 code revisions were, however, of an entirely different magnitude. These choices typically would be among dozens of courts, not just two or three. The revisions became part of the Bankruptcy Code enacted in 1978 and went into effect on October 1, 1979.

Through the 1980s, big bankrupt companies and their lawyers exercised their new powers of choice to pick courts that offered various advantages. About a third of the cases were filed in a court located somewhere other than where the company was headquartered. That forum shopping was not particularly alarming to those who managed the bankruptcy system. The bankruptcy courts, laws, and rules of procedure are all federal. Theoretically, at least, they are the same throughout the United States. Forum shoppers certainly could gain some advantage by their choices, the system managers thought, but not much.

The Competition Emerges

Beginning in 1990, the bankruptcy forum shopping produced an unexpected dynamic. That year, the single-judge backwater bankruptcy court in Wilmington, Delaware, began attracting corporate giants. Within six years, nearly 90 percent of all large public companies filing bankruptcy in the United States filed in Delaware. The sudden change surprised and alarmed bankruptcy lawyers and judges throughout the United States—and federal policymakers.

In 1997, the National Bankruptcy Review Commission recommended elimination of the venue provision the big companies were relying on to get to Delaware. Delaware's two determined senators, however, prevented the commission's venue recommendation from coming to a vote in Congress. By the end of 1998, it was clear that Congress would take no action on bankruptcy venue. The bankruptcy system had accepted Delaware as its new leader.

Delaware's new bankruptcy industry came at the expense of bankruptcy lawyers practicing in major cities throughout the rest of the country. Those lawyers began pressing their local bankruptcy judges to respond to Delaware's competitive threat. Courts in several major cites modified their local rules and practices to compete for large public company bankruptcies.

This response to Delaware was possibly unprecedented. In other circumstances, courts have sometimes expressed views or made rulings that attracted cases. In the 1980s, for example, the liberal Texas state courts attracted the cases of workers injured on North Sea Oil rigs. In the early 1990s, U.S. district judge Jack Weinstein attracted gun and tobacco plaintiffs from all over the United States to his court in Brooklyn. But those were merely situations in which judges expressed views that attracted cases. Judges were not changing their views in order to compete with other courts for cases.

Some of the changes that resulted from the bankruptcy court competition were for the better. Judges who had thought of themselves as emperors presiding over federally allotted domains suddenly found that they had to treat lawyers and litigants with courtesy and respect. If the judges didn't, the "customers" would go elsewhere. The judges became more responsive and accessible. They scheduled hearings for the convenience of the lawyers and litigants, not merely for their own. They published rules and guidelines explaining what they wanted from the lawyers, and they committed to what they would do in response. One effect was to make the bankruptcy reorganization process more predictable, generally to the benefit of everyone involved.

The pressures of competition did not, however, stop at the boundaries of propriety. The lawyers, corporate executives, banks, and investment bankers who chose the courts for their cases—the "case placers"—had the power to make winners or losers of the courts. The case placers wanted more money for themselves and freedom from the restrictions of bankruptcy law and procedure. In cities across the United States, they pressed the judges to see how much each judge was willing to give them.

Slowly but surely, the entire bankruptcy system began shifting in response to the case placers' wishes. Professional fees, which had fallen sharply since the 1980s, began to increase. The courts relaxed conflict of interest standards and granted lawyers and financial advisers unprecedented releases and indemnification from liability for their own wrongdoing. The jobs of executives—including those who led their companies into financial disaster—became more secure, and the courts allowed their companies to pay their executives huge bonuses, supposedly to retain the failed executives' valuable services. Deals made among the case placers were sacrosanct, even if they violated the rights of other parties. Procedures designed to protect small investors and the public were abandoned.

Even before the nation's bankruptcy courts began emulating Delaware's reorganization methods, evidence of those methods' failure had begun to accumulate. Delaware-reorganized firms failed at rates substantially exceeding those for firms reorganized in other courts. The failures of individual firms were of course noticed, and efforts were made to explain them. But in the complex, sprawling world of big-case bankruptcy, the pattern of failure—and in particular, Delaware's role—went unnoticed. When it finally came to light in the spring of 2000, the reaction was one of disbelief and denial. By then, the competition was so far along in altering the practices of the bankruptcy courts and the attitudes of bankruptcy lawyers, judges, and academics that it seemed impossible to turn back. As the evidence accumulated, however, it became increasingly evident that turning back was the only viable alternative.

International Bankruptcy Court Competition

In the 1990s, the frequency and size of multinational bankruptcies also increased, with cases such as Bank of Credit and Commerce International (BCCI) and Maxwell Communications. The newly bankrupt giants discovered that the competing U.S. bankruptcy courts welcomed the cases of companies from anywhere on earth. Those in a position to place the cases of multinational companies generally preferred the U.S. courts because U.S. bankruptcy law permitted the debtor's executives to remain in control during bankruptcy. The laws of most other countries put creditors in control. From a Brazilian cable television company to a Greek shipping concern, multinational companies—and some foreign companies with virtually no connection to the United States—began filing their bankruptcies in the United States.

International forum shopping was, however, subject to a limitation not present in domestic shopping within the United States. Courts anywhere in the United States were bound by decisions of the Delaware bankruptcy court, but courts outside the United States were not. A Delaware bankruptcy court decision had only as much authority outside the United States as the courts of other countries were willing to give it. This sharply limited what the competing courts could accomplish for those who brought them the cases.

Coincidentally, an international reform movement that sought to remove that limitation was already well under way. "Universalists" were seeking to bind the nations of the world by treaty or model law to honor the decisions of the courts of a multinational debtor's "home country." In a universalist world, a multinational debtor's home country court would apply home country law to people and events all over the world. Other countries would precommit to honor the home country's decisions.

The universalists could not explain what they meant by a multinational's "home country," and it was apparent that, however the universalists defined that attribute, multinationals could easily change it. As a result, the growing universalist movement threatened to replicate the problems of domestic forum shopping and court competition on a global scale in a far less controlled environment.

Why Do the Judges Compete?

Most people are surprised to hear that bankruptcy judges want big cases. Bankruptcy judges are appointed for 14-year terms. The federal government pays each an annual salary of $142,324 and, if they leave office after even a single 14-year term, a full federal pension. Attracting big cases changes neither the salary nor the pension. The judges who attract the cases generally end up with heavier case-loads than those who do not. Big cases mean more work.

Not all judges do want the cases. Those who do, want them for any of four reasons. The most obvious are personal. A judge who presides over the reorganizations of large public companies has the opportunity to work with the leading professionals in the fields of bankruptcy and finance. When the judge does so, the judge is the most powerful person in the room. Millions and sometimes even billions of dollars turn on his or her decision. The status that power confers extends beyond the courtroom.

Celebrity comes along with the power. The judges' decisions are reported in the media. Judges in the biggest cases have standing invitations from professional organizations to travel to resort cities at the organizations' expense to give speeches and be honored. If they return to law practice, which many do, clients with big cases will seek them out. When a bankruptcy judge dies, the obituary will likely mention the big cases over which the judge presided—assuming, of course, there were any.

The most important reasons that the judges want the big cases, however, are more subtle. Each bankruptcy judge is a member of a community. In any large city in the United States, there are 100 or more lawyers and other professionals specializing in bankruptcy practice. Those professionals interact daily as they resolve cases in the local bankruptcy court. The professionals in a city typically form an association that meets regularly for lunch and occasionally for multiday conferences. Many of the members become close friends.

When a bankruptcy judgeship becomes available, the community seeks to install one of its own. More often than not, the effort succeeds. As with any position of leadership, the one chosen incurs a debt to his or her supporters. Those supporters expect a certain amount of loyalty. If a judge forgets how he or she got the job, the judge will be reminded if and when the judge seeks a second term.

The committee that passes on reappointments will probably survey the members of the local bankruptcy bar regarding the quality of the judge's prior service.[25] A recent study found that more than 8 percent of the bankruptcy judges who applied for reappointment during the period 1998 to 2002 were not reappointed.[26] Others won reappointment but only after their competence had been challenged and they had been "put through the wringer."[27]

For bankruptcy professionals, bankruptcy venue is a bread-and-butter issue. If a big St. Louis company—such as TWA, Purina Mills, or Solutia—files in St. Louis, leading St. Louis bankruptcy lawyers are likely to get the key roles in the case and the big fees that come with them. If the case is big enough, virtually every bankruptcy lawyer in St. Louis will have a client. If instead the company files in some other city, bankruptcy lawyers in that city will get most of the work and the money. If most of the cases from a city go elsewhere, the career prospects in that city may be limited. And if the lawyers in a city view their judges as the cause of that problem, things can get ugly.

Consider, for example, the three-judge bankruptcy panel in Boston, Massachusetts. Boston is a corporate headquarters city, making it a natural venue for bankruptcy cases. Since 1982, 24 Boston companies have filed for bankruptcy reorganization—the sixth highest number for any bankruptcy court in the nation. Had those companies filed in Boston, that city would have been the third busiest bankruptcy court—behind only Delaware and New York—and one of the best places in the United States to practice bankruptcy law.

As matters unfolded, however, only four of the 24 (17 percent) filed in Boston (see table 2).

I interviewed several Boston bankruptcy lawyers about their situation. As they saw it, the quality of Boston's bankruptcy judges was not the problem. The problem was that the Boston judges refused to join in the competition for cases—even after years of prodding. For example, the competing courts in other cities had been willing to grant liquidating retailers broad exemptions from state and local taxes and regulations on going out of business sales.

In 1998, Boston bankruptcy judge William C. Hillman not only refused to go along but published an opinion committing himself to that position.[28] Thereafter, a bankrupt retailer had a simple choice: file in Boston and have at least a one-third chance of having to pay taxes and abide by regulations or file in a competing court and be excused from both.

Bankruptcy lawyers—from Boston and other cities—complain about the "unpredictability" of the Boston judges. What they mean is that the Boston judges refuse to commit—through the adoption of complex case rules or in some other manner—to the manner in which they would handle the big cases if they got them. Each judge is predictable in that he or she has approved certain provisions in first-day orders and will likely approve the same provisions again. The problem is that the three judges do not approve the same provisions. In Boston, which first-day order a filer gets depends on the luck of the draw.

The Boston lawyers who complain most vociferously about the Boston judges seem to agree that they are not bad judges. The lawyers give one of the three, Judge Carol J. Kenner, lower than average marks.[29] But the First Circuit Court of Appeals seems to disagree; it reappointed her to a second term as a bankruptcy judge in 1998 and to a prestigious place on the circuit's Bankruptcy Appellate Panel.

Nor did Boston's problems begin with these three judges.

TABLE 2.   **Boston-Based Firms Filing Bankruptcy since 1980**

1982 KDT Industries	1995 Bradlees, Inc.	2001 ACT Manufacturing
1986 Towle Manufacturing	**1997 Molten Metal**	2001 Casual Male
1989 Bay Financial	2000 Bradlees, Inc.	2001 Polaroid Corporation
1991 Hills Department	2000 CareMatrix	2001 Waste Systems
Stores	2000 GC Companies	International
1992 Child World, Inc.	2000 Learnout &	2002 CTC Communications
1992 Prime Computer	Hauspie	2002 Genuity, Inc.
1992 Wang Laboratories	**2000 Trend-Lines**	2002 Network Plus
1993 Healthco International	2000 Stone and Webster	2002 SLI, Inc.

Source: Data from Lynn M. LoPucki's Bankruptcy Research Database.
Note: Firms filing in the Boston Bankruptcy Court are shown in bold.

Boston was a shop-out city before any of the three were appointed. In the late 1980s, lawyers told my coresearcher, Bill Whitford, and me in interviews that big companies didn't file in Boston because the Boston court would not approve first-day-order provisions the New York court would.

The problems with the Boston judges are subtle. But in an era of rampant, routine forum shopping, they were enough to turn Boston big-case bankruptcy practice into a desert. As one lawyer put it: "I've come to accept the fact that I'm not going to have cases here." The situation must be unpleasant for the Boston judges, and one has to wonder how long they will be able to hold out. (Judge Kenner recently resigned.)

In addition to Boston, seven other cities have shop-out rates too high to be fairly attributed to mere chance.[30] Alexandria, Virginia, lost 11 of 13 cases (85 percent) to forum shopping; Bridgeport, Connecticut, 10 of 11 (91 percent); Columbia, South Carolina, five of five; Columbus, Ohio, nine of ten (90 percent); Fort Lauderdale, Florida, five of five; Philadelphia, Pennsylvania, seven of seven; and West Palm Beach, Florida, five of five. These are the lawyers and judges the competition left behind. To feel their pain, one has only to imagine the mood at the first monthly bar luncheon after yet another big local company chose to file in Delaware or New York.

The process by which pressure to compete is brought to bear on the judges is brutal and intimidating. The lawyers who place cases are among the most powerful and prestigious of the bankruptcy bar. They publicly laud the judges who give them what they want and harshly criticize those who do not. Some of the latter become pariahs of the national bankruptcy bar—judges considered so bad they drive the cases away. Lawyers—and other judges—malign them as "toxic judges."

Forced to a simple choice between popularity and integrity, most judges would choose integrity, even under these conditions. But the choice is seldom presented so starkly. A judge can easily suppose him- or herself clever enough to achieve popularity and maintain integrity simultaneously. But the game is played over a long period of time, and the pressure of competition is relentless.

As the judges are put to choice after choice, the changes occur in increments, each too small to be recognized for the erosion of integrity it is. To corrupt the bankruptcy system, it was not necessary to corrupt all of the bankruptcy judges. Once a few judges succumbed, the cases flowed to them, rendering the remaining judges irrelevant.

1

New York's Game: 1980–86

Were [transacting business in the jurisdiction] enough [to make venue proper] large corporations would be free to roam the entire country in search of venues which might provide them with what, in their opinion, would be a more favorable hearing.

—United States Court of Appeals for the First Circuit (1982)

For decades before 1980, big company bankruptcies had been rare. Some said it was because modern firms were "too big to fail." The bankruptcy lawyers saw it differently. Bankruptcy was not a financial condition. Bankruptcy was a legal proceeding. Firms filed bankruptcy when bankruptcy was in the interests of the people who made the decision: top management. Under the antiquated, Depression-era law then in effect, bankruptcy seldom was. Large public companies were supposed to file under Chapter X of the Bankruptcy Act. That chapter required the managers to surrender control of the firm to a court-appointed trustee. There were ways of getting around the law, but they were awkward and risky.

The bankruptcy lawyers complained about the trustee requirement. After a decade of study and debate, Congress gave in. In 1978, it enacted a new, "modern" bankruptcy code that gave top managers the right to remain in control of their firms during bankruptcy. The House committee that reviewed the bill was remarkably frank about the reasons for the change.

Debtors' lawyers that participated in the development of a standard for the appointment of a trustee were adamant that a standard that led to too frequent appointment would prevent

debtors from seeking relief under [the reorganization law] and
would leave the [law] largely unused except in extreme cases.[1]

In other words, Congress concluded that if top managers could not
remain in charge during bankruptcy, those managers would not
take their firms into bankruptcy at all.

The new law took effect October 1, 1979, and the procession of
big cases began a few months later. Three big firms filed in 1980.
The annual number of big firm filings climbed steadily through the
decade, reaching 16 in 1989. Each of those cases was a bonanza for
the law firms involved, with fees in the millions and often the tens
of millions of dollars. The largest of those filings—by Johns
Manville—alone generated court-awarded fees and expenses of
$82 million. Before the new code, silk-stocking law firms in New
York and elsewhere had shunned bankruptcy practice as sleazy
and unprofitable. In the years following enactment, those same
firms began building and advertising their bankruptcy departments.

The National Science Foundation Study

In 1986, Bill Whitford and I received a grant from the National Science Foundation to study big bankruptcy reorganization cases. Bill
was a colleague of mine on the University of Wisconsin Law School
faculty. Neither of us knew much about big bankruptcy reorganizations, but we figured we could learn.

The Securities and Exchange Commission helped us compile a
list of every case filed in the United States by or against a public
company with assets of $100 million or more. Over the next four
years, Bill and I read what had been written about the cases in the
financial press, obtained and analyzed the plans of reorganization,
conducted about 120 interviews with lawyers in the cases, and con-
structed a database. Ultimately, the study covered all cases filed
after October 1, 1979, in which the court confirmed a plan by
March 15, 1988—a total of 43 cases.

In looking over our list of cases, we noticed that many of them

had been filed in New York. That did not seem odd. New York is
the financial center of the United States, and many of the country's
largest firms are headquartered there. But as we learned more
about the firms that filed in New York, it became apparent that
many of them had only the most tenuous connections to that city.
The Johns Manville Corporation, for example, filed in New York
shortly after building and moving into a $40 million headquarters
building in Colorado and changing its place of incorporation to
Delaware. The center of Manville's operations was in Colorado;
the firm had no apparent connection with New York at all. HRT,
a chain of retail stores with its headquarters and center of operations in California, and Towle Manufacturing, a firm with nearly
all of its operations in Massachusetts, also filed in New York.
Eventually it dawned on us that many of the firms we were studying were forum shoppers.

Forum Shopping

Literally, "forum shopping" means only that a party to litigation is
choosing among courts. As previously noted, the law sometimes
deliberately allows such choices. Rarely do those choices threaten
the legal system. Most parties use their freedom to choose courts
convenient for themselves. If the courts they choose are particularly inconvenient for other parties or witnesses, the chosen courts
can transfer the cases to more convenient courts.

Nevertheless, the phrase "forum shopping" is generally used as
a pejorative. The phrase implies that the party choosing the court
is by that choice seeking some unfair advantage. The advantage
sought is usually a judge or jury biased (the squeamish may read
"inclined" each time this word appears) in some manner that will
benefit the party.

Laws are deliberately vague and subject to interpretation. They
leave plenty of room for judges to do what they think is right, best,
or expedient. The judges' decisions may be reversed on appeal. But
appeals are expensive and difficult to win, so losing parties seldom
take them. Even if reversal occurs, the new decision will more

likely be the result of the appellate court judges' biases than law. Good lawyers know that the identity of the judge is a crucial determinant of the outcome of the case, and they seek the judge who will be best for their client.

Judicial biases are not subtle. In the courtrooms of federal judges (and death penalty opponents) Marilyn Hall Patel and William Ingram, for example, death penalty cases are likely to remain pending for over a decade, while in the courtrooms of federal judges (and death penalty proponents) Manuel Real and Edward Rafeedie, death penalties are likely to be approved in as little as two years.[2] Debtors filing for Chapter 13 bankruptcy in San Antonio, Texas, in the early 1990s generally had to pay 100 percent of their debts, while debtors filing the same kind of case in Dayton, Ohio, generally had to pay only 10 percent of their debts.[3] The supply of such examples is virtually unlimited.

One might expect lawmakers to respond to bias by tightening the instructions to judges on how they should rule. If done effectively, that would insure the law's ideal: rules that are the same for everyone. Instead, the law's response is so peculiar that most people do not even connect it with the bias problem. Courts randomize the assignment of judges.

Most courts consist of a "panel" of judges to whom the clerk of the court can assign a particular kind of case. The number of judges on a panel commonly ranges from two to 20 or 30. Each clerk has some mechanism for assigning cases randomly among the members of the panel. For example, in the courts of Florida's Eighth Judicial Circuit, where I practiced, the clerk used tokens. Each was inscribed with the division letter of a particular judge. The clerk mixed a large number of those tokens in a drawer. When someone filed a case, the clerk reached into the drawer—while looking at the ceiling—and drew one of the tokens. The clerk assigned the case to the judge whose division letter appeared on the drawn token. Today, clerks more frequently use computers to make random assignments, but the principle remains the same.

Any effort to evade the randomness of the draw is considered a serious ethical breach. That does not keep some lawyers from trying. A lawyer may be able to evade the draw by filing the case with a particular judge at the judge's home on the weekend. To do that, the lawyer must assert some "emergency" requiring that the case be filed before the clerk's office opens on Monday morning. Another technique is to assert that a newly filed case is so closely related to a case already assigned to the desired judge that the new case should be assigned to that judge without a draw. Sometimes a feared judge goes out of the draw temporarily because the judge is ill or overloaded with cases. Lawyers wait for these opportunities to file. The lawyers learn about them from friends who work in the clerks' offices.

Another way to beat the draw is to file several cases and then dismiss all but the one assigned to the desired judge. For example, Geoffrey Feiger is a Southfield, Michigan, plaintiff's lawyer famous for his successful representation of Dr. Jack Kevorkian, who assisted suicides in the 1990s. When Feiger sought to challenge a ruling of the Michigan Supreme Court in a federal district court, he filed 13 lawsuits. On the thirteenth, Feiger must have drawn the judge he wanted. He dismissed the first 12, leaving just that one pending. When the court figured out what he had done, the court sanctioned Feiger, imposing a $7,500 fine.[4] In another case, Mayer Brown & Platt, the prominent Chicago firm, was sanctioned by a Cook County circuit court. A partner and an associate of the firm filed five identical complaints in an attempt to draw one of three preferred judges. In imposing a total of $5,000 in fines, the judge expressed dismay that Mayer Brown "would cheapen itself in this fashion."[5]

What is peculiar about random judge assignments as a remedy for judicial bias is that the remedy does nothing to cure or even mitigate the problem. Random assignment makes judges no less biased. What it does is distribute the effects of judges' biases randomly among litigants. Every litigant has an equal chance of falling victim to every kind of bias. As the editors of the *Harvard Law Review* put it: "Forum shopping violate[s] fair play by allowing parties to circumvent fate."[6]

To prevent parties from circumventing their fate with respect to judges, the system must do more than prevent them from choosing among the members of a panel. The system must also prevent them from choosing among panels. The choice of a city is the choice of one panel of judges over another. That is merely a stochastic circumvention of fate but nevertheless an important one. If the city chosen has only a single judge, the choice of city is a choice of judge, just as surely as in the scheme Geoffrey Feiger used.

Preventing litigants from choosing among judges by choosing among cities is more difficult than preventing them from choosing among judges within a city. Cases can't be randomly assigned to cities; they must be heard in cities that are reasonably convenient to the parties, their lawyers, and the witnesses. But the most convenient city for a particular case may be difficult to determine, even after a case is well under way. That is particularly true in big bankruptcy cases. At the time a big bankruptcy case is filed, even the debtor may not know who will be an active participant. The uncertainty provides cover for lawyers who choose courts for their judges' biases but claim they have chosen them for the geographical convenience of the parties.

The Bankruptcy Venue Game

Bill Whitford and I decided to look further into bankruptcy forum shopping. What we found was a highly permissive venue statute, an imaginative array of strategies for taking advantage of the statute, and a high judicial tolerance for those who simply ignored the statute and filed their cases wherever they pleased.

In the mid-1980s, approximately 300 bankruptcy judges were distributed among approximately 200 panels in the 98 federal court districts. In less populated areas, the panel often consisted of a single judge. In large cities, there were usually three or four. The panel in Los Angeles was the largest with eight; New York had five.

The bankruptcy venue statute, which has not changed since 1978, recognizes four connections between a debtor and a court, any of which makes the court a proper venue for the debtor's bankruptcy. The four connections are that the court is (1) at the "domicile or residence" of the debtor, (2) at the debtor's "principal place of business," (3) at the location of the debtor's principal assets, or (4) where the bankruptcy case of an affiliate is already pending. The first of these choices, domicile or residence, would later play a major role in the forum shopping. That role is explained in chapter 2. In the 1980s cases Bill and I studied, however, it played no role at all.

Principal Place of Business

Imagine the "principal place of business" of a major corporation and you may get an image of a big industrial plant with an executive office building at the front. But even by the 1980s, that image was largely obsolete. Major U.S. corporations typically did business at numerous locations, whether those locations were industrial plants, chains of hotels or restaurants, or airline hubs.

If the bankruptcy courts were writing on a clean slate, they might have interpreted "principal place of business" to refer to the largest of those operations or the one through which the most business was done. But "principal place of business" is what the lawyers call a "term of art"—a phrase that originated in the English language but has a different meaning when used as legal jargon. Long before it appeared in the bankruptcy venue statute, "principal place of business" had been interpreted to mean the headquarters of the firm—the so-called nerve center from which the firm's operations were directed.

Now the image you get of a firm's "principal place of business" may be a gleaming skyscraper bearing the firm's name. Many firm headquarters fit that image. But the nerve center of a firm can be little more than the office of the chief executive, remote from the rest of top management. Move the chief executive officer and you at least arguably move the principal place of business. AM International, for example, had most of its operations in the Chicago area. But in the five years before it filed its first bankruptcy in 1982, the firm moved its headquarters from Chicago to Cleveland to Los Angeles and back to Chicago. The purpose of these moves was not to manipulate venue but merely to accommodate a series of chief executive officers who did not want to move to Chicago. Each managed the business from his or her home city. Another of the 43 firms we studied, Evans Products, moved its headquarters from Portland, Oregon, to Miami, Florida, about a year before filing in Miami. Evans Products had been taken over by Miami financier Victor Posner. Posner lived in Miami and chose to run the Oregon firm from his home city.

Some of the firms we studied did move their headquarters to manipulate venue. Tacoma Boatbuilding owned and operated a shipyard in Tacoma, Washington. The shipyard was the firm's sole place of business. Not surprisingly, prior to the financial difficulties that brought Tacoma Boatbuilding to bankruptcy, the firm's head-quarters were at the shipyard.

Tacoma is one of the approximately 200 cities in the United States that has both a bankruptcy court and a clerk's office. That court was certainly Tacoma Boatbuilding's natural venue. But Tacoma is in the Ninth Circuit, and the Ninth Circuit Court of Appeals at that time required firms to pay interest on their secured debts while the firms remained in bankruptcy. Tacoma Boatbuild-ing wanted to file in Second Circuit, where the Second Circuit Court of Appeals made debts of the kind Tacoma Boatbuilding owed interest free.

Tacoma Boatbuilding rented a small office in Manhattan, declared that office the firm's headquarters, waited the 90 days a new connection must exist before it is recognized for venue pur-poses, and filed its bankruptcy case in New York. The banks objected to New York venue, but Judge Burton R. Lifland ruled in favor of the company. The case stayed in New York. Among other advantages, Tacoma Boatbuilding was not required to pay interest on about $5 million in bank loans—interest the company would have been required to pay if the case had been transferred to Wash-ington.[7] Through the entire episode, Tacoma Boatbuilding contin-ued to list Tacoma, Washington, as its "principal executive offices" on the annual reports the firm filed with the Securities and Exchange Commission. Nobody seemed to have noticed.

Baldwin-United was another big debtor that sought to choose its bankruptcy court by moving its headquarters. That company was a Cincinnati, Ohio, conglomerate that had begun life as a piano maker. When Baldwin-United filed in 1983 with $9 billion in assets, the firm was by that measure the largest ever to file bankruptcy. Six months before filing, Baldwin-United named Victor Palmieri, a well-known distressed property liquidator, as its chief executive officer. Instead of moving to Baldwin-United's Cincinnati headquarters, Palmieri moved into New York offices of Baldwin-United, saying that New York "was a good location for negotiation with the various Baldwin creditors."[8] Because Palmieri was in New York and directed the firm's operations from New York, New York was arguably both the nerve center of the company and a proper venue for the firm's bankruptcy filing. Baldwin-United filed in New York.

That was not, however, the end of the story. A group of creditors wanted the case heard in Cincinnati. When negotiations that might have avoided the filing broke off, the creditors raced to the Cincinnati bankruptcy court and filed a creditors' petition—just minutes *before* Baldwin-United filed in New York.

When the same bankruptcy is filed in two courts, the court in which the first filing was made decides which court keeps the case. That was the Cincinnati court. When Baldwin-United learned that the creditors had won the race to the courthouse, it faced a choice. Baldwin-United could have argued to the Cincinnati judge that he should transfer the case to New York. But the firm had already insulted the Cincinnati panel by setting up the New York "headquarters" and filing there. By arguing to the Cincinnati judge for a transfer to New York, they would have risked offending him personally. Baldwin-United dropped its New York filing and let the Cincinnati judge hear the entire case.

Principal Assets

Most of the 43 studied firms filed in the court of their headquarters city. Of the seven that did not, only Towner Petroleum relied on the location of its principal assets as the sole basis for venue. Until a few years before it filed, Towner had been an Ohio company. In an expansion that led to the firm's financial difficulties, Towner moved its headquarters to Houston, Texas. When it filed bankruptcy a few years later, it chose the court in Oklahoma City, Oklahoma. Towner's bank lenders objected to Oklahoma City as the venue. The Oklahoma City court kept the case, agreeing with the debtor that more of the firm's oil and gas properties were in the Western District of Oklahoma than in any other district.

Manipulating the location of its assets to establish venue is not, for most big firms, a practical option. But for some it is. One of the studied cases was Seatrain Lines, a firm whose principal assets were six oil tankers Seatrain operated in the Alaskan coastal trade. By basing the tankers in different ports, Seatrain Lines could probably have made any of those ports the location of its principal assets. Seatrain chose to file at its headquarters in New York, but because of the mobility of its principal assets, it was actually choosing among numerous available courts.

A firm can change the location of the firm's principal assets without moving any of them. To illustrate, Dreco Energy, another of the studied firms, was a Canadian corporation. Just a few years before bankruptcy, Dreco's headquarters, its principal assets, and most of its employees were in Canada. Canadian bankruptcy law was then and is now less favorable to corporate debtors than U.S. bankruptcy law. Dreco established a new headquarters in Houston, Texas; sold some of its Canadian assets; and discharged some of its Canadian employees. By the time it filed for bankruptcy in Houston, it had more assets and employees in the United States than in Canada. After bankruptcy, the firm reestablished its Canadian headquarters and, through acquisitions and divestitures, within a few years again had more Canadian assets and employees than U.S. ones.[9] Dreco Energy had, in a very real sense, come to the United States to file bankruptcy and then returned to Canada.

Case of an Affiliate Pending

Businesses—consisting of people and things—exist in the real world. Corporations do not. Corporations are figments of the legal imagination. For a few hundred dollars you can have one of your own, complete with a certificate from the secretary of state of the state of your choice attesting to your corporation's existence. You are then entitled to claim that your corporation is a person separate from yourself. Most courts in most situations will respect this otherwise outlandish claim. Your corporation may even have constitutional rights independent of your own. By virtue of the "existence" of your corporation, you can gain a variety of legal advantages that would not otherwise be available.

Large public companies typically consist of a parent corporation and dozens of wholly owned "subsidiary" corporations. The single group of managers that runs the entire company designates particular subsidiaries as the owners of particular assets. For example, a major airline may have a corporate subsidiary that owns the aircraft, another that owns the real estate, a third that employs the flight crews and conducts operations, a fourth that owns the airline's accounts receivable and borrows money against them, and a fifth that owns and operates a feeder airline. Together, the parent and these five subsidiary corporations constitute a "corporate group." Formally, each of the corporations will have its own officers and directors, but those officers and directors are likely to be the same people who are officers and directors of all of the corporations in the group. Look at this airline and you will see only a single business. But when the law looks at the same airline, it sees six corporations, each with its own assets, liabilities, employees, officers, and directors. Incorporation is a game of make-believe for adults.

Even the Supreme Court of the United States plays. In one recent case the Court referred to the directors as "changing hats" when they sat as directors of the various corporations in the group.[10] The Court was not, as you might suspect, using that term to make fun of the game before skewering the players. It was explaining why it would recognize each of the corporations as a separate person with separate rights.

Some of the corporations in a group can be in financial difficulty when others are not. But most of the time, difficulties that affect one member of a group affect most or all of them. Corporate groups cannot, however, file bankruptcy. Only corporations can. Each corporation in the group pays an $800 filing fee and files its own petition. To put the hypothetical airline just discussed into bankruptcy, its lawyers would probably file six petitions. The court would then enter an order "consolidating" the six cases into one for purposes of administration. The "existence" of separate corporations would affect the entitlements of creditors. A creditor that loaned money to one of the six corporations would have a claim against only that corporation's assets. But for most purposes, the court would simply ignore the individual corporations and treat the group as if it were the debtor. The same lawyers would almost certainly represent all six corporations, and the same executives would manage the company as a whole.

Each of the corporations in a corporate group is by definition an "affiliate" of the others. If one affiliate is in bankruptcy, the venue statute authorizes the other affiliates to file in the same court. Allowing a corporation to file bankruptcy in the court where the bankruptcy of an affiliate is already pending may at first sound like good common sense. Dividing the bankruptcy of a single airline between two or more bankruptcy courts would be inefficient.

But the right to file bankruptcy where the bankruptcy case of an affiliate is pending looks less sensible once one sees what clever lawyers can do with it. Eastern Airlines was one of the country's major carriers when it filed for bankruptcy in 1989. At the time of Eastern's filing, its headquarters and the bulk of its operations were in Miami, Florida. But for strategic reasons, Eastern did not want to file there.

Eastern was a corporate group, with various subsidiary corporations performing different functions for the airline. One of those affiliates, Ionosphere, Inc., operated Eastern's hospitality lounges in airports. Ionosphere had less than $2 million in assets—one-twentieth of 1 percent of Eastern's $3.7 billion in assets.[11] Ionosphere, Inc., was also solvent and therefore probably not even in need of bankruptcy. But Ionosphere, Inc., had connections to New York that made it eligible to file in the New York bankruptcy court.

On the day of the filing, Eastern's lawyers took two petitions to the New York bankruptcy court. First, they handed the clerk the petition for Ionosphere, Inc. At the moment the clerk stamped it filed, Ionosphere's case was pending in the New York bankruptcy court. Six minutes later, the lawyers handed the clerk the petition for Eastern Airlines. New York was a proper venue for Eastern's filing because the case of an Eastern affiliate—Ionosphere—was pending there.

This technique is commonly used. When Dallas-based LTV Corporation sought to file in New York in 1986, it first caused a New York–based subsidiary—Chateaugay Corporation—to file in New York. Chateaugay, like Ionosphere before it, reportedly was not even in need of reorganization.[12]

Lawyers refer to the first filing in each of these sequences as the "venue hook"—something perhaps like the grappling hooks that attacking tall ships used to bind themselves to their prey. A venue hook enables a corporate group to pull itself into any court in which any of its constituent corporations can set the hook. For large corporate groups, that can include almost any bankruptcy court in the United States.

In 2001, Enron used a venue hook to get into the New York court. Enron Corporation was an Oregon corporation with both its principal place of business and its principal assets in Houston, Texas. Enron's hook was Enron Metals & Commodity Corporation, a subsidiary that was eligible to file in New York because it had its principal place of business there. At the time the Enron group filed in New York, the group had 25,000 employees, over 7,500 of whom worked at the firm's headquarters in Houston. Enron Metals & Commodity Corporation had 57 employees in New York and owned one-half of 1 percent of Enron's assets.[13] But when it comes to venue hooking, size does not matter.

Where Were the Judges?

That legal rules constrain judges and make them do things is a magnificent illusion but an illusion nonetheless. There may indeed be a rule that tells a judge to do X, but with a little effort the judge can always find a rule that tells the judge not to do X. Judging is not following the rules but rather deciding which rules to follow.

The bankruptcy venue statute can be fairly read to authorize all of the slick tricks previously described, but another bankruptcy venue statute authorizes their undoing. That statute instructs the bankruptcy court where a case is pending to transfer the case to another district whenever transfer is "in the interest of justice or for the convenience of the parties."[14] That is, even though the debtor files in a proper venue, the court can transfer the case to a better venue.

Such transfers were what the Bankruptcy Rules Committee had in mind when it adopted the current rules in 1974. George Treister, a member of that committee, reports that committee members realized they were authorizing a wide choice of venues for business filers. They wanted to afford a wide choice so that the debtor could put the case in the best venue, expecting that if the debtor used its freedom to put the case in any other venue, the judges would correct the problem by transferring the case. The committee failed to anticipate that the judges would want the cases badly enough to retain them even in inappropriate venues. At the time, there had only been a few large cases, and the existing venue provisions had not been abused.

Transfers of big bankruptcy cases are rare, even in the face of obvious abuse. Parties seldom ask for transfers, and when they do, the judges seldom grant them. The judges' reluctance results partly from practical considerations and partly from self-interest.

The practical problem is that when the debtor files in a court, the case quickly grows roots there. Immediately on filing the case, the debtor makes "first-day motions" to the court, usually seeking authorization to borrow money on an emergency basis, to use collateral belonging to secured creditors, to pay employees and critical suppliers, and to employ lawyers and financial advisers. The judge typically must rule on these motions within a few days, in the process devoting hours—maybe dozens of hours—to becoming familiar with the case. Another public official, the United States

Trustee, appoints a creditors' committee. The committee hurriedly interviews and hires professionals so it can participate in the early, crucial stages of the case. For the largest cases, the court must make special logistical arrangements, including setting up meeting spaces, creating web pages devoted to the case, and maybe even hiring additional court personnel. Creditors, landlords, and other parties in distant cities hire lawyers in the court city. The court cannot rule on a request for a change of venue immediately on receiving it. Those who will argue for and against the change need time to prepare.

If some party makes a request to transfer the case to another city, the court will likely hear the request a month or two after the party files it. If the court were to grant a request for a change of venue, the rooting process described here would repeat in the new city. By the time that the transfer occurred, the effect would be to inconvenience just about everyone involved.

The other reason bankruptcy judges don't transfer big cases was discussed in the introduction. Many judges don't want to give up the cases. That may be because a judge seeks the high visibility big cases bring, because the judge wants to bring business to his or her local legal community, or because the judge fears the criticism he or she will get for letting the cases go.

Thus, even though the bankruptcy judges have the power to nullify the debtors' manipulation of the venue requirements, the judges rarely do it. Those who choose courts on behalf of the debtors have the final say.

What Shoppers Want

When Bill Whitford and I realized that forum shopping would be an important facet of big-case bankruptcy, we began asking our interviewees about it. Most readily admitted that shopping was pervasive in big bankruptcy cases, but they differed in their descriptions of what the shoppers were after.

The most frequently cited objective was to get "good judges" who had experience with large reorganizations. Probably the second most cited goal was to get a court convenient to both the debtor and the debtor's lawyers. But the lawyers also reported a dark side to the shopping. Debtors were seeking judges likely to rule in their favor on key issues, and lawyers were seeking courts that would not cut their fees.

Venue hooks and headquarters moves were used to increase the odds that cases would "stick" in various cities throughout the country. But the most blatant shopping during the period of our study brought cases to New York. Six of the 43 cases we studied were filed in a city that was neither the location of the debtor's headquarters nor the location of the debtor's principal operations. Five of the six were filed in New York. Whatever forum shoppers were after was most available in New York.

During the period of our study—as remains true today—most of the leading bankruptcy professionals were located in New York. That includes not just the bankruptcy lawyers but also the workout departments of money center banks, accounting firms, and financial advisers. New York's success in attracting cases in the early 1980s fed on itself. Because the cases were in New York, the professionals there had the experience, and their experience drew more cases. New York has long been the headquarters city for many of the largest U.S. firms. As a result, New York had also been the head-quarters city for many of the bankrupt firms Bill and I studied. For both the professionals and the managers, Manhattan's Foley Square was often a convenient place to go to bankruptcy court.

That is not, however, the entire story. A large bankruptcy infra-structure, such as exists in New York, requires a steady flow of cases. Cases would come only as long as the New York bankruptcy court remained an attractive place to reorganize. That put pressure on the court.

The lawyers told us that three factors besides good judges and convenient courts were important enough to attract or repel cases: extensions of exclusivity, attorney fees, and first-day orders. "Exclusivity" is short for the debtor's exclusive right to file a plan of reorganization during the first 120 days of the case and such extensions of that 120-day period as the court may allow.

The debtor's objective in a bankruptcy case is usually to win confirmation of a plan of reorganization. The plan "restructures" the bankrupt firm's obligations, reducing the amounts of the debts, providing for payment over longer periods of time, transforming creditors into shareholders, or forcing other concessions from creditors. The bankrupt firm negotiates the plan with representatives of its creditors, but like nearly all negotiations, those negotiations take place in anticipation of what will happen if the parties do not reach agreement.

That is where exclusivity comes in. As long as the court continues to grant extensions of exclusivity, what happens in the absence of agreement is that the debtor remains in bankruptcy and continues to pay nothing to its creditors. The creditors cannot move the case forward because the creditors cannot propose a plan. That barrier is removed if the court lifts exclusivity. The creditors can then file a plan, and when the court confirms it, the debtor must begin repayment. Extensions of exclusivity—granted or anticipated—prevent the creditors from moving the case forward without the debtor's agreement; their effect is to confer bargaining leverage on debtors.

During the period of our study, the New York bankruptcy court extended exclusivity until the debtor struck a bargain with the creditors in 12 of 13 cases (92 percent). Other courts extended exclusivity for that long in only 22 of 30 cases (73 percent). The effect was that in New York debtors could negotiate with greater confidence that the court would not pull the rug out from under them by lifting exclusivity. With only one exception, the New York cases went forward on the debtor's terms or not at all.

Fees were another important consideration. The key professionals representing the debtor and the creditors in a bankruptcy case are paid from the assets of the bankrupt firm. But if the firm is insolvent—as most bankrupts are—the bite of those fees may be felt more by the creditors than the debtor. What assets an insolvent debtor has left after paying the fees belong to the creditors. A dollar more in fees to the debtor's lawyer may simply mean a dollar less in payments to creditors. To keep the debtor from spending too much of the creditors' money on fees, bankruptcy law requires that the court approve fees as reasonable and necessary before the debtor makes payment. To justify their fees, the lawyers must keep detailed records of the time they spend on the case and the particular tasks on which they spend it. They submit these time records to the court along with their applications for payment. Theoretically, the judge examines the application carefully, cuts the amounts of the fees when appropriate, and authorizes the debtor to write the checks.

As a practical matter, a bankruptcy judge can determine the reasonableness of fees only in the most general sense. Figure 1 illustrates the problem. This is one page in a fee application that runs more than 100 pages. The page contains a tremendous amount of information but not much that would be useful in trying to second-guess the lawyers as to the reasonableness of the charges. The application from which it was taken was for one of four professional firms in the case, and the application covered only a little more than the first 100 days of the case. In a big case, all the fee applications together are likely to run to hundreds or even thousands of pages.

Even if a judge read them all, the judge still could not evaluate the reasonableness of the fees. Meaningful evaluation—if it can be done at all—requires sophisticated computer analysis. In some cases, the court authorizes employment of a professional fee auditor who does such an analysis, but more often, the court does not. Cutting lawyers' fees is not a career-enhancing activity for other lawyers (what goes around comes around) or bankruptcy judges (who may need the support of the lawyers who practice before them to be reappointed).

The fee cutting that actually occurs is mostly cosmetic. If a lawyer makes the mistake of billing for more than 24 hours in a single day—lawyers have been caught doing so in some cases—the court may catch it and cut the hours back to 24.[15] But occasionally fees are cut in two more significant ways. First, the court may decide that the quality of a lawyer's work was poor and arbitrarily slash some major portion of the fee. Lawyers enjoy this kind of crit-

PROFESSIONAL	DATE	HOURS	DESCRIPTION
FLICS	07/13/99	.30	E-MAILS RE: PREPARATION FOR DIP AND EXCLUSIVITY HEARING (.20); TELEPHONE CONVERSATION WITH R. YOUNG RE: SAME (.10).
FLICS	07/14/99	.90	REVIEW DRAFT AFFIDAVIT RE: EXCLUSIVITY MOTION (.30); REVIEW ISSUES RE: PRESENTATION FOR 7-20 MEETING (.60).
YOUNG	07/14/99	3.60	TELEPHONE CALL WITH E. SCHWARTZ RE: STATUS OF MOTIONS AND NEED FOR WITNESSES (.30); TELEPHONE CALLS WITH M. FLICS RE: SAME (.20); TELEPHONE CONVERSATIONS WITH W. LOVY RE: AFFIDAVIT IN SUPPORT OF EXCLUSIVITY (.20); REVIEW DIP OBJECTION (.50); TELEPHONE CALLS WITH M. FLICS RE: SAME (.70); TELEPHONE COVERSATIONS WITH D. BLOOM AND T. NOULLES RE: SAME (.50); MEETING WITH W. LOVY RE: SAME (.40); REVIEW COLLECTED CASE LAW RE: SAME (.50); REVISE SCHOPFER AFFIDAVIT RE: EXCLUSIVITY (.30).
LOVY	07/14/99	3.70	DRAFT AFFIDAVIT IN SUPPORT OF DEBTOR'S MOTION TO EXTEND EXCLUSIVE PERIOD FOR FILING PLAN (1.70) ; RESEARCH LEGAL BASIS FOR OBJECTION OF BLACK WARRIOR TELECOMMUNICATIONS TO NEW DIP FINANCING (2.00).
YOUNG	07/15/99	5.20	TELEPHONE CALLS WITH W. LOVY RE: OBJECTION TO DIP FINANCING (.60); TELEPHONE CALLS WITH M. FLICS RE: SAME (.50); TELEPHONE CALL WITH OPPOSING COUNSEL RE: SAME (.30); REVISE RESPONSE TO OBJECTION (2.30); REVIEW UNDERLYING BLACK WARRIOR AGREEMENTS (.80); TELEPHONE CALLS WITH T. NOULLES AND EILERS RE: SAME (.70).
LOVY	07/15/99	1.00	RESEARCH LEGAL BASIS FOR OBJECTION OF BLACK WARRIOR TELECOMMUNICATIONS TO NEW DIP FINANCING (1.00).
FLICS	07/16/99	1.80	CONFERENCE WITH R. YOUNG RE: DIP OBJECTION AND PREPARE FOR HEARING (.50); REVIEW REPLY RE: DIP OBJECTION (.40); TELEPHONE-R. YOUNG RE: SAME (.10); REVIEW EXCLUSIVITY MATERIAL IN PREPARATION FOR HEARING (.80).
YOUNG	07/16/99	3.40	REVISE RESPONSE TO OBJECTION TO DIP FINANCING (.80); TELEPHONE CALLS WITH M. FLICS AND W. LOVY RE: SAME (.50); MEETING WITH M. FLICS RE: HEARING ISSUES FOR DIP FINANCING (.50); REVIEW WALSH LETTER RE: FINANCING (.40); MEETINGS WITH W. LOVY RE: TASKS FOR HEARING (.80); TELEPHONE CALLS WITH T. NOULLES RE: DIP OBJECTION (.40).

Fig. 1.   One page of a fee application

icism about as much as other people do and steer a wide berth around any court inclined to do it. Second, some courts are reluctant to approve fees in excess of particular hourly rates. For example, through the 1980s, the Philadelphia bankruptcy court refused to approve fees in excess of $200 per hour for senior partners, while the bankruptcy court in New York was approving fees as high as $450 an hour. Not surprisingly, Philadelphia got none of the 43 cases in our study—and hasn't had a big case since then, either. (One of the two Philadelphia judges who imposed the $200 limit was denied reappointment in 2000, apparently solely on the basis of adverse comments received during the public comment period.)[16]

A variety of factors cause the fees of New York bankruptcy lawyers to be, on average, higher than the fees of bankruptcy lawyers in other cities. Firms' costs are higher in New York, and so are the costs of living for the lawyers the firms employ. To maintain their images as premier providers of legal services, the New York firms have tried to hire the best and the brightest on graduation from law schools and, some believe, have grossly overpaid for them. In some major cities, the cost of representation by the best local bankruptcy lawyers may be half or less what it is in New York. If the comparison is between the cost of bringing New York lawyers to St. Louis and using St. Louis lawyers in St. Louis, the differential is even greater. Lawyers travel first class, and they bill for travel time.

New York lawyers did handle cases outside New York in the 1980s. But when they did, they often stirred resentment. In each case, the New York lawyers' fees—and their reputations—were at risk. For example, Levin & Weintraub was one of the leading bankruptcy firms in New York when it represented Evans Products as debtor in the Miami bankruptcy court in 1986. After ruling against the firm's client on the merits, Bankruptcy Judge Thomas C. Britton cut Levin & Weintraub's fees by one-third, noting in a published opinion that the quality of the work of Levin & Weintraub's opponent in the case was "markedly superior" to that of Levin & Weintraub.[17] To avoid these risks, the New York lawyers tried, whenever possible, to bring the cases to New York.

Not all courts were as provincial as the one in Miami. Realizing that the New York lawyers had substantial control over the flow of cases, some courts signaled in published opinions that New York lawyers would be welcome in their districts. For example, the Oklahoma City bankruptcy court had three of the 43 cases in our study, making it the second most popular court. One of the judges of that court wrote that "outside counsel may charge rates normally charged clients in their respective regional areas for counsel time expended in these proceedings."[18] A Denver bankruptcy judge approved the payment of "New York rates" to some New York lawyers,[19] and the bankruptcy judges in Nashville opined that a New York firm practicing in the court would not be confined to Nashville, Tennessee, rates.[20]

That the New York bankruptcy court would pay New York rates—and not unduly hassle the lawyers about their fees—went without saying. Had the New York court done otherwise, New York would not have been the leading venue.

The third factor crucial to the flow of cases was first-day orders. In the view of some of the lawyers we interviewed, the practicalities of operating a business in bankruptcy reorganization were often in conflict with the requirements of the Bankruptcy Code. In New York, the code yielded to the practicalities; in Boston, and other cities, judges were inclined to the opposite view. This clash was less evident in the 1980s than in recent years, and so further discussion of it will be postponed to chapter 6.

The Judge at the Center

During the period of our study, the Manhattan division of the United States Bankruptcy Court for the Southern District of New York was a five-judge court. One judge stood out. Burton R. Lifland was a bankruptcy lawyer in New York before he became a member of the court in March 1980. Ten days after taking office, Judge Lifland drew the bankruptcy case of Penn-Dixie Industries, one of the 43 cases in our study. Before the end of 1985, he had eight of the 43. No other judge had more than three.

Judge Lifland quickly became both a bankruptcy celebrity and a center of controversy. Lifland was the judge who handled the big cases. Some of the lawyers we interviewed described him as "pro-debtor," and *Forbes Magazine* echoed that charge in 1991.[21] "Pro-reorganization" is probably a more accurate term, because Lifland's primary goal seemed to be that the company survive the bankruptcy case.

Judge Lifland had at that time an unusual style. Some bankruptcy judges set matters for hearing and let the approaching day of reckoning provide the incentives for negotiation. Judge Lifland rarely set matters for hearing. Instead, he pressured the negotiators to settle the case. In most instances that meant threatening to lift exclusivity, cut lawyers' fees, or take unspecified action that would make the lawyers sorry they hadn't settled. Of course, the terms of the settlements Judge Lifland imposed were generally favorable to those who brought him the cases.

Judge Lifland wanted the big cases, and the debtors' lawyers wanted him to have them. In the early 1980s, New York was the most attractive bankruptcy venue in the country, and Burton Lifland was the most attractive judge in that venue.

How he got the case assignments remains both a mystery and an object of suspicion. When the Eastern Airlines case was assigned to Judge Lifland in 1989, Amy Dockser of the *Wall Street Journal* referred to Lifland's "knack for landing atop the biggest cases" and noted:

> While [Eastern's] choice of New York seemed predictable, the selection of Judge Lifland raised some eyebrows because of the uncanny way he has wound up assigned to the most important and visible bankruptcies. A number of bankruptcy lawyers question whether the lottery system of assigning cases among the seven judges in New York is entirely random.[22]

Despite the existence of a random draw—or "wheel," as it was known in New York—the clerk initially assigned six of the 13 New York cases in our study to Judge Lifland and later reassigned two more of the 13 to him when the initially assigned judges were unable to complete them. The odds that eight of 13 cases would be randomly assigned to a single judge on a five-judge court are only a little better than one in 1,000.

When Professor Ted Eisenberg and I circulated a paper reciting these odds, we drew an angry public reply from Cecelia Morris, then clerk of the New York bankruptcy court and now a U.S. bankruptcy judge in New York.[23] Morris pointed out that the court was not at full strength during the period due to a death, a resignation, and some conflicts of interest that prevented particular judges from hearing particular cases. Using the terms of the judges supplied to me by the Administrative Office of the U.S. Courts and deleting the judges that Judge Morris indicated in her reply were unavailable to receive particular assignments, I calculated that the average number of available judges at the time of the 13 initial assignments and three reassignments that delivered eight cases to Judge Lifland was slightly higher than four.[24] Ted, an accomplished statistician, calculates the odds of a particular judge on a four-judge court getting eight of 13 cases by random draw at six in 1,000.

The End of an Era

When Bill Whitford and I began our study, New York was at the height of its prominence. At the time, that prominence seemed both natural and inevitable. With all the key players there, how could New York not be the leader in big-case bankruptcy?

The surprising answer came sooner than anyone expected. Judge Lifland's extraordinary run ended in 1985, amid rumors about improprieties in case assignments. The following year, 1986, was the last good year for the New York bankruptcy court. It got four of the 10 big cases filed that year, a 40 percent market share. From 1980 through 1986, New York's market share of big-case bankruptcy averaged 32 percent. Beginning in 1987, New York's popularity declined. Over the next nine years (1987–95) the New

York court still averaged a respectable 17 percent market share. But in 1996, a lean year for big bankruptcy nationally, New York got not a single one of the 15 cases filed.

Delaware had by that time replaced New York as the big bankruptcy capital of the United States. And only a short time after that, the Delaware court's prominence seemed equally natural and inevitable.

The Rise of Delaware: 1990–96

The war is over and Delaware has won. The "Delawarization"
of bankruptcy law appears complete.

—Robert K. Rasmussen and Randall S. Thomas (2001)

Throughout the entire decade of the 1980s the U.S. bankruptcy court in Wilmington, Delaware, presided over only a single large public company bankruptcy. The company, Phoenix Steel, had all of its operations in Delaware. In November and December 1990, the court attracted two more big public company cases in quick succession—United Merchants and Manufacturers and Continental Airlines. In the six years that followed, Delaware attracted many more, and that court's market share grew steadily. In 1996, 13 of the 15 large public companies filing bankruptcy in the United States (87 percent) filed in Wilmington. Starting from nothing, the United States Bankruptcy Court for the District of Delaware had, in just six years, become the bankruptcy capital of the United States.

Figure 2 shows the annual progression by which Delaware came to dominance. Big-case bankruptcy boomed nationally from the late 1980s into the early 1990s. Most of the bankruptcies filed during this period resulted from defaults on junk bonds issued in the 1980s. The national boom peaked in 1991, just after Delaware began attracting cases. But as filings in the rest of the United States declined, the number in Delaware continued to rise.

Delaware's sudden rise to near-complete dominance of big-case bankruptcy raised a number of questions. Most bankrupt companies had a bankruptcy court conveniently available to them in the

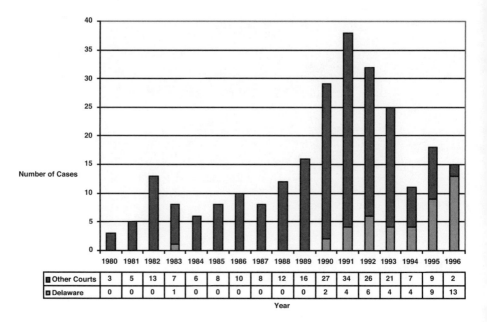

	1980	1981	1982	1983	1984	1985	1986	1987	1988	1989	1990	1991	1992	1993	1994	1995	1996
■ Other Courts	3	5	13	7	6	8	10	8	12	16	27	34	26	21	7	9	2
▫ Delaware	0	0	0	1	0	0	0	0	0	0	2	4	6	4	4	9	13

Fig. 2.   Number of big public firm bankruptcies by year,
1980–96. (Data from author's Bankruptcy Research Database.)

city of their headquarters. Why were they choosing a court hundreds, or in some cases thousands, of miles away? What did they
seek to gain? Even more directly relevant to the subject of this
book, why was the Delaware court providing it? Was the Delaware
court simply minding its own business, being the best court it
could, when it was suddenly discovered by bankrupt companies
hungering for efficiency and competence? Or was the court pan-
dering to lawyers and executives who sought a court that would let
them take advantage of other parties to the case in ways their home
court would not allow?

The Delaware judges have been careful never to comment publicly on their methods or motives. But Delaware's record in other
areas of law sheds light on what the Delaware bankruptcy judges
may have been up to.

Delaware as Onshore Haven

Despite its onshore location, the state of Delaware is a haven, engaged in many of the same businesses pursued by offshore havens such as Bermuda, the Cayman Islands, the Cook Islands, Gibraltar, the Jersey Islands, the Netherlands Antilles, and Mauritius. Havens are states or countries that turn lawmaking into a business and prey on their neighbors. Their lawmaking differs from that of other governments in that the laws havens make are not for their own citizens. Haven laws are for foreign clients. Havens are law "exporters."

When successful, the laws of a haven provide its foreign clients with some advantage at home. They may lower the client's taxes in the client's own country, protect the client from its creditors at home, make secret that which would be public under the laws of the client's home country, or free the client from some home country regulation.

To obtain the advantages of a haven, the client typically must feign some attachment to the haven: the client incorporates in the haven country, deposits funds in the haven country (deposits that may remain there for only an instant), declares the haven its "headquarters," flies the haven's flag on its ships, or establishes an office in the haven country. The attachment is only feigned in that the physical operation of the client's business changes little, if at all. The same people continue to work in the same places. As part of the feigning ceremony, the client pays a fee to the haven government, the business of a haven resident, or both. The clients pay gladly because the fees are only a small fraction of the benefits the haven confers. Those benefits come at the expense of the client's home country, whose government collects less in taxes or whose citizens have fewer rights against the haven's clients.

Havens are generally small states or countries that provide their services to the residents of large ones. For a haven, small size has four advantages. First, havens can extract only limited amounts of money from other countries before the governments of those countries react. Those limited amounts may be bonanzas to the small countries that become havens but insignificant to larger countries that might otherwise have been tempted to become havens. Second, haven activity is usually deceitful. The haven pretends to be legislating neutrally, oblivious to the wealth transfer from the client's home country to the client. Such pretending is easier in a small, close-knit community that depends economically on haven activity than in a larger community where the economy is more diverse. Third, a haven can legislate more opportunistically when the class of persons or businesses affected by the legislation exists only outside the haven country. If members of the class also exist inside the country, they will object to the legislation. The haven can exempt its own citizens from the operation of any law, and havens sometimes do so. But that spoils the appearance of neutrality, reducing the chances that other countries will recognize and give effect to the haven's law. Finally, in any large country, many citizens will be vulnerable to foreign pressures. The victims of a haven will bring pressure against those citizens to force their haven government to end the haven activity. In a small country devoted largely to haven activity, citizens vulnerable to foreign pressures are less likely to exist.

Delaware is naturally suited to being a haven. In 1990, Delaware had a population of only 660,000, ranking it forty-sixth among the fifty states. The large bulk of that population is concentrated in Wilmington, a tight-knit community capable of acting relatively in unison. Even more important, Delaware has a great, ironclad contract—the U.S. Constitution—that grants Delaware the right to exploit the other 49 states. That is, the Constitution requires other states to give "full faith and credit" to the "public acts, records, and judicial proceedings" of Delaware.[1] What Delaware does or decides, the other states are constitutionally obligated to honor. To prevent the other states from protecting themselves from Delaware by federal legislation, Delaware has two members in the United States Senate. (This is the same number as California, which has 45 times Delaware's population.) Finally, Delaware is conveniently located between the United States' financial capital (New York) and its political capital (Washington). Wilmington is easily accessi-

ble from both by Amtrak and from the rest of the United States
through the Philadelphia airport. People can do business in
Delaware without having to stay.

As described in the prologue, Delaware got its start as a haven
over a century ago, in the business of incorporation. Some 60 percent to 80 percent of all large public companies incorporated in the
United States are incorporated in Delaware. "Incorporation" is, of
course, a mere legal fiction. To incorporate in Delaware, the company need have no employees, assets, offices, or operation there.
All a company need do to gain the benefits of Delaware incorporation is to send documents and money to Delaware's public officials.
The main benefit of Delaware incorporation is freedom from
restriction by the corporate laws of other states and countries. The
"internal affairs" of a corporation are governed by the law of the
state or country of incorporation. For a Delaware corporation,
that means Delaware law, regardless of where in the world the corporation actually does business.

Incorporation havens such as Delaware, Bermuda, or the
Netherlands Antilles constantly compete for the incorporation
business. Like other competing businesses, they must be sensitive
to the interests and preferences of their clients. Delaware's clients
are the people who decide where large public companies incorporate. Those clients include corporate promoters, managers, and
corporate lawyers. The haven designs its laws to favor them. The
principal benefit to a haven that sells corporate charters is the filing
fees and franchise taxes the corporations pay. In 2004, Delaware's
filing fees and franchise taxes totaled $653 million, about 27 per-
cent of the state's budget.[2]

Delaware is also in the usury-facilitation business. That is,
Delaware provides a haven for credit card issuers, who charge residents of other states interest rates prohibited by the laws of those
other states. In 1978, the United States Supreme Court ruled that a
national bank located in Nebraska could issue credit cards in Minnesota and charge the Minnesota residents the rate of interest per-
missible under Nebraska law even though Minnesota law prohibited that rate as usurious.[3] Two years later, Congress "leveled the

playing field" by authorizing state-chartered banks to do the same thing.[4] As a result, banks need only comply with the usury laws of their own states, even while lending money to the citizens of other states.

Citibank, the nation's largest credit card issuer, immediately searched out the state that permitted banks to charge the highest rate of interest. That state was South Dakota, and the interest rate allowed was 24 percent. When Citibank contacted South Dakota officials about the possibility of "moving" to South Dakota, the state was bowled over by the prospect of the hundreds of jobs it would bring.[5] South Dakota dropped its usury law entirely so that Citibank could charge residents of other states as much as Citibank wanted.[6] Of course, Citibank didn't move its entire operations to South Dakota, just its credit card billing operations.

Seeing South Dakota's success, Delaware decided to compete for the business. Although Delaware was not the first to enter the business, Delaware succeeded by doing it better. (This statement is true of virtually every haven business Delaware has undertaken.) Delaware not only repealed its usury law, it invited Chase Manhattan Bank and J. P. Morgan & Company to participate in drafting what became Delaware's Financial Center Development Act of 1981 (the "FCDA")—a law designed to induce credit card issuers to set up in the state.[7] The law was not ideologically pro-competition; it prohibited the credit card issuers from conducting a general banking business in Delaware in order to protect Delaware's indigenous banks.[8] Instead, the law was exactly what its title suggested: a law to bring business to Delaware. If banks did their credit card billing from Delaware, those banks became employers of Delaware citizens; tenants of Delaware landlords; customers of Delaware businesses; and, not incidentally, Delaware taxpayers. This was fundamentally the same thing that Alabama was doing when it attracted factories but without the smokestacks.

Delaware's FCDA was wildly successful. Eighteen money center and regional banks from New York, Pennsylvania, Maryland, Georgia, North Carolina, and Virginia established Delaware bank subsidiaries.[9] Included among them was MBNA, which by 2002 had become Delaware's largest private employer.[10] In 2004, Delaware's Bank Franchise Tax was expected to bring in 6 percent of the state's revenues.[11]

Asset protection trusts are another haven business now under cultivation in Delaware. Since the early 1980s, thousands of Americans have put trillions of dollars in offshore "asset protection" trusts in traditional havens such as the Cayman Islands, Bermuda, the Jersey Islands, and the Cook Islands. The principal purpose and function of these trusts are to enable clients to beat their home country creditors. The typical client is a medical doctor in the United States who has decided to cancel his or her malpractice insurance and instead put assets where malpractice judgment creditors can't get at them. U.S. courts invalidated such trusts at every opportunity,[12] but for reasons beyond the scope of this book, the trusts were nevertheless largely effective in defeating the rights of U.S. judgment creditors.[13] The offshore asset protection trust industry flourished.

In 1997, Alaska adopted a law validating asset protection trusts established in that state.[14] Advocates of the law argued that the offshore trusts were big business and were going to happen anyway, so why shouldn't Alaska get part of the benefit? Just a few months later, Delaware followed with an asset protection trust law of its own.[15] In the first five years, investors set up 100 Delaware asset protection trusts with more than $2 billion in assets.[16] The direct benefit to Delaware from the existence of those trusts is probably small, but asset protection trusts are only one of many haven businesses in which Delaware is engaged.

Seeking to build on its success in attracting incorporations, Delaware has recently engaged in efforts to sell corporations on the idea of litigating in Delaware. Among those efforts was the mailing of a glossy brochure touting a survey commissioned by the United States Chamber of Commerce.[17] In that survey, in-house lawyers for large public companies ranked the Delaware state courts first in the nation on each of ten criteria. The survey shows corporations clearly satisfied with their treatment in the Delaware courts. The survey's criteria included "punitive damages" and "timeliness of summary judgment/dismissal"—two issues dear to the virtual hearts of American corporations.

By 1990, Delaware was already well established in the business of selling law, legal status, and litigation to the rest of the United States. Delaware's expansion into the bankruptcy reorganization of large public companies was a logical next step. Delaware already had the confidence of the large public companies that were filing for bankruptcy. Seventy-three percent of the large public companies that have filed bankruptcy in the United States since 1992 were incorporated in Delaware.[18]

Later, when Delaware succeeded in winning the corporations' bankruptcy reorganization business, lawyers and judges in the rest of the country complained that the Delaware bankruptcy court was taking "their" cases. Delaware's preexisting relationship with the corporations provided crucial political cover. Delaware's defenders argued that the companies were not located at their headquarters or their centers of operations—Montgomery Ward in Chicago; Trans World Airways, Inc., and Purina Mills, Inc., in St. Louis; Birmingham Steel Corporation in Alabama; and Polaroid Corporation in Massachusetts. Each of these corporations, the defenders asserted, was located in Delaware because each was a Delaware corporation. That is, each came into existence as the result of an official act of the state of Delaware—the grant of the corporation's charter.

The defenders could also plausibly argue that Congress had authorized Delaware corporations to file their bankruptcies in Delaware. The bankruptcy venue statute provides that "a [bankruptcy] case . . . may be commenced in . . . the district in which the domicile, residence, principal place of business . . . or principal assets . . . of the person or entity [are] located."[19] By 1990, lower courts and commentators had split on whether the state of incorporation was the "domicile or residence" of a corporation,[20] and no appellate court had addressed the matter at all.[21]

In the 1980s, Helen Balick was Delaware's only bankruptcy judge. In two cases decided in 1988, *Ocean Properties*[22] and *Delaware & H.R. Co.*,[23] she held that any corporation incorporated in Delaware was eligible to file for bankruptcy there. Whether Judge Balick was right on the law really didn't matter. What mattered was what she would do when Delaware corporations filed bankruptcy in Delaware. If Judge Balick took the cases, there was nothing the debtors' home courts could do about it, and no appeals court would be likely to interfere. Consistent with that reality, Judge Balick merely stated her opinion and made no attempt to justify it. In *Ocean Properties,* for example, she merely said that "[s]ince the Debtors are Delaware corporations, venue in this District is proper . . . ." With her firm declarations that Delaware corporations were entitled to file for bankruptcy in Delaware, Judge Balick had put out the welcome mat.

Continental Airlines

Continental Airlines' second bankruptcy case, filed in 1990, was Delaware's big break. With assets of $5 billion, Continental was nearly twenty times the size of any company that had previously filed for bankruptcy in Delaware. If Delaware could succeed with Continental, more cases would follow.

Judge Balick recognized the opportunity and seized it. First, she took extraordinary measures to prevent the Houston bankruptcy court from taking the Continental case from her. Once the case was firmly in her grasp, she showered the debtor with every imaginable benefit. By the time Judge Balick confirmed Continental's plan in April 1993, she and Delaware were major players in the world of big-case bankruptcy. If any doubts remained that Judge Balick was seeking to attract large public company bankruptcies to Delaware, the Continental Airlines case should have put them to rest.

Continental's story begins in 1981, when Frank Lorenzo took control of the company through his Texas Air Corporation. Continental was then a union airline, paying "high-tier" wages and competing against "low-tier"-wage, nonunion airlines such as Southwest. Continental was already in serious financial difficulty when Lorenzo bought it. Lorenzo set out to solve Continental's financial problems by cutting labor costs. After two years of wrangling, the powerful Machinists' Union struck. Six weeks later, in September 1983, Lorenzo put Continental into bankruptcy in Houston. He repudiated all of Continental's labor agreements, shut the airline down, locked the union pilots out, and began assembling a nonunion labor force.

The unions fought bitterly, but the Houston bankruptcy court sided with Continental on virtually every important issue. Shielded from its creditors, Continental resumed operations with a new, nonunion workforce and logged three straight years of profits before emerging from bankruptcy in 1986.

Flush from that success, Lorenzo tried it again. He bought Eastern Airlines, another high-tier-wage airline in financial difficulty. In 1989, Lorenzo put Eastern into bankruptcy in New York. This time the case went miserably, dissipating $3.5 billion in assets and ultimately ending in almost complete piecemeal liquidation. The Eastern case become a symbol of all that critics thought was wrong with big-case bankruptcy reorganization. The principal charge was that indulgent judges—Judge Burton R. Lifland in the Eastern case—gave failed debtors too much leeway to continue operations.[24]

From the beginning of the case, Eastern's unions pressed for the appointment of a trustee. Lifland was reluctant. But in April 1990, after the examiner reported that Lorenzo's Texas Air had taken $285 to $403 million of Eastern's assets and the creditors' committee joined the unions in requesting a trustee, Lifland relented.[25] He ordered the appointment of a trustee and then added insult to injury by naming Martin Shugrue—an airline executive that Lorenzo had fired just over a year earlier—to the post. That put Shugrue fully in control of the airline for the duration of the bankruptcy case. Even if Eastern survived, Lorenzo would never regain control. Frank Lorenzo had trusted his airline to the New York bankruptcy court, and the court had taken it from him. For that breach of trust, the New York bankruptcy court would pay dearly.

In the meantime, Continental was back in financial difficulty. Lorenzo bailed out by selling his interest in Continental to SAS

(Scandinavian Airlines System). Just four months later, in December 1990, Continental had to decide where to file its second bankruptcy case. To Continental's management, the usual courts seemed unappealing. Continental's first bankruptcy was still pending before Judge R. F. Wheless in Houston. In the early years of that case Judge Wheless had treated Continental well, ruling in Continental's favor on nearly every matter of importance. After confirmation, however, the relationship had soured. The low point was probably when Judge Wheless referred to Continental—on the record—as "Attila the Hun." What caused the souring, one lawyer told me, was that Wheless started getting the personal bankruptcy cases of Continental's former pilots. Continental wouldn't let them go back to work. Continental didn't want to do a second bankruptcy in front of Wheless.

The court in Denver, Colorado, a Continental hub, had just come down hard against lawyer conflicts of interest in the Amdura case.[26] The New York court already had the case of Continental's affiliate, Eastern Airlines, and the case was going spectacularly badly. If Continental filed in New York the odds were high the case would be assigned to Judge Lifland to be administered along with Eastern. Judge Lifland ordinarily was a pro-debtor, pro-reorganization judge. But Judge Lifland had appointed a trustee in the Eastern case, and Continental's executives may have feared the New York court would do the same to them. In addition, Eastern and Continental were fighting over the System One reservation system, and Lifland's examiner in the Eastern case had already taken Eastern's side in the dispute.[27] Continental needed someone who would fight Lifland's examiner.

Continental initially hired a prominent New York bankruptcy firm to handle the case. Despite the problems with New York as a venue, that firm prepared the papers for filing there. But at the last minute, Continental switched law firms and itself came up with the idea of filing in Delaware.

The big issue was whether Continental could break free of the Houston bankruptcy court. Continental had strong ties to Houston; the company had been headquartered there for more than a decade and had had a hub there for even longer. Continental's only tie to Delaware was incorporation there. Continental didn't even fly to Delaware.

The Houston court had confirmed Continental's plan in 1986, so the bulk of Continental's first case was over. But Judge Wheless had retained jurisdiction and was still hearing a number of post-confirmation matters. Technically, at the time Continental filed in Delaware it was already in bankruptcy in Houston. And the fact that Houston was Continental's home court made matters worse.

The Bankruptcy Rules, applicable to all bankruptcy courts nationwide, were clear. "If petitions commencing cases under the [Bankruptcy] Code are filed in different districts by . . . the same debtor . . on motion filed in the district in which the petition filed first is pending . . . the court may determine . . . the district . . . in which the case or cases should proceed."[28] In other words, even if Continental was entitled to file a second case in Delaware while the first remained pending in Houston, Judge Wheless still had the power to determine where that second case would be heard. Continental filed in Delaware anyway, hoping that nobody would object.

Somebody did. Continental owed American General, a Texas insurance company, about $40 million. Since 1985, Continental and American General had been engaged in bitter litigation over the terms of the loan. When Continental filed in Delaware, American General hired Houston bankruptcy lawyer Hugh Ray. On December 18, 1990—15 days after Continental filed in Delaware—Ray filed a request with the Houston bankruptcy court to transfer the Delaware filing to Houston.

On the following day, December 19, Continental filed its own request with the Delaware bankruptcy court. Continental asked Judge Balick to enjoin Ray from proceeding with his request in Houston. Courts rarely grant such a request. If the Delaware court could enjoin lawyers from proceeding in the Houston court, the Houston court could enjoin lawyers from proceeding in the Delaware court. Such bullying had little potential for solving a venue problem. It had lots of potential for making matters worse by stripping both courts of lawyers.

Judge Balick not only granted Continental's request, she did it at lightning speed. She began a hearing on the request at 9:00 the morning the request was filed and issued her injunction before night fell. The injunction read in part as follows.

> [I]t sufficiently appearing by plaintiffs' Verified Complaint, brief and otherwise that defendants have applied to another bankruptcy court, seeking an order of that court to transfer the venue of these cases or to dismiss them, in circumstances where that court lacks jurisdiction to do so, and that such proceedings thus constitute an unwarranted attempt to interfere with the statutory exclusive jurisdiction of this Court over these debtors and these proceedings . . . .
>
> IT IS ORDERED:
>
> 1. Defendants [American General] and their respective officers, directors, agents and attorneys . . . are hereby temporarily restrained from taking, initiating or participating in any of the following actions without first obtaining . . . the prior approval of this court.
>
> (a) . . . [T]aking any steps whatsoever in support of . . . American General's . . . pending application . . . to request . . . the . . Houston Bankruptcy Court . . . to transfer the venue of [Continental's Delaware case] to that Court . . .[29]

Judge Balick directed that a copy of her order be delivered to Judge Wheless the following day.

At first, Judge Wheless was merely amused. At the hearing on Ray's motion, Judge Wheless laughed and said to Ray: "I understand you can't even talk." New York lawyer Robert Rosenberg, who represented the creditors' committee and wanted the Continental case to remain in Delaware, assured the court: "[H]e has been enjoined." At one point in the hearing, Judge Wheless asked if Judge Balick was also going to take over the claims disputes that still remained pending from the first Continental case. To Ray, it sounded like Wheless would be happy to be rid of them.

Seeing little hope that Judge Wheless was going to fight for the Continental case, Ray settled. The deal was complicated. American General agreed that Continental's second bankruptcy would stay in Delaware. In return, Continental would join with American

General in obtaining a quick determination of American General's $40 million case in the Delaware Chancery court. Judge Balick would have no role in deciding the amount of American General's judgment.

Part of the deal was that Continental and American General would join in requesting an unusual order from Judge Wheless. The order would recite that the Houston court did have jurisdiction over Continental's second case and had determined "in the interests of justice and for the convenience of the parties" that the case should stay in Delaware.[30] By claiming the case and transferring it instead of merely denying American General's request for transfer, Judge Wheless would have given Judge Balick greater control. The transfer would have given Judge Balick the right to decide any requests for a change of venue that other creditors might make in the future; a mere denial would have left that control with Judge Wheless.

The deal specified that Judge Wheless's order would be served only on the creditor's committee—who didn't want to move the case—and not on the thousands of Continental Airlines creditors who might want to move it and would be precluded from doing so by the order. Unless they read about it in the newspaper, those thousands of creditors would not even know they had been foreclosed.

On January 9, 1991, Hugh Ray and Paul Welsh, a Delaware lawyer representing Continental Airlines, met with Judge Wheless to obtain his signature. Judge Wheless hit the ceiling. In a letter to Judge Balick dated the same day, Wheless expressed his anger at being asked to sign the order "under these circumstances." Judge Wheless wrote that he "did not feel it appropriate for me to make [the Delaware venue] determination when *I* was not in fact making *any* determination one way or another and I did not wish to cut off the right, if any, of any other party to move to transfer the case" (emphasis in original). Judge Wheless said in the letter that he "declined to sign the order," suggesting instead that American General simply withdraw its request to transfer the Delaware case to Houston.[31] Continental waived the signing of the Houston order and concluded the American General settlement without it.

American General was out of the venue fight, but the fight wasn't over. On January 18, 1991, nine days after Judge Wheless refused to sign the American General order, the O'Neill Group of Continental Airlines pilots filed its own request with the Houston court to transfer the Delaware case to Houston.[32] The hearing on that request was set for Monday, March 18, 1991. Continental responded essentially the same way they had with American General.

On March 13, with only five days remaining before the scheduled venue hearing in Houston, Continental's lawyers called Randolph J. Haines, the O'Neill Group's Phoenix, Arizona, attorney. The lawyers told Haines they were asking Judge Balick to enjoin Haines from proceeding with the Houston hearing and that the hearing on their request would be held the following day, March 14—in Delaware.

In 1991, only a few Delaware lawyers did bankruptcy work, and all had roles in the Continental case already. Haines could not find a Delaware lawyer to represent him before Judge Balick. He asked Continental's lawyers to request that Judge Balick allow him to participate in the Delaware hearing by telephone. The following day, Continental's lawyers called back to tell Haines that Judge Balick had issued the injunction. As to Haines's request to participate in the hearing by telephone, Continental's lawyers explained that they had passed the request along to Judge Balick. She had denied it. Her reasoning was that local rules in Delaware prohibited out-of-state lawyers from participating in Delaware cases without retaining local Delaware counsel. It was a complete Catch-22.

As Ray had done before him, Haines immediately appealed Judge Balick's injunction to the Delaware district court. This time, however, all of the Delaware district court judges had conflicts that prevented them from hearing it. The appeal was assigned to a Philadelphia district court judge. The following day, Friday, March 15, the Philadelphia judge heard the appeal by telephone. He indicated that he would rule before the Houston hearing scheduled for Monday morning.

Haines was now just two steps—and perhaps only two days—from moving the Continental case to Houston. If the Philadelphia judge vacated the injunction over the weekend, "Attila the Hun's" fate would be in Judge Wheless's hands on Monday morning. On Saturday, Continental called Haines with a settlement offer worth more than $22 million.[33] The parties settled litigation that had been pending for six years and finalized the settlement before the Monday hearing. Haines withdrew his request for a change of venue, and the Continental case stayed in Delaware. Judge Balick had won the fight for the Continental case.

A year after Judge Balick successfully enjoined proceedings in Judge Wheless's court, she tried the same thing against Judge Frank Easterbrook, a Seventh Circuit Court of Appeals judge then sitting as a district judge. This time, Judge Balick met her match. The Kendall Company was one of several defendants in patent litigation pending before Judge Easterbrook in early 1992. If a defendant in such litigation files bankruptcy—as Kendall did on May 20, 1992—the litigation can't proceed against that defendant until the issues between the two courts are sorted out. If insufficient time remains to sort them out before the litigation comes to trial, the plaintiffs often dismiss the bankrupt defendant from the litigation and continue against the other defendants. The bankrupt defendant escapes liability, even if it was in sufficiently good financial condition to pay.

As a strategy, companies that are defendants in multiparty litigation may time the filing of their bankruptcy case to gain such a dismissal. That is apparently what Kendall was trying to do. But instead of dismissing Kendall from the patent case, Judge Easterbrook set a hearing to determine whether he could require Kendall to go to trial. Repeating essentially what she had done in Continental Airlines, Judge Balick enjoined the lawyers from participating in Judge Easterbrook's hearing.

On May 28, 1992, the day after Judge Balick issued her injunction, Judge Easterbrook responded with an eleven-page opinion, in which he referred to Judge Balick's injunction as "preposterous," "unfathomable," and "rogue."[34] He issued an injunction of his own. Judge Easterbrook's injunction prohibited Kendall Company and "all acting in concert with them" from attempting to enforce

Judge Balick's order, ordered Kendall's lawyers to withdraw their request for the injunction Judge Balick had already granted, and ordered the lawyers Judge Balick had ordered *not* to appear before him to appear before him.[35] Put to a choice, the lawyers violated Judge Balick's order to comply with Judge Easterbrook's.

With the Continental case firmly in hand, Judge Balick used it to gain national visibility as a pro-debtor, pro-reorganization judge. She tried four major matters and ruled in Continental's favor on all four. First on Judge Balick's chopping block were the lessors who owned 104 of Continental's aircraft. By law, aircraft lessors are virtually exempt from the effects of a bankruptcy reorganization. Unless the airline brings its payments to lessors current within 60 days of the bankruptcy case filing and agrees to continue making them, the lessors are entitled to repossess the aircraft.[36]

The applicable statute simply says "lessor."[37] Desperate for a way around the law, the lawyers who represented bankrupt airlines had come up with an argument. Congress, they claimed, had intended the law to apply only to "acquisition" lessors, not "sale and leaseback" lessors. The argument was rejected in 1990 by a Florida bankruptcy court in the Braniff Airlines bankruptcy;[38] by the bankruptcy, district, and appeals courts in the Pan Am bankruptcy;[39] and by the district and appeals courts in Continental Airlines.[40] Judge Balick accepted the argument in the Continental Airlines case—apparently the only time any judge ever did. That was the first of the four major matters she tried in Continental. Her decision was reversed by the Third Circuit Court of Appeals in May 1991.[41] But by that time, Continental had settled with most of the lessors on terms that deferred its payments until September 1991.[42] Because Continental still had another issue it could raise even after the appeal—that its "leases" were actually mortgages in disguise—Continental was able to continue settling with aircraft lessors even after it lost the appeal.

Next on Judge Balick's chopping block were a group of bondholders secured by aircraft and equipment. The Bankruptcy Code entitled them, as secured creditors, to "adequate protection" against decline in the value of their collateral during the bankruptcy case.[43] Ordinarily, bankrupts provide adequate protection to secured creditors by making cash payments in amounts equal to the depreciation in collateral value. Continental made intensive use of that collateral over the two and half years of the case. By the end, the secured creditors calculated the decline in value of collateral at $117 million, and Continental calculated it as at least $22 million.[44]

By a series of procedural maneuvers Judge Balick sent the secured creditors home with nothing at all. Two and a half months into the case, the secured creditors filed a request for adequate protection. Ordinarily, a bankruptcy court will rule on such a request within 30 to 60 days. Judge Balick held the hearing—the second of the four major matters—six months after the request.[45] Then she delayed her ruling for almost an additional year. On August 27, 1992, Judge Balick ruled that (1) the secured creditors had properly raised the issue of adequate protection by directly requesting it— they did not have to request a lifting of the automatic stay (the automatic stay is an injunction against any action to collect a debt from a bankrupt which automatically comes into existence on the filing of every bankruptcy case); (2) however, the collateral had not declined in value by July 1, 1991, the last date covered by the evidence presented at the hearing, so no adequate protection payments were yet due. The secured creditors responded by requesting adequate protection for the period after July 1, 1991 and, in an abundance of caution, they also requested a lifting of the automatic stay. Judge Balick did not rule on these two motions until the day she confirmed Continental's plan of reorganization, April 16, 1993.[46] On this third major matter, she ruled that (1) any decline in collateral value that occurred during the two and a half years of the case had occurred between July 1, 1991, and August 27, 1992— before the secured creditors' motion to lift the automatic stay; (2) secured creditors could recover only for decline in collateral value that occurs after they requested a lifting of the automatic stay; and (3) because the decline in this case occurred before the secured creditors' request for a lifting of the automatic stay, they were entitled to nothing. The second point of this ruling was, of course, directly contrary to what Judge Balick had ruled on August 27, 1992.[47]

Judge Balick included her ruling on the secured creditors' requests as part of her order confirming Continental's plan—the fourth major matter she heard in Continental. The effect of the inclusion was to make it virtually impossible for the secured creditors to appeal the ruling. The secured creditors tried anyway. In refusing to hear their appeal the district court commented that the secured creditors would probably have won on the merits.[48] But the court refused to reach the merits because the order denying adequate protection was part of the unappealable confirmation order. The bottom line was that Continental got the use of about $350 million worth of aircraft for two and a half years, without having to pay a dime.

To top matters off, Judge Balick had one more go at the dueling injunctions game. Recall that Continental had declined to file in New York in part because the New York court's examiner had already taken Eastern's side in the fight between Eastern and Continental over System One. To resolve that dispute, Eastern filed an adversary proceeding before Judge Lifland in New York. Continental filed the same case before Judge Balick in Delaware. Eastern's lawyers filed an emergency motion with Judge Lifland at 9 A.M., seeking an order temporarily restraining Continental from proceeding before Judge Balick (a "TRO"). The hearing was set for noon. As one of the lawyers for Eastern described the battle:

> At Judge Lifland's request, Eastern gave facsimile notice of the hearing to [Continental's] lawyers. In [the] three hours [between the notice and the hearing], Continental sprinted to Judge Balick and got her to enter an ex parte TRO precluding Eastern from going forward on its TRO motion. It was signed 11:50 a.m.
>
> We go forward at 12 p.m. [Their lawyers] argued we were in violation of Balick's TRO. Judge Lifland was not very happy. He accused everybody of gamesmanship. He strongly suggested the TRO entered by Balick be voluntarily dissolved. He entered a

mediation order. They negotiated a voluntary dismissal of the TRO in Delaware but continue to keep an advantage over us. If the mediation broke down, the case would be in front of Balick before Lifland.[49]

Balick had faced Lifland down and given her side—Continental—the advantage in negotiations. Helen Balick was looking like the toughest, most pro-debtor bankruptcy judge in America.

Playing Delaware

The bankruptcies of 41 large public companies were filed in Delaware from 1991 through 1996. New York bankruptcy lawyers filed the large majority of those cases. The same New York lawyers continued to file cases in New York and in the jurisdictions where the debtors were headquartered. It was as if the New York lawyers were playing a piano and the courts were the keys. If they wanted a particular decision, they chose the court that would give it to them.

The cases filed in Delaware in 1990 and 1991 fit no simple pattern. The first case—a month before Continental Airlines—was United Merchants and Manufacturers. The *Deal* reported that United Merchants chose Delaware "because it was concerned about how its bonds would be treated in the Southern District of New York."[50] In January 1990, New York bankruptcy judge Burton Lifland made a ruling in the LTV bankruptcy that limited the claims of bondholders who had exchanged their bonds for new ones in anticipation of bankruptcy.[51] The bondholders in LTV had made the exchange and the bankruptcy had been filed in New York, so they were stuck. The only thing the LTV bondholders could do was to appeal. But future bondholders who wanted to make such exchanges probably could avoid the problem simply by avoiding the New York bankruptcy court. All it took was a deal between the bondholders and the debtors that the debtors would file in some other court. United Merchants and Manufacturers apparently made such a deal with its bondholders.

United Merchants was represented by New York bankruptcy

lawyer Michael Cook. Cook filed the case in Delaware. In June 1990, the *New York Law Journal* identified four other exchange offers "known or rumored to be in trouble" as a result of the LTV decision: Interco, Inc.; Southland Corporation; Western Union Corporation; and West Point–Pepperell, Inc.[52] None of the four risked filing in New York while the LTV decision remained standing. Interco filed in St. Louis, and Southland filed in Dallas. Western Union and West Point–Pepperell filed in New York but only after Judge Lifland's decision was overturned on appeal by the Second Circuit in April 1992.[53]

Ironically, it was creditors who filed the third big case in Delaware. The bondholders who filed the involuntary petition against Harvard Industries did so before Judge Balick went on her pro-debtor rampage in Continental. After Harvard, creditors would not file another case in Delaware until 2000.

The fourth big case, giant Columbia Gas, was odd in two respects. First, the company was actually based in Delaware, making Delaware a natural venue. Second, Columbia Gas was one of the longest cases of the decade, taking more than four years from filing to confirmation. (Only seven of the 449 large public company bankruptcy cases filed and concluded after 1989 [1.5 percent] remained pending for longer periods.) Judge Balick's handling of the case demonstrated that the Delaware court's true commitment was to the service of case placers rather than speed. The debtor in Columbia Gas requested and received nine extensions of its exclusive right to file a plan of reorganization.[54] Some of those extensions were hotly contested. Nevertheless, the case ended only when the debtor was ready to bring it to a close. At the same time, the Delaware court was making its reputation for speed in other cases. The difference, of course, was that in those other cases, the case placers *wanted* speed.

Delaware's fifth filer was Days Inns of America, Inc. Days Inns was among the first large public companies to file under Chapter 11 with the intent to sell its entire business in a section 363 sale. By indicating its amenability to this kind of sale, the Delaware court opened an entirely new market for its services.[55]

With four big cases in 1991, Delaware was already one of the leading big-case bankruptcy courts in the nation. New York was the leader, with eight cases that year. Delaware was tied with Los Angeles for second place. Delaware had not yet, however, had its first prepackaged case.

Prepacks

To the extent that Delaware's early success was based on any particular kind of case, it was on prepackaged bankruptcies—"prepacks" for short. A nonprepackaged bankruptcy begins with the filing of the case. During the case, the debtor makes full financial disclosure to the creditors and then files a plan for restructuring its debt. The creditors vote on the plan. Then the court decides whether to confirm the plan. If it does, the case is over. If the court does not confirm the plan, the debtor can try again with a different plan. The entire process occurs under court supervision. As doubts about the proper procedure arise along the way, the court resolves them.

The same basic steps occur in a prepack but in a different order. The debtor begins by sending a proposed restructuring plan and disclosure statement to creditors, along with a ballot for voting on the plan. As creditors vote in favor of the plan, they are also agreeing to be bound by it. No court action is necessary to bind those creditors. If creditors holding more than a specified proportion of the debt—usually 90 percent or 95 percent—accept the plan, no bankruptcy filing is necessary. The debtor can pay the accepting creditors in accord with the plan and, because the dissenting creditors hold only a small portion of the debt, can pay the dissenters in full.

If, as is more likely, the acceptance rate is lower than the 90 percent to 95 percent necessary to implement the plan without court action, but is at least half in number and two-thirds in dollar amount, the debtor files a bankruptcy case. Along with the petition, the debtor files the plan, the disclosure statement, and the ballots. The case is referred to as "prepackaged" because these key documents are delivered to the court all at the same time.

Provided that the disclosure statement was adequate, that the plan is in compliance with the requirements of the Bankruptcy Code, and that the balloting was properly conducted, the bankruptcy court can confirm the plan on the basis of prefiling vote. Confirmation makes the plan binding on all creditors, including those who voted against it. This power to bind creditors who voted no or didn't vote at all is what distinguishes a prepackaged bankruptcy from an out-of-court settlement. Out of court, the dissenting creditors would be paid in full; in a prepack they are paid whatever the majority chose to accept. From filing to confirmation, the prepackaged case may take as little as about 30 days.

From the debtor's perspective, prepacks have at least three advantages. First, by conducting the vote before filing, the debtor might discover that a sufficient number of its creditors will agree to the plan that the debtor need not file bankruptcy at all. Second, if the debtor does have to file bankruptcy, the case—and the accompanying embarrassment—will be brief. Third, in a prepack, the debtor has more control over the plan negotiation and approval process. No case has been filed, so there is no court to interfere. In addition, some think that professional fees and other expenses of administration are lower in prepacks because the crucial stages of the process occur "out of court." That, however, remains to be proven.

The disadvantage of a prepack from the debtor's perspective is that the court is not available to guide the parties in drafting their plan and disclosure statement and conducting the voting. If the court later finds the procedure or disclosure inadequate, the parties must repeat the entire disclosure and voting process.[56] If that occurs, alliances may fall apart, costs may increase by millions of dollars, short-term investors who bet on quick confirmation may suffer losses, and the viability of the company may be threatened. In the minds of the debtors' executives and lawyers, starting over is not really an option.

Because the judge comes into the prepackaged case only after the plan and disclosure statement have been distributed and the vote on the plan has been taken, the judge has only two choices.

The judge can approve what has been done or make the parties start over. Faced with such a drastic alternative, judges tend to be less demanding regarding disclosure and the conduct of voting in prepackaged cases.

To draft documents for what might become a prepackaged case, bankruptcy lawyers want to know the judge's standards for approval and satisfy them. In a court with four or five judges applying different standards, however, that might mean knowing all the judges' standards and satisfying the most stringent as to each issue. By comparison, the one-judge court in Delaware had tremendous appeal. To draft for Delaware, the lawyers had only to know and comply with Judge Balick's standards.

Contrary to popular belief, Delaware neither invented nor pioneered the use of prepacks. The Bankruptcy Code Congress enacted in 1978 specifically authorized the filing of prepackaged cases. No large public company made use of the procedure until the junk bond defaults of the late 1980s. Crystal Oil filed the first large public company prepack in Shreveport, Louisiana, in 1986. Four other large public companies filed prepacks—in Dallas (Southland Corporation), New York (JPS Textile Group), Camden (Trump Taj Mahal Funding), and Cleveland (Edgell Communications)—before Delaware got its first (Memorex Telex) in January 1992.

Memorex Telex's Delaware reorganization was a disaster. A month after confirmation, it was apparent that the reorganization had failed. In less than two years, Memorex was back in bankruptcy. What the market noticed about the Memorex case, however, was not the reorganization's failure but the speed and ease with which Judge Balick had confirmed the plan—a near-record time of 32 days from filing. (The record for a big prepack is 31 days, set just a month before Memorex by the Cleveland bankruptcy court in the Edgell Communications case; the median time for big prepacks is 44 days.)

Theoretically, the bankruptcy court in a prepackaged case tests the plan and disclosure statement by the same standards as in a non-prepackaged case. Upon the filing of a case, the United States trustee appoints a creditors' committee.[57] The committee retains attorneys, accountants, and/or financial advisers.[58] Those advisers assist the committee in determining whether the disclosure was adequate, the voting procedure was fair, and the plan complies with Bankruptcy Code requirements including a requirement that "confirmation of the plan is not likely to be followed by the liquidation, or the need for further financial reorganization, of the debtor."[59]

In reality, the procedure required by law cannot be condensed to 30 days, and the Delaware court was making no serious attempt to do that. (Chapter 6 elaborates on this abandonment of required procedure, which occurred both in Delaware and in other competing courts.) What the court was doing was relying on the professionals. If the debtor's professionals delivered a plan, a disclosure statement, and a set of ballots and no one objected, the court simply assumed that the procedure had been adequate and the plan was sound. After all, the professionals were among the most respected law and investment banking firms in the world. The plans were negotiated between representatives of the debtor and its creditors. How could anything be wrong?

By refusing to look behind "the agreement of the parties," the Delaware court became essentially a rubber stamp for prepacks. From the professionals' perspective, a rubber stamp was ideal; the parties who put the plan together got precisely what they wanted. From the court's perspective, wielding a rubber stamp took a lot less time and effort than examining cases on the merits. And because rubber stamping was attractive to the professionals, it brought more cases to the Delaware court.

At the time, other courts were still judging the merits of prepackaged cases and sometimes forcing renegotiations. In late 1990, Dallas bankruptcy judge Harold Abramson refused to confirm Southland Corporation's prepackaged plan because the vote had not been fairly conducted. (Among other things, the creditors had been given only eight business days to read the 300-page disclosure statement and vote on the plan.)[60] Judge Abramson ordered a new vote. Before the ballots went out, Southland settled with the objectors. Once the objections had been withdrawn, creditors approved the modified plan, and the court confirmed it 120 days after the filing of the case. Although the delay had been brief, the renegotiation had been risky for the company and costly for the shareholders and major bondholders who had put the plan together and chosen the court.[61] The professionals blacklisted the Dallas bankruptcy court, and that court is still waiting for its second large public company prepack.

Since 1993, Delaware has completely dominated the competition for prepacks, getting 27 of the 35 cases filed (77 percent). If the case was prepackaged, Delaware was the place to go. As table 3 shows, not only did Delaware dominate prepacks, by number of cases, prepacks provided 39 percent of Delaware's caseload from 1993 through the end of 1996.

Another Judge for Delaware

From 1989 to 1992, the annual number of big-case bankruptcy filings in Delaware had increased from zero to six. Delaware's six filings in 1992 surpassed New York's five, making Delaware the nation's leading big-case bankruptcy court. Based on Delaware's increased caseload, Congress awarded Delaware a second bankruptcy judge. The Third Circuit Court of Appeals selected Wilmington bankruptcy lawyer Peter J. Walsh for the job. He took office in February 1993.

From Delaware's point of view, the bankruptcy court got its second judge just in time. Even a short time later, case filing levels might no longer have warranted the second judge. Nationally and

TABLE 3.   Distribution of Cases by Type Filed, 1993–96

	Delaware	Other Courts	Total
Prepackaged	12 (39%)	8 (20%)	20 (28%)
Not prepackaged	19 (61%)	33 (80%)	52 (72%)
Total	31 (100%)	41 (100%)	72 (100%)

Source: Data from Lynn M. LoPucki's Bankruptcy Research Database.

in Delaware, the numbers of big reorganization cases were declining. New filings peaked at 39 in 1991 and fell to 32 in 1992, 26 in 1993, and only 11 in 1994. Delaware's share of those cases increased from 10 percent in 1991 to 36 percent in 1994, but Delaware's number of new cases declined from six in 1992 to five in 1993 and four in 1994. The cases filed in Delaware in 1993 and 1994 required less judicial attention because all but one (AM International) were prepacks.

With Walsh's appointment, Judge Balick became the chief judge of the district, in charge of case assignments. She assigned Judge Walsh his first big case in February 1994—the second filing of Memorex Telex.

Appointment of a second judge doubled the capacity of the Delaware bankruptcy court. But the effect on the court's competitiveness was problematic. One of the principal attractions of the Delaware court—and the source of much of its advantage over New York—had been predictability. In New York a judge was assigned randomly on the wheel, from a panel of five; in the one-judge court in Delaware the filer had been assured of getting Balick. With Judge Walsh's appointment, that had to change.

Each bankruptcy court controls the manner in which cases are assigned among members of the court.[62] That meant the Delaware court was not legally required to assign its large reorganization cases randomly, as virtually every other bankruptcy court in the nation did. Chief Judge Helen Balick took advantage of that flexibility. She assigned large cases individually, on the basis of relative workloads. About half the cases went to Judge Walsh. Judge Balick's unusual assignment procedure seemed innocuous at the time, but that perception would change.

Judge Walsh adopted many of Judge Balick's case management techniques and proved popular with forum shoppers. Delaware's share of the declining market continued to grow. In 1995, Delaware got nine of the 20 big cases filed in the United States (45 percent); in 1996 it got 13 of 15 (87 percent). In just seven years, Delaware's share of the big-case bankruptcy market had risen from zero to 87 percent. The court had made the difficult transition from one judge to two without scaring the customers off. By the end of 1996, the two-judge court in Delaware was the leader in both prepackaged and nonprepackaged cases and had become the bankruptcy capital of the United States. Whatever one might think of Delaware's or Judge Balick's methods, the accomplishment was remarkable. In seven years, she had attracted a major industry to her state.

3

The Federal Government Strikes Back

The reaction I'm hearing from judges is that it's very frightening
that a bankruptcy court may be cast in a bad light and that light
will then be reflected on all other bankruptcy courts.

—Wisconsin bankruptcy judge Robert D. Martin (1997),
commenting on the withdrawal of the reference in Delaware

To get its 87 percent market share in 1996, the Delaware bankruptcy court sucked the lifeblood out of bankruptcy practice in the
rest of the nation. The number of big cases filed in any given city
had never been large, but each one was a bonanza for lawyers in
the city chosen. In each case, tens or hundreds of clients sought
local lawyers to represent them. Everyone got a piece of the action,
and the top bankruptcy lawyers in the city got rich. For bankruptcy
lawyers, having a big case come to town was a modest version of
winning the lottery. By 1996, the odds of a big case coming to most
cities seemed to be approaching the odds of winning the lottery.

That year, only two cities other than Wilmington were winners.
Kennetech Windpower filed in Oakland, California, and Best Products filed in Richmond, Virginia. By the end of 1996, bankruptcy
lawyers throughout the rest of the United States were grumbling.
For reasons already explained, the bankruptcy judges in some cities
were grumbling with them.

Delaware's sudden success embarrassed those public officials
most directly responsible for the operation of the court system.
Americans pride their government as being one of "laws, not
men." Bankruptcy is governed by the same federal law in every district. Minor differences in procedure can be authorized by local

77

rule or practice. But differences that induced $700 an hour lawyers and the CEOs of their clients to fly to distant cities where the clients also had to retain local counsel raised eyebrows. Significant differences can exist in the Courts of Appeals' interpretations of particular provisions of the Bankruptcy Code. But those kinds of differences would result in the accumulation of cases in a circuit— not in a single court. The accumulation of 87 percent of all big-case bankruptcy reorganizations in a two-judge court in Wilmington, Delaware, suggested that something untoward was going on. As a prominent Chicago bankruptcy lawyer, Gerald Munitz, put it, the forum shopping "demeaned the entire system by suggesting that the bankruptcy courts were for sale."[1]

National Bankruptcy Review Commission

Amid growing concern over the rogue Delaware court's sudden rise to power, two federal agencies launched counterattacks in 1996. The first salvo came from the National Bankruptcy Review Commission Congress had established in 1994. The nine-member commission's task was to review the bankruptcy laws and practices to determine whether changes should be made. The commission was not established with Delaware in mind; it simply happened to be operating when Delaware splashed onto the scene.

Conscious of the national backlash against Delaware, the commission held a public hearing in February 1996 on the subject of venue and forum shopping. By June 1996, the commissioners had pretty well made up their minds. They framed their tentative decision as a question for further discussion: "Should the current venue system be modified to prohibit corporate debtors from filing for relief in a district based solely on the debtor's incorporation in the state where that district is located or based solely on an earlier filing by a subsidiary in the district?" The Delaware State Bar Association retained Alesia Ranney-Marinelli, a bankruptcy partner in the New York office of Skadden, Arps to respond.

Ranney-Marinelli drafted a Report of the Delaware State Bar Association to the National Bankruptcy Review Commission in

Support of Maintaining Existing Venue Choices. The report argued that big firm bankruptcy cases had no "natural venue." The firms and their creditors were spread across wide areas of the United States, making any choice of venue somewhat arbitrary. Venue at the place of incorporation, like venue at the firm's headquarters or center of operations, is somewhat arbitrary, but unlike the latter places, the place of incorporation is clear and easy to ascertain. If the commission was unhappy with particular practices or decisions that drove the forum shopping to Delaware, the report said, the commission should recommend legislation abolishing those practices or reversing those decisions.

That was essentially the conclusion Bill Whitford and I had reached in our study of forum shopping in the 1980s. From a policy viewpoint, forum shopping was a mixed bag. In the 1980s, the New York court was popular in part because it had slow dockets and would approve high attorney fees. On the other hand, many of the forum shoppers were legitimately seeking to avoid real problems with their local courts. Some judges did not have the knowledge or the temperament to preside over billion-dollar bankruptcies. Some were rude, arrogant, and inconsiderate of business realities. Delaware brought a whole new approach to big-case bankruptcy, one in which the company and its lawyers were treated as customers. Delaware pioneered the "omnibus" hearing that made it convenient for out-of-town lawyers to participate in Delaware cases. (The alternative was separate hearings on each matter, which might require the lawyers to travel to Delaware every few days.) The judges heard first-day matters on the first day of the case, stayed after five to finish important matters, and issued memos on how they would handle particular kinds of matters. From a public policy viewpoint, all these things were good.

The best reconciliation of these opposing effects, I believed at that time, was to measure the effects through empirical research, restrain the courts from practices shown to produce negative effects, but continue to allow choice among courts to gain the positive effects. When the commission held a public hearing on the venue proposal, I appeared on my own behalf and expressed this opinion. In essence, I was arguing to regulate the forum shopping and allow it to continue.

Unpersuaded, the commission made two venue recommendations. The first was to eliminate place of incorporation from the list of venue choices. Because nearly all Delaware filers relied on place of incorporation as their basis for venue, the effect would have been to knock the Delaware bankruptcy court back into obscurity. The second recommendation was to eliminate the use of subsidiaries as venue hooks. Under the recommended procedure, subsidiaries would still have been able to file in the court where the bankruptcy of their parent company was pending, but parent companies would no longer have been able to file in the court where the bankruptcy of their subsidiary was pending. The effect would have been to eliminate one of the two main devices by which debtors shopped into New York. (The other device was to set up a skeleton "headquarters" in New York.) In their final report, the commissioners assured readers that their recommendation "was not directed at the bankruptcy courts of New York, those in Delaware, or in any other specific bankruptcy venue."[2] Of course, no one actually believed them.

Judicial Conference

The second salvo in the government's counterattack came from the Judicial Conference of the United States. The Judicial Conference is the policy-making body with respect to the administration of the U.S. courts. To the extent that the federal courts are like a business, the Judicial Conference is its board of directors. The chief justice of the United States Supreme Court presides over the 27-member conference, and the chief judges of the thirteen courts of appeals sit on it.[3]

In 1996, the Judicial Conference Committee on the Administration of the Bankruptcy System requested that the Federal Judicial Center—the research, education, and planning agency of the federal judicial system—study whether "the bankruptcy case venue statutes and procedural rule should be amended" in light of the forum shopping to Delaware.[4] The making of this request conveyed to the Delaware bankruptcy court that it had been noticed—at the highest levels of government.

Gordon Bermant, an experienced and respected researcher employed by the Federal Judicial Center, drew the task. Bermant reviewed the literature, sent questionnaires to the bankruptcy judges, gathered and analyzed empirical data on the shopping pattern and its effect on the parties, and interviewed key participants.

Bermant delivered the Federal Judicial Center's report on January 10, 1997. The survey of bankruptcy judges found slightly more in favor of a change in the venue rules (37 percent) than opposed (34 percent). Twenty-five percent checked "Don't know," and the remaining 4 percent left the answer space blank. Those who favored change generally made comments that left no doubt it was Delaware they were concerned about. Still, the opposition to Delaware among the bankruptcy judges was hardly overwhelming.

The report documented that the forum shopping was principally to Delaware and included large numbers of prepacks. It criticized this pattern based on evidence that the "average creditor . . . was usually inconvenienced by a Delaware filing in relation to a filing at the principal place of business."[5] But it seemed almost to laud the pattern based on evidence that Delaware processed cases faster than other bankruptcy courts.[6] The report noted the accusation that debtors went to Delaware because the court was "debtor-friendly" but said that further research, particularly regarding the set of orders routinely entered on the first day of each bankruptcy case—known as "first-day orders"—would be necessary to know whether the accusation was correct.[7]

One paragraph of the report, however, was sensational. The paragraph described how Judge Balick divided the cases between Judge Walsh and herself.

Some Chapter 11 cases are filed in Delaware according to the following practice. Before filing, debtor's local counsel telephones Judge Balick, in her role as chief judge, to inform her of an impending filing and indicate the day, or range of days, during which the debtor wishes to file. Judge Balick assesses the current

Chapter 11 caseloads of Judge Walsh and herself, including which judge was assigned the last large case. On that basis, with a goal of keeping Chapter 11 workloads more or less even, Judge Balick decides whether she or Judge Walsh will take the case. She informs the lawyer by telephone of her decision. If she is to take the case, then she tells local debtor's counsel of the date on which she will have enough time to hear and decide first-day motions. If she decides that Judge Walsh is to take the case, she tells debtor's counsel to contact Judge Walsh to confirm a filing date on which he will have enough hearing time. The judges will adjust their schedules to meet debtors' needs. Debtor's local counsel may prepare a document on law firm stationery addressed to the assigned judge. If the debtor does not file on the day originally scheduled, the originally assigned judge will take that case whenever it is filed. The letter specifies the first-day motions debtor intends to make. This list of first-day motions is dated and hand-delivered by debtor's local counsel to the assigned judge the day before the case is filed. (District court rule 83.5 requires out-of-district counsel to associate with local counsel. Thus, it is always local counsel who contact Judges Balick and Walsh.) [8]

Ostensibly, this practice merely let the debtor know which judge would be assigned to the case *when* the debtor filed. But viewed in the context of intercourt competition, the practice let the debtor know which judge would be assigned *if* the debtor filed in Delaware. If the debtor did not want the judge assigned, the debtor could avoid that judge simply by filing in another district. Delaware was a two-judge court, but unlike in other two-judge courts, Delaware filers were not at the risk of the draw.

Revelation of the Delaware practice shocked the bankruptcy community nationwide. To my knowledge, no other bankruptcy court in the United States allowed counsel to phone in and find out what judge would be appointed in a case that had not yet been filed. The telephone call to Judge Balick is what is known as an *ex parte* communication, that is, a communication by one party to litigation without notice to opposing parties and an opportunity to be heard. Ex parte communications are, as one court recently put it: "anathema in our system of justice."[9] Specifically, the Code of

Judicial Conduct for United States Judges—which expressly applies to bankruptcy judges[10]—provides that "[a] judge should . . . neither initiate nor consider ex parte communications on the merits, or procedures affecting the merits, of a pending or impending proceeding."[11] Assuming that the ex parte communications in Delaware occurred exactly as described in the Bermant report, their legality would depend on whether the "procedures" of assigning the case to a judge, scheduling the first-day hearings with that judge, and ultimately filing (or not filing) the case in Delaware were "procedures affecting the merits."

In conducting prefiling conferences, Judge Balick certainly failed to comply with Canon 2 of the Code of Judicial Conduct, which requires that "[a] judge should avoid impropriety and the appearance of impropriety in all activities." For months before the Bermant report was issued, rumors had been circulating in the bankruptcy community that the meetings with Balick concerned much more than scheduling. Some referred to it as "negotiating into Delaware." What actually took place in those prefiling conferences has never been revealed. Apparently no record was made, and no party has ever been called to testify.[12]

Delaware's opponents were delighted with the revelations. The court system would have to respond, and whatever the response, it would not be good for Delaware. The question remaining was what that response would be.

Judge Farnan Revokes the Reference

Seventeen days after release of the Bermant report, Joseph J. Farnan, Jr., chief judge of Delaware's United States District Court, revoked the automatic reference of Chapter 11 cases to the Delaware bankruptcy court. To understand the significance of that revocation, one must first understand the automatic reference. The reference is a relic of past battles over the status of the bankruptcy court. Prior to 1972, bankruptcy "referees" appointed by the district court processed bankruptcy cases. The Bankruptcy Rules adopted in 1972 changed the job title to "bankruptcy judge." Most of the same people stayed. In some districts this meant that they began wearing robes and using the elevators, parking lots, and dining rooms that had previously been reserved for "real" judges.[13] In 1978, Congress shifted the power to appoint bankruptcy judges to the president and elevated the bankruptcy court to a status that was in most respects equal to that of the district court. Again, most of the same people stayed on. As a result of these job upgrades, people who had recently been the district judges' direct subordinates—the equivalent of magistrates—were now virtually their equals. The status-conscious district judges and their sympathizers on higher federal courts were deeply offended. Chief Justice Warren Burger took the unprecedented step of lobbying Congress against the upgrade provisions of the 1978 law but won only minor concessions before the bill passed.

What the chief justice could not do by persuasion, the Supreme Court did by fiat. In its 1982 decision in *Marathon Pipeline*,[14] the Court declared Congress's entire delegation of jurisdiction to the bankruptcy courts unconstitutional, supposedly plunging the bankruptcy courts into a constitutional crisis. The Supreme Court set a deadline by which Congress was to recalibrate the prestige and power of the bankruptcy courts or those courts would cease to exist altogether. Calling the Court's bluff, Congress let the deadline pass. The Judicial Conference—which had no rule-making authority—responded by promulgating the "emergency rule." That rule gave the district judges jurisdiction over the bankruptcy cases and authorized the district judges to "refer" them to the bankruptcy judges if they chose to do so. Nearly all of the district judges did. But that still didn't give the bankruptcy judges the authority to enter a binding order. If any party objected to a bankruptcy judge's decision, the district judge had to come back in.

In 1984 Congress backed down from the confrontation by enacting legislation similar to the emergency rule.[15] That legislation gave the bankruptcy cases to the district court.[16] The district court could keep the cases or refer them to the bankruptcy court, as it chose.[17] This arrangement was acceptable to the district judges because it made clear that the district court was in control and hence "above" the bankruptcy court. The arrangement was acceptable to the bankruptcy judges because they knew the district judges did not want the bankruptcy cases.

As soon as Congress put the new arrangement in place in 1984, every district court in the nation entered an order referring all bankruptcy cases filed in the district to the bankruptcy court.[18] These orders are known as the "automatic reference" because with respect to any particular case, the reference occurs automatically upon the filing of the case with the district court. Even though nothing had been done to resolve the "constitutional crisis," once the prestige of the district judges had been vindicated the crisis ceased to be of much concern to anyone.

Under the 1984 resolution, district judges could, at least in theory, decline to refer all bankruptcy cases, any group of cases, or any particular case. Since 1984, a handful of orders had been entered by district courts retaining particular cases. The best known retention was that of Richmond, Virginia, district judge Robert Mehrige. In 1985, he retained the case filed by drugmaker A. H. Robins in response to hundreds of thousands of Dalkon Shield product liability claims. But until Judge Farnan's order in January 1997, no district court had ever withdrawn the reference with respect to all of a court's Chapter 11 cases.

Judge Farnan's only explanation for withdrawal of the reference—that "a significant increase in the number of bankruptcy cases has occurred and that it is appropriate and necessary that judges of the district court participate in the handling of such cases"[19]—was unconvincing.[20] The number of big[21] Chapter 11 cases had risen from nine in 1995 to 13 in 1996, but omitting the prepacks (in which the court would do little) the number had fallen from nine in 1995 to eight in 1996. The total number of Chapter 11 cases filed in Delaware had also fallen—from 246 in 1995 to 217 in 1996.[22] The bankruptcy dockets were moving well, and the bankruptcy judges had not asked for assistance. *BCD News and Comment,* a savvy bankruptcy newsletter that stays in close touch with bankruptcy professionals, put it more bluntly: "No one believed [withdrawal of the reference] was because of the bankruptcy court's heavy caseload."[23]

Judge Farnan has never clarified his reasons for revoking the reference. He did not seem to like or respect Balick. Farnan had not even consulted her before entering an order withdrawing the reference of most of her court's work. The *National Law Journal* ventured the opinion that withdrawal of the reference was punishment for the prefiling contacts described in the Federal Judicial Center report.[24] Some speculated that the case takeover was part of an attempt to justify the need for an additional district judge in Delaware. Others interpreted it as an attack on the bankruptcy court, intended to end the forum shopping. Yet others saw Farnan's move as merely intended to moderate the shopping and thereby deflate the political backlash against what was going on in Delaware.

Whatever the intent, entry of the order stunned the bankruptcy community. The Delaware bankruptcy court had been cut down in its moment of triumph. Shoppers went to Delaware for the two bankruptcy judges; now they were being told they might get any of three district judges who knew nothing about bankruptcy. A prominent North Carolina bankruptcy lawyer summed up the problem.

> Whatever a district judge's expertise in handling civil and criminal trials, he cannot be expected to administer a large corporate reorganization case efficiently and effectively without first making a few mistakes. The judicial knack for the Chapter 11 process—the art of nurturing a living, albeit troubled, business, understanding the peculiar group dynamics and knowing how to foster a consensual reorganization plan—is not fully intuitive and certainly is not learned by trying drug cases or complicated patent cases. District judges are not used to the emergency hearings and frequency of motion practice that typify Chapter 11 cases. No responsible debtor's counsel would want his client's Chapter 11 case to serve as a learning experience or training vehicle for a Delaware district judge.[25]

Filers had overwhelmingly rejected the bankruptcy courts of the rest of the country in favor of Delaware, only to have Delaware suddenly disappear. Judge Farnan entered the order on January 17, 1997, effective February 3. MobileMedia Communications filed in Delaware before the deadline, and Judge Balick assigned the case to Judge Walsh. On February 7, Jayhawk Acceptance filed in Dallas. Then the entire bankruptcy community collectively held its breath and waited to see what would happen next.

Return of the Delaware Bankruptcy Court

Almost immediately after revoking the reference, the district judges began signaling that their intent was not to bring forum shopping into Delaware to a halt. The court appointed an 11-member committee of local bankruptcy practitioners to address the concerns of the bankruptcy bar and told the committee that district judges would continue the bankruptcy court practice of making instant "bench" rulings on many matters because of the "time-sensitive nature of bankruptcy."[26] The district judges said they were not interested in rewriting substantive bankruptcy law in the jurisdiction and that, except for the new method of case assignment, they would continue to follow established bankruptcy court procedures.[27] Initially, Judge Farnan would make the case assignments, but the long-term goal would be random assignments.[28]

The wait to see whether big cases would continue to flow to Delaware was lengthy. Some midsize forum shoppers tested the new waters in Delaware over the ensuing months. But after Jayhawk, only a single large public company filed for bankruptcy anywhere in the United States for five months. The single company to file was Harvard Industries, an auto parts manufacturer that filed in Delaware on March 8, 1997. Harvard Industries might have filed in Delaware thinking that the revocation of the reference did not apply to it. Harvard had gone through a Delaware bankruptcy in 1991, and Judge Balick had presided. Harvard Industries might have assumed that Judge Farnan would assign the refiling to Judge

Balick. He didn't. He assigned it to District Judge Sue L. Robinson instead.

Four months later, on July 7, 1997, Montgomery Ward broke the ice again by filing in Delaware. Montgomery Ward was a high-visibility retailer with assets of $5 billion. The case was assigned to Bankruptcy Judge Peter J. Walsh. Four more cases followed quickly. Three of the four were assigned to district judges (Judge Balick got the fourth). The assignment of cases to district judges made it clear that withdrawal of the reference was not merely symbolic. The district judges were actually going to do bankruptcy cases.

Once the bankruptcy community got over the initial shock of district judges presiding over bankruptcy cases, the new regime was reasonably well received. The district judges got good marks from the lawyers for their handling of bankruptcy cases[29] and generated slightly lower refiling rates than their bankruptcy counterparts.[30] Perhaps presiding over bankruptcy megacases wasn't all that difficult.

If Judge Farnan's intent was to moderate the flow of cases to Delaware until the heat was off—without killing the flow entirely—he employed the perfect device. Only 8 of the 15 big cases filed in 1997 (53 percent) went to Delaware. In 1998, the proportion fell to 13 of 31 cases (42 percent) but then rebounded to 28 of 44 cases (64 percent) in 1999 and 45 of 79 cases (57 percent) in 2000. Delaware's momentum was so great that neither district judge nor random draw could entirely staunch the flow. In September 1997, a *BCD News and Comment* headline proclaimed that "In Delaware: Business Is Back."

In November 1997, nine months after Judge Farnan withdrew the reference, Judge Balick announced her resignation. When I suggested in print that Judge Farnan's withdrawal of the reference might have been the cause,[31] she broke her usual pattern of speaking only through court opinions by firing off a letter to the editor denying it.[32]

To replace Balick, the Third Circuit Court of Appeals choose Philadelphia bankruptcy lawyer—and Delaware outsider—Mary

F. Walrath. The court's choice of Walrath was widely viewed as an attempt to rein in the Delaware court. Commentators said that her status as an outsider may have helped Walrath get the job and that her appointment was intended to "buck the [Delaware] culture."[33] But once on the bench, Judge Walrath continued the traditions that had made Delaware attractive for forum shoppers.[34]

Business was back but not at 1996 levels. At Delaware's new, lower market share, the political pressure to do something about Delaware abated. In early 1998, the district court quietly began assigning the bulk of the big cases to Bankruptcy Judges Walsh and Walrath; at the end of that year, the district judges quit taking big bankruptcy cases altogether. Farnan's order withdrawing the reference still stood, but it had no practical effect. The press did not even notice the change.

Judge Farnan's order withdrawing the reference remained in effect for exactly four years, until February 3, 2001.[35] By that time, efforts to change the venue statute had dissipated, and the competition for big bankruptcy cases had entered a new stage. Delaware lawyers who had previously been content to serve as local counsel were insisting on larger roles in the cases. Firms from other parts of the United States began opening Delaware offices. In the short run, lawyers could fly in from Cleveland or Dallas or ride the Metroliner from New York. But in the long run, it seemed inevitable that lawyers who lived and worked in Delaware would dominate Delaware bankruptcy practice and Delaware bankruptcy practice would dominate U.S. bankruptcy practice. The big-case bankruptcy community had accepted Delaware's domination.

Tsunami in Delaware

By the end of 2000, the Delaware court faced a new and perhaps more serious challenge. As shown in figure 3, the numbers of big-case bankruptcies filed in Delaware—and the rest of the country—had skyrocketed in 1999 and 2000. Delaware's market share had not increased materially since 1997, but the numbers of companies filing in Delaware were much larger. In September 1999, the district

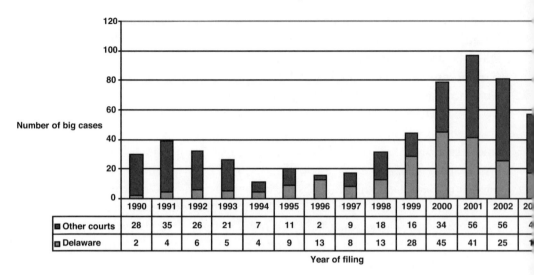

Fig. 3. Number of big public firm bankruptcies by year, 1990–2003. (Data from author's Bankruptcy Research Database.)

court resumed taking bankruptcy cases just as quietly as it had discontinued taking them in early 1998. In 2000, the number of big cases filed in Delaware was three times the number filed in 1996. If Delaware's two bankruptcy judges had needed help in 1996—as Judge Farnan had written in his order—they triply needed that help in 2000.

The usual method of handling case overloads in the federal courts is to bring in "visiting judges" from districts where the caseloads are lighter. Delaware had been receiving assistance from visiting judges for years, but in late 1999 and 2000, the Delaware court began assigning big cases to them. In addition to the district judges, at least six visiting judges—John C. Akard from the Northern District of Texas, Randall Newsome from the Northern District of California, Erwin Katz from the Northern District of Illinois, Judith H. Wizmur from the District of New Jersey, Judith K. Fitzgerald from the Western District of Pennsylvania, and Judge Ronald Barliant from the Northern District of Illinois—were hearing big cases in Delaware.[36] Even so, the court could not keep up with the swelling caseload. The judges could no longer reliably enter first-day orders on the first day of the case, hearings had become difficult to get, and Delaware's renowned speedy dockets were slowing. The court was slowly but surely being overwhelmed by the gigantic case flow it had induced. In January 2001, one lawyer complained anonymously that "[f]ee petitions aren't getting ruled on. The clerk's office is hopelessly behind. For the life of me, I don't get [why people are still filing in Delaware]."[37] Delaware needed more bankruptcy judges.

Desperately Seeking Judgeships

The Judicial Conference, which recommends additional judgeships based on workloads, was unsympathetic. In 1997 Delaware bankruptcy workloads justified an additional bankruptcy judge. But the Judicial Conference declined to include Delaware's judgeship in its recommendations,[38] saying that it believed Delaware's upward filing trend could change drastically due to "anticipated changes in interest rates, the national economy, and tax laws."[39] The explanation was absurd. The Judicial Conference was a group of judges, not economic soothsayers. Delaware's prosperity in big-case bankruptcy was the product of neither economic conditions nor tax laws. Nationally, big-case filings were at historic lows in 1997. Delaware's prosperity was the product of forum shopping. The Judicial Conference was signaling that the decision was not about caseloads. The conference seemed to be saying that if the Delaware bankruptcy judges wanted to attract more cases they could work longer hours and do those cases themselves. Delaware was being punished for embarrassing the system.

The National Bankruptcy Review Commission issued its Final Report recommending that Congress put an end to the forum shopping in October 1997. The following spring, Professor Ted Eisenberg and I released a study on the nature of the forum shopping. Probably the most important finding in that study was that the shopping did not result simply from the attractiveness of

Delaware. The shop-out rates for a few courts—Bridgeport, Connecticut; Santa Ana, California; and Boston, Massachusetts—were very high, while the rates for others—New York, Phoenix, and Denver—were very low.[40] This pattern suggested that there was a push as well as a pull to the forum shopping. Differences existed among the other courts that made some of them acceptable to filers and others not. We concluded that

> To the extent that forum shopping responds to problems with home fora, reducing the level of shopping may exacerbate those problems. Assume, for example, that one or more judges in a district enter unduly restrictive first-day orders, making it difficult to reorganize in the district. If debtors' lawyers respond by filing their cases in another district, the problem largely dissipates. If a solution to forum shopping does not address the underlying problem, some businesses will fail unnecessarily.[41]

By its September 1998 meeting, the Judicial Conference's attitude toward the situation in Delaware seemed to have shifted. Addressing the recommendations of the National Bankruptcy Review Commission, the Conference "urged that Congress defer action on the recommended change in the venue statutes until there is additional published scholarship on the subject, because the data now available do not clearly support the need for any statutory change."[42] Early the following year the Conference recommended that Delaware receive an additional bankruptcy judge.[43]

The Conference's action was merely a recommendation to Congress. The next step in obtaining Delaware's third bankruptcy judgeship was for the recommendation to be enacted into law. An omnibus bankruptcy reform bill was then pending before Congress, and the congressional leadership decided to attach the bankruptcy judgeships to it. For Delaware, it would turn out to be a costly decision. For a variety of reasons having nothing to do with Delaware, the omnibus bankruptcy bill teetered on the brink of adoption for several years, never quite making it. While the bill teetered, the Delaware bankruptcy court continued to struggle with its surging caseload.

The Delaware bankruptcy judges could have dealt with the tsunami by transferring cases to other courts. Bankruptcy courts can make such transfers "in the interest of justice or for the convenience of the parties."[44] That would have been a reasonable course if the judges were interested in doing a good job and nothing more. But if they were trying to build an empire, they would need more judges. The only way to get those judges was to keep working an overload until the Judicial Conference and Congress gave in and admitted that Delaware's need was permanent. The Delaware judges acted as if they were trying to build an empire. Which, of course, they were.

Riding Herd on the Visiting Judges

The forum shoppers sought speed and predictability. Those were difficult qualities for the Delaware bankruptcy court to provide through a pickup team consisting of two bankruptcy judges, four district judges, and a half dozen part-time visiting judges who had volunteered to come in from other districts to help.

A crucial element of predictability is knowing that if one files a case in Delaware, the case will remain there. Forum shopping is risky. If one files in a distant court and that court transfers the case back to the local court, time has been lost, and issues might have to be relitigated. Perhaps more important, the shopping attempt implies criticism of the local court. Upon the shopper's return to the custody of its local court, it is not beyond imagination that there might be retribution. Before they commit to a court, forum shoppers want to know that the court won't send them back.

The Delaware court did send cases back. In its 1996 defense of Delaware, the State Bar Report listed 19 cases the Delaware court had transferred to courts at the debtors' "center of gravity."[45] But those were relatively small cases. As the demand for Delaware's services increased and the number of judges in Delaware remained constant, the size of the cases the Delaware court transferred increased. The rumor was that by 2001 Delaware was only really interested in billion dollar cases.[46] The data on transfers are consistent with that rumor. Of the large public company cases filed in Delaware since 1990, the court has transferred only 4 (2 percent). The largest was Harrah's Jazz, a New Orleans casino that reported assets of $767 million. Of the 90 largest cases filed in Delaware to date, not a single one has been transferred. Truly big companies don't have to worry.

That Delaware wouldn't send big cases back came into question for a few days during the week of April 2, 2001. On Monday, visiting judge Randall Newsome was conducting first-day hearings in Delaware in the case of W. R. Grace. Newsome is a highly regarded judge who began his career in Cincinnati, where he presided over the giant Baldwin-United case in the 1980s. Later, he moved to Oakland, California. In April 2001, Newsome was in Delaware as a much-needed volunteer.

W. R. Grace was a $2.5 billion firm with an asbestos problem—a messy kind of case that would last a long time and generate huge professional fees. Although Grace was incorporated in Delaware, Newsome noticed that the firm was headquartered in nearby Columbia, Maryland. Speaking from the bench, Newsome ordered the lawyers to brief him on why he should not transfer the case to the Maryland bankruptcy court. During the same week, Newsome made similar requests to the lawyers in two other big cases: Worldtex and Borden Chemicals.[47] (Neither was nearly as large as W. R. Grace.) Friday of that same week, Judge Newsome received four envelopes from Chief District Judge Sue Robinson. Three contained orders removing him from the W. R. Grace, Borden Chemical, and Worldtex cases and transferring those cases to other judges. The fourth was an order revoking the automatic reference that had been reinstated only four months earlier.

The district judges were back in the business of hearing bankruptcy cases. The explanation for revocation contained in the order was essentially the same as that given by Judge Farnan four years earlier: the bankruptcy court was in need of help with its caseload. This time the explanation rang truer: the bankruptcy court desperately needed help. But they had also needed help four months earlier when Judge Robinson had reinstated the reference.

None of the orders attempted to explain the transfer of Newsome's cases, and nobody involved was willing to do so on the record. But an anonymous bankruptcy lawyer from the hinterlands expressed metaphorically what bankruptcy lawyers and judges across the country were thinking.

> It seems that Judge Newsome is the new St. Thomas Moore and the Delaware District Court is King Henry VIII. If you even think about venue, off with your head. I have this image of the clerk sitting there with a little judicial ejection button underneath the desk. If anyone mentions the V-word, it's ejection.[48]

A retired judge, also quoted anonymously, added:

> But you have to be fair to the district judges, too. It's their district. It's an economic thing. A lot of money flows to Delaware because of these cases. It supports a cottage industry of local counsel. The money goes to everything from cabs, to the train station, to hotels. You can't get a hotel room there some nights, and who goes to Delaware? It's very important to them. You've got to look at all sides. As a visiting judge, you have to be sensitive to the local culture.[49]

The Newsome affair was one of several events that have occurred since Judge Farnan's revocation of the reference in 1997 that have shed new light on his motivations. From the district court's adoption of the bankruptcy court's procedures, to its quiet return of the bankruptcy cases to the bankruptcy judges, to its intervention in W. R. Grace, it had become progressively clear that Judge Farnan's apparent rebuke of the bankruptcy court had merely been a way of defusing the political backlash. Since the entry of the revocation order, the district court had been working to preserve Delaware's dominant position in big-case bankruptcy. The district judges were in on it.

Birch Telecom provides another illustration. That Kansas City company filed a prepack in Delaware on July 29, 2002.[50] The case was assigned to visiting bankruptcy judge John C. Akard. Judge Akard was critical of Birch Telecom's management and hinted that he might not confirm its plan. Birch responded by filing a request with the Delaware district court to withdraw the reference with respect to Birch's case. Judge Farnan did so; assumed jurisdiction over the case; and, in only 13 days from the request, confirmed Birch's plan.

Whether Judge Akard was acting improperly or unreasonably in Birch's case was not the issue. Judges act improperly and unreasonably every day in courts throughout the United States. The remedy is to appeal at the end of the case, which may, after a year or two, lead to a new trial. Only in Delaware bankruptcy does the appellate court swoop in like a department store manager who discovers that a clerk has been bickering with one of the customers and immediately give the customer what he or she wants.

4

Failure

Study Attacks Delaware Bankruptcy Court
—Headline in the *National Law Journal* (March 2002)

In the spring of 2000, UCLA law student Sara Kalin and I made a shocking discovery. The companies that had reorganized in Delaware from 1990 through 1996 were failing at an alarming rate.

The discovery came as the result of two accidents. The first occurred in the final months of the study Bill Whitford and I had done in the 1980s. Bill and I were studying the reorganization process from filing to confirmation. We were not collecting data on what happened to the companies after they emerged from the process, but the names of the 43 companies in our study were firmly etched in our minds. As we prepared to publish our findings in the early 1990s, we noticed some of those names in the newspapers again. Firms that had emerged from bankruptcy only a few years earlier were filing again. As the numbers of these refilings grew, we decided to count them. By the time we published the last article in our study in 1993, Bill and I identified 12 of the 38 emerging firms from our study (32 percent) as having refiled.[1]

The discovery surprised us. Refilings were supposed to be rare. The law required that, before confirming a plan, the bankruptcy judge find that confirmation was "not likely to be followed by . . . the need for further financial reorganization."[2] It appeared that the judges' findings had been wrong in almost a third of the cases.

I resolved to look into the refiling problem further, but other matters always seemed more pressing. Two years later Professor Edith Hotchkiss of Boston College published a study on the subject. She found that 32 percent of public firms emerging from bankruptcy "reenter bankruptcy or privately reschedule their debt."[3] Because she counted both refilings and out-of-court workouts and still reached a total of only 32 percent, I assumed that if she had counted separately she would have found a refiling rate considerably lower than the 32 percent Bill and I had found. Perhaps the cases Bill and I had studied had been a bad batch.

The LoPucki-Kalin Study

Although I could never find the time for a refilings study, each semester I tried to interest my seminar students in doing one. In the spring of 2000, one did. Sara Kalin tracked down the refiling data on each of the 188 large public companies that emerged from a bankruptcy court anywhere in the United States from 1983 through 1996. For each, she determined whether the emerging firm had filed a second bankruptcy by February 20, 2000. The task was difficult because about 30 percent of the firms changed their names at least once, some merged or were acquired in transactions that raised issues of how to count, and many dwindled in size until they could no longer be tracked in newspapers. Essentially, what Sara had to do was to use Securities and Exchange Commission filings, newspaper reports, bankruptcy services, business directories, court records, web sites, and other sources to track each of the companies from its emergence from bankruptcy to its ultimate fate. For some, that was more than a decade. I reviewed Sara's documentation with respect to each of the cases.

Among other contributions, Sara's seminar paper identified the period of enhanced risk of refiling shown in figure 4. The probability that any given public company will file bankruptcy in a given year is 0.77 percent. But for a company that has already been through bankruptcy, the refiling risk is higher, beginning at 1.6 percent in the first year, peaking at 4.4 percent in the third year, declin-

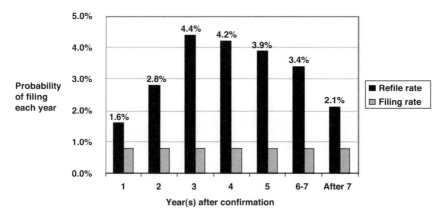

Fig. 4.   Refiling and filing rates by year after plan confirmation.
(Reprinted from Lynn M. LoPucki and Sara D. Kalin, "The Fail-
ure of Public Company Bankruptcies in Delaware and New
York," 54 *Vanderbilt Law Review* (2001): 247.)

ing slowly to 3.4 percent in the sixth and seventh years, and falling
to 2.1 percent after the seventh year.

Sara's project had nothing to do with Delaware. She did not collect data on the locations of the cases she studied. But those locations were already in my Bankruptcy Research Database (BRD).
The second accident occurred just a couple of months after I added
Sara's data to the BRD. In scanning the data, we noticed that most
of the refilers had initially reorganized in Delaware or New York.

By the summer of 2000, the bankruptcy community was well
aware of the forum shopping to Delaware and New York. They
were also aware that substantial numbers of companies emerging
from bankruptcy reorganizations were refiling. (A Chapter 11 case
followed by another Chapter 11 case was widely referred to as a
"Chapter 22.") But no one had noticed the connection between the
two phenomena. To the contrary, legal scholars were lauding the
forum shopping as healthy competition and Delaware as the best
bankruptcy court in the United States.[4]

The correlation between reorganizing in Delaware or New York
and later returning to bankruptcy was dramatic. Considering all
188 cases, Delaware's refiling rate (32 percent) was more than three

times that of all courts other than Delaware and New York (10 percent). New York's rate (28 percent) was similar to that of Delaware. (More detail on these refiling rates is shown in table 4.) The difference in the proportion of Delaware-reorganized firms refiling and the corresponding proportion for other courts was statistically significant at the .01 level, meaning that the odds of so great a difference occurring by chance were less than one in 100. (I will use "other courts" to refer to all courts other than Delaware and New York.)

In one important respect, these refiling rates made Delaware's performance look better than it was. Because the Delaware cases had been filed toward the end of the period covered by our study, the Delaware- reorganized companies had had less time in which to fail. To adjust for this problem, we recomputed our statistics, considering only companies that emerged from 1991 through 1996—the first years when companies were also emerging in Delaware. The recomputation included 127 of the original 188 cases. Delaware's recomputed refiling rate was 30 percent, as compared with 23 percent for New York and only 5 percent for all other courts. Measured simply by numbers of refilings, Delaware's refiling rate was six times that for other courts. Although based on fewer cases, this difference too was significant at the .01 level (see table 5).

The 30 companies that emerged from Delaware reorganization in the period 1991–96 were the reorganizations on which Delaware had made its reputation as the nation's best bankruptcy court.

TABLE 4. Refiling Rates by Court, 1983–96

Court	Number of Firms Emerging	Number of Firms Refiling	Percentage Refiling	Refilings per Year Followed (%)
Delaware	31	10	32	8.6
New York	36	10	28	5.2
Other courts	121	12	10	1.7
Total/Average	188	32	17	3.1

Source: Lynn M. LoPucki and Sara D. Kalin, "The Failure of Public Company Bankruptcies in Delaware and New York: Empirical Evidence of a 'Race to the Bottom'," 54 *Vanderbilt Law Review* (2001): at 249.

They were Delaware's great successes. But by February 20, 2000, nine of those 30 reorganizations had already failed. A reassessment of the Delaware court's performance seemed to be in order.

My study with Kalin reached essentially two empirically based conclusions. The first was that firms emerging from Delaware and New York reorganizations were significantly more likely to refile than firms emerging in other courts. The second was that the elevated refiling rates were a product of intercourt competition. As we explained in the study, this second conclusion was based on four sets of findings.

First, Delaware produced high rates of refiling during its period of competitive success in the 1990s. Second, New York produced high rates of refiling during its period of competitive success in the 1980s. Third, the New York refiling rates declined after New York's period of competitive success. Fourth, the judge that made New York competitive in the 1980s had higher refiling rates than his colleagues on the New York court.[5]

That judge was Burton R. Lifland. His refiling rate for companies emerging in the 1980s was 57 percent.[6]

UCLA released our findings and conclusions in July 2000. At the same time, we posted the complete study on the UCLA Law School web site, including the names of the companies and the dates of every filing and refiling. Release of the data meant that no one would have to take our word for anything. Our study involved no

TABLE 5. Refiling Rates by Court, 1991–96

Court	Number of Firms Emerging	Number of Firms Refiling	Percentage Refiling	Refilings per Year Followed (%)
Delaware	30	9	30	7.9
New York	22	5	23	4.8
Other courts	75	4	5	1.1
Total/Average	127	18	14	3.1

Source: Lynn M. LoPucki and Sara D. Kalin, "The Failure of Public Company Bankruptcies in Delaware and New York: Empirical Evidence of a 'Race to the Bottom'," 54 *Vanderbilt Law Review* (2001): at 250.

sampling. It included every case in which a large public company debtor emerged from bankruptcy during the relevant period. Skeptics could check any item of data used in the study. They could reorder the data and recalculate the study in any way they chose. Everything was in the open. If our facts were wrong, we could be sure someone would tell us.

Reaction to the Initial Study

Our study, like the many bankruptcy empirical studies I had done before, was a study of human activity. Not surprisingly, the humans engaged in that activity—bankruptcy lawyers and judges—think they know a thing or two about what they themselves are doing. As a result, those humans tend to read such studies not so much for what they might learn from them as to judge them based on the readers' own experiences.

This phenomenon supports only two possible reactions to a newly released study, both bad. If the results conflict with the reader's personal experience, the reader concludes that the study is wrong. If the results accord with the reader's experience, the reader concludes that the study was unnecessary; it didn't tell the reader anything he or she didn't already know.

As a researcher, I much prefer the "it's wrong" reaction. If readers "knew that already," the study is quickly forgotten. Being told one is wrong can be unpleasant, but it has the potential to spark discussion, lead to controversy, and ultimately change people's minds.

We did get a little of the we-knew-it-already reaction. Bankruptcy Judge Russell Eisenberg wrote me that "[w]e all knew pretty well in advance what you would have found . . . ." But overwhelmingly, the reaction of bankruptcy practitioners was that the study just had to be wrong. A few days after we posted it, the *Delaware Law Weekly* reported that "[a]t least two local analyses are in progress to challenge the [LoPucki/Kalin] study."[7] One of the analysts was the prominent Delaware bankruptcy firm Richards, Layton & Finger. The article did not identify the other.

Three weeks later, the *National Law Journal* reported that "[Mark Collins of Richards, Layton & Finger] and other Delaware bankruptcy experts say that they will set the record straight with a written response to the LoPucki study that will review each of the refilings."[8] That response never came.

At the time we released our study, Harvey R. Miller was head of the bankruptcy department at Weil, Gotshal and Manges, the largest and most prestigious bankruptcy department in the country. A few months after the release, Miller, working with two Weil, Gotshal associates, obtained our data and began his own reanalysis. Miller filed numerous cases in New York and Delaware and strongly believed in the quality of those two courts. Yet in the article he published in 2002, Miller agreed with our conclusion "that the recidivism rates for both traditional and prepackaged and prenegotiated reorganizations are higher in Delaware than in all other jurisdictions minus the Southern District of New York."[9]

The Weil, Gotshal lawyers had used our data as their starting point. Had those data been materially wrong, these researchers were certainly in a position to notice. Later a doctoral candidate at the University of Chicago confirmed our results using data he compiled independently.[10] Within a few years, the bankruptcy world had accepted the fact that Delaware and New York had higher refiling rates than other jurisdictions—at least through 1996. What remained to be resolved was why—and what it meant.

Was Delaware at Fault?

Based on the data, Kalin and I attributed the elevated refiling rates to court competition. In our article, we speculated about the nature of the link. Intense examination of a few of the failed cases revealed that the Delaware court had adopted a laissez-faire approach to the confirmation of plans. If the major parties to the case—typically the debtor and a committee purporting to represent creditors—were in agreement, the court would confirm the plan without serious examination or analysis. Some of the plans presented had little chance of success.

The parties seemed to be presenting these shaky plans to avoid having to deal with the debtors' very formidable problems. Addressing the problems would have put the parties in conflict with each other. In those conflicts there would have been winners and losers. The companies' weaknesses would have been exposed. Managers might have been fired and the amounts owing to creditors slashed. For all parties, the day of reckoning would have arrived.

Better, the parties seemed to be thinking, to reach an agreement that papered over the companies' problems—a deal that ended the bankruptcy quickly, let the deal makers keep their jobs, promised creditors full or substantial repayment, and allowed all the professionals to claim victory. If the day of reckoning came knocking again—as it ultimately did in 54 percent of the Delaware cases—that would be later, perhaps on someone else's watch. It would be someone else's problem.

Consistent with these speculations, leading bankruptcy lawyers such as Harvey Miller,[11] Kenneth N. Klee,[12] and J. Ronald Trost[13] were complaining that distress debt traders were buying the bonds of bankrupt companies; forcing quick, ineffective reorganizations; and then cashing out before the companies inevitably crashed again. As Miller put it: "[T]hey get the debt, and then they sell the debt into the public markets and they're gone and then you have the same problem."[14]

Bankruptcy lawyers readily agreed that the Delaware judges were rubber-stamping plans (of course, the lawyers put it more delicately) but disagreed that the rubber stamping made the judges responsible for the ensuing refilings. Absent objection, the lawyers said, rubber-stamping the plans was what the judges were supposed to do. "The court is . . . permitting the parties-in-interest . . . to adjust their own debts," said Delaware bankruptcy lawyer John McLaughlin; "that's the way it's supposed to work."[15] Leading Delaware bankruptcy lawyer Laura Davis Jones explained that "[c]onfirmations of Chapter 11 cases in this district are thoroughly analyzed by professionals and advisers on all sides of table before the plans are presented to the court."[16] Harold Novikoff of

Wachtell, Lipton added: "It's difficult to go back and blame it on the judge when the plan was the result of extensive negotiation by sophisticated, well-advised parties."[17] Weil, Gotshal's Harvey Miller summed up: "You can't expect a judge to become a prosecutor. People come into court arm-in-arm singing 'We Shall Overcome.'"[18]

The debate quickly turned to whether it was even possible for judges to evaluate plans. Pittsburgh bankruptcy judge Bruce McCullough, who occasionally served as a visiting judge in Delaware, was skeptical.

> You must have seen some of these plans. Some of them are as big as the New York telephone book. How is a judge who is foreclosed from participating in the reorganization ever going to read that plan and find anything wrong with it? . . . I don't care how smart you are, you wind up talking to yourself, challenging your own assumptions and driving yourself crazy. The judge isn't going to be allowed to call in and examine a bunch of expert witnesses. That's not a typical judge's role. It may be the judges' responsibility, but as a practical matter they can't do it.[19]

Another highly respected bankruptcy judge, Barbara Houser, agreed.

> A judge is bound by the record that is presented. If you have good lawyers, they will present a record that establishes feasibility. If the judge reviews the disclosure statement and things leap out, I think the judge will ask questions. But if you have good lawyers and they're doing their job right, the likelihood of things jumping out is pretty slim. Lawyers may disclose assumptions, but in the absence of discovery or something being flagrant on its face, it's hard for a judge to know what's a wild assumption and what's not.[20]

St. Louis bankruptcy lawyer David Lander put it more bluntly: "If nobody's complaining, the notion that the judge should do his or her own feasibility analysis is crazy."[21] The reality, Harvey Miller said, was that "[i]f the banks say 'you have to carry so much debt' management will ultimately say okay . . . . Those deals go through.

Whether those plans are feasible or not is not ever really subjected, in my view, to an objective analysis."[22]

There were a few who disagreed. Los Angeles bankruptcy judge Lisa Fenning not only thought it was possible for the judge to second-guess the parties, she reported doing it.

> I frequently questioned the assumptions [underlying the financial projections]. If I thought there was a real question, I gave a heads up at the disclosure hearing that, even if everyone was in agreement, I would require testimony at the confirmation hearing. Occasionally, I required them to provide different scenarios varying a couple of the key assumptions in their projections . . . . Public companies have plenty of money to run scenarios.[23]

The direction the debate had taken surprised me. As Ken Klee, a UCLA Law School colleague and leading practitioner, put it: "Case law—not 100 percent, but almost 100 percent—says that in order to confirm a plan the judge has to find that [the Bankruptcy Code's feasibility requirement] has been satisfied. They have an affirmative obligation, even if nobody objects."[24]

At the end of each reorganization case, the judge signs a confirmation order. That order makes a finding of fact that "confirmation of the plan is not likely to be followed by the . . . need for further financial reorganization."[25] The judges I interviewed admitted that making that finding was a prerequisite to confirming a plan. Each of the judges required the proponent of each plan to provide evidence to serve as the basis for the finding—either by signed affidavit or testimony in open court. Those procedures had been followed for more than a decade before Delaware began attracting cases.

Now, after more than a decade of signing confirmation orders, Delaware's defenders were saying the whole confirmation process had been a sham from the beginning. The judges weren't doing what they purported to be doing—holding hearings, considering the evidence, and determining the likelihood of plan failure—because they couldn't.

The biggest problem with the judges-can't-judge-feasibility

defense was that it did not explain why refiling was a problem only in Delaware and New York. If the sophisticated judges in Delaware and New York couldn't determine feasibility, it would seem to follow logically that the unsophisticated judges in other courts couldn't either. And if the other judges couldn't determine feasibility, why didn't the other judges have a refiling problem?

When UCLA released our study in July 2000, Delaware's bankruptcy business was booming. That year, 45 large public companies chose the Delaware court for their bankruptcies, bringing the total number since 1990 to 136. Delaware's system for processing big cases was the envy of most other courts. When the clerk of some other court got his or her first big case, that clerk often called Delaware's clerk, David Bird, for advice.

Delaware's two bankruptcy judges were highly respected and among the most experienced in the world in large public company bankruptcies. Only a few judges in New York had done as many cases. When a judge in one of the other courts drew a large public company bankruptcy, it was usually the judge's first and rarely more than the judge's third. Other court judges were amateurs. The amateurs simply couldn't be doing a better job than the pros. There had to be some other explanation for the refilings.

Delaware's Defenses

Delaware's defenders accepted as axiomatic that the high refiling rates could not be the fault of the court. As Harvey Miller argued: "The similarity of recidivism rates in these two sophisticated jurisdictions [Delaware and New York] indicates that it is not the bankruptcy court that is the cause of subsequent failures . . . ."[26] Defenders offered several speculations as to what might be.

Professor Douglas Baird of the University of Chicago Law School suggested that the high refiling rate might not be a "Delaware or New York effect" but merely a "Balick/Lifland effect."[27] Others echoed that view.[28] The evidence, however, provided no support: Delaware's other bankruptcy judge, Peter J. Walsh, completed six cases during the 1991–96 period, and four of them later refiled. (The four were Morrison Knudsen [2001, as Washington Group], Memorex [1994], Grand Union [1994], and Westmoreland Coal [1995].) On the face of it, his record was worse than Judge Balick's.

Some argued that the Delaware and New York courts were running higher failure rates because they were trying to rescue companies that other courts would have left for dead. This argument found similarly little support in the data. Including all cases filed and disposed of from January 1, 1990, through December 31, 1996, only 30 of 38 large public companies that filed in Delaware (79 percent) emerged; whereas 99 of 117 that filed in other courts (85 percent) emerged. This difference in rates was not statistically significant. Nevertheless, it suggested that Delaware filers were not only more likely to fail *after* their reorganization, they were also more likely to be liquidated *during* their reorganization. A larger percentage of Delaware-reorganizing companies was failing during the bankruptcy case, and then a larger percentage was failing afterward.

Perhaps the most brazen argument put forth on Delaware's behalf was that Delaware's refilings were not failures but merely the unfortunate, inevitable by-product of smart risk taking. Thus University of California, Berkeley, law professor Jesse Fried, in commenting on a draft of our paper, said: "I'm not sure that prepacks should be counted as bankruptcy filings for your purpose because they are essentially cheap, out-of-court workouts. There seems to be little cost . . . and so what is the big deal if they fail?"[29] Putting the same point more formally, Vanderbilt University law professors Robert K. Rasmussen and Randall S. Thomas wrote:

> [The] second reorganization proceeding [following a prepack] should not be considered a failure of the first bankruptcy proceeding. The first proceeding was designed to separate out those firms that need a full-blown Chapter 11 proceeding from those that do not. . . . The fact that a full-blown Chapter 11 proceeding follows a prepackaged bankruptcy cannot thus be viewed as a failure of the system.[30]

That argument, however, came almost exclusively from academics; practitioners rarely made it. The one exception I was able to find appeared in an article in *Bankruptcy Court Decisions (BCD)*. The article quoted a "well-known New York bankruptcy attorney" (who had requested anonymity) saying essentially what Fried, Rasmussen, and Thomas had said. But Michelle Johnson, author of the *BCD* article, added that "most turnaround professionals are completely outraged at an answer like that."[31] ("Turnaround professionals" are managers who specialize in bankrupt or near-bankrupt companies. They manage during the crisis and leave when it is over.) Johnson went on to quote Bettina Whyte of Alix Partners—a leading bankruptcy turnround firm—saying "I think [refiling is] a crime practically. All the money spent on the first bankruptcy is lost. The morale and confidence of people is lost. The reputation and brand name, especially the consumer name, is lost. Vendors are very hesitant the second time around . . . . The chances of a company getting out [of bankruptcy] a second time are substantially reduced."[32]

The losses companies suffer as a result of failed prepacks are substantial. In response to Rasmussen and Thomas's argument I did a small study to estimate those losses. The study included all nine companies that had by that time emerged from Delaware reorganization as public companies and refiled. (All of the refilings were within five years of plan confirmation in the initial case.) For each, I determined the amount of the operating losses reported for the period between bankruptcies—after confirmation but before the filing of the second petition. Those operating losses averaged 18 percent of the entire value of the company as reported on the company's last financial statement prior to the first filing. Operating losses are generally hard cash, and prepetition financial statements generally overvalue the companies' assets, so the 18 percent figure is a very conservative estimate of the losses that occurred between bankruptcies. For the five prepacks included in the study the average operating loss was even higher: 23 percent. To calculate the losses from failed reorganization one would also have to add the cost of the additional bankruptcy. Refiling was far too expensive to be efficient.[33]

Three other possibilities that might have exculpated Delaware could not be so easily dismissed. First, prominent Phoenix bankruptcy attorney Tom Salerno argued that lower refiling rates in other courts did not mean those other courts had lower failure rates. The failed reorganizations from other courts, he proposed, might be more likely to be resolved in out-of-court workouts or liquidations, rather than in returns to the bankruptcy courts.

Second, several commentators asserted that the companies filing in Delaware and New York were bigger, more complicated, or otherwise more difficult to reorganize, making a higher refiling rate for those companies understandable.

Third, Professors Rasmussen and Thomas argued that because Delaware cases were faster, they were probably cheaper. The savings on professional fees in the larger number of cases that didn't result in refiling might be more than enough to offset the business losses on the few that did. I was skeptical, but without some data on the magnitude of professional fees I couldn't be sure.

My article with Kalin was published in the March 2001 issue of the *Vanderbilt Law Review*. The issue included two replies. One was by Professors Rasmussen and Thomas, the other by Professor David Skeel of the University of Pennsylvania Law School. In their replies, the three raised many of the issues just discussed. The issue also included a response in which I argued some of the points Rasmussen, Thomas, and Skeel had raised and agreed that others would require further research. By the time that issue was published, I was already well along on a follow-up study.

The Follow-up Study

The follow-up study focused on two of Delaware's potential defenses: (1) that refiling rates did not adequately reflect failure rates and (2) that Delaware had higher refiling rates only because the companies filing there were more difficult to reorganize.

Because this follow-up study would require sophisticated regression analysis, I invited Joseph W. Doherty, the associate director of the UCLA Law School's Empirical Research Group, to join me as a coinvestigator.

For the follow-up study, we narrowed the group of companies examined to those that were public after bankruptcy as well as before. Public companies must disclose their financial statements; private companies seldom do. Examining only public companies would mean that we could consider more possible explanations because we would have more information on each company. Narrowing the study to public companies emerging from 1991 to 1996 reduced the number of cases from 188 in the first study to 98 in the second. Of those 98 companies, 26 had reorganized in Delaware, 16 in New York, and 56 in other courts. More companies would have been better, but the 98 included every large public company that reorganized in the United States during the relevant period and remained a public company after reorganization.

The follow-up study had another advantage over the initial study. By the time we stopped collecting data for the follow-up study, each of the reorganized companies had been out of bankruptcy for at least five years. By counting only refilings that occurred in the first five years (later refilings were less likely the fault of the court) we could eliminate the methodological problems that came from comparing failure rates for firms that had been out for different lengths of time. Together, these changes in method brought the pattern of reorganization failure into sharper focus.

The follow-up study showed that the differences in refiling rates were even greater than Kalin and I had reported. Of the 26 large public companies emerging from Delaware reorganization, Doherty and I found that 11 (42 percent) had refiled within five years. The corresponding figures were three of 16 (19 percent) for New York and two of 56 (4 percent) for other courts. Companies reorganized in Delaware had refiled at more than ten times the rate for companies reorganized in other courts. These differences in refiling rates were statistically significant at the .001 level, meaning there was less than one chance in 1,000 that so big a difference in filing rates would have occurred by chance.[34]

To investigate Tom Salerno's assertion that other court reorganizations failed without producing refilings, we looked at what happened to each of the 98 emerging companies in the five-year period after confirmation. We found that 28 of the companies (29 percent) had been absorbed into other companies by merger or simply liquidated. The liquidations were clearly failures. The mergers, however, included some that should be considered failures—mere sales of the assets of businesses that were unable to continue operations—along with others that should be considered successes. To achieve a rough separation of the two kinds of mergers, we calculated the total income of the company between its emergence from bankruptcy and its merger. If the income was positive, we classified the reorganization as a success; if it was negative—the company had lost money for the entire period from bankruptcy to merger—we classified it as a failure. Based on these classifications, we counted six of Delaware's 26 reorganizations (24 percent) as resulting in complete business failure within five years after reorganization. The corresponding failure rate for New York–reorganized companies was about the same: four of 16 (25 percent) failed. But among companies reorganized in other courts, only seven of 56 (13 percent) failed. Delaware and New York reorganizations were nearly twice as likely to result in complete business failure as were reorganizations in other courts.[35]

Some reorganized companies refiled without completely failing; others completely failed without refiling. To get a comprehensive picture of reorganization failure, we counted the numbers of companies that refiled or completely failed in the five years after bankruptcy. We found that 14 of the 26 Delaware reorganizations failed (54 percent). The corresponding figures for New York and other courts were five of 16 (31 percent) and eight of 56 (14 percent). Delaware reorganizations were almost four times as likely to fail as reorganizations in other courts.[36]

As a fourth measure of failure, we calculated the average annual earnings of each emerging company in the five years after bankruptcy. The average of those averages, for all firms emerging from Delaware reorganization, was a 9 percent loss. For New York the corresponding figure was a 3 percent loss; for other courts it was a 1 percent profit. Delaware-reorganized companies were failing at least in part because their business losses—unlike the business losses of companies reorganized in other courts—continued after their reorganizations were complete.[37] (See table 6.)

From these data Joe and I concluded that Delaware reorganizations did not merely result in more refilings, they also resulted in more reorganization failure. No matter how one measured failure, Delaware had more of it than other courts. A lot more.

Joe and I then turned to the second defense of Delaware—that the court had higher failure rates because it got the hardest cases. The defenders—mostly bankruptcy lawyers who did cases in Delaware and New York—argued that the Delaware and New York cases were harder because the companies were larger and the cases more complex. Harvey Miller, for example, wrote that the "higher percentages of recidivism may be attributed to the complex and sophisticated Chapter 11 cases that gravitate toward Delaware and New York"[38]

To the extent that the argument was based on company size, it was easily refuted. The companies reorganizing in Delaware were larger than those reorganizing in other courts. Lumping the Delaware companies together with those reorganizing in New York, the difference was even statistically significant. But until we

TABLE 6. Failure Rates by Court, Large Public Companies Emerging 1991–96

	Delaware	New York	Other courts
Refilings	11 (42%)	3 (19%)	2 (4%)
Business failures	6 (24%)	4 (25%)	7 (13%)
Reorganization failures	14 (54%)	5 (31%)	8 (14%)
Earnings	–9%	–3%	1%
Number of cases for this court	26	16	56

Source: Lynn M. LoPucki and Joseph W. Doherty, "Why Are Delaware and New York Bankruptcy Reorganizations Failing?" 55 *Vanderbilt Law Review* (2002): 1933–85, at 1939, 1942, 1944, 1945.

published our initial study showing higher failure rates in Delaware and New York reorganizations, nobody had ever argued that big companies were harder to save than small ones. Numerous studies had shown just the opposite: plan confirmation rates for small companies were in the neighborhood of 20 percent to 35 percent, while plan confirmation rates for large companies exceeded 90 percent.[39]

Because we were comparing relatively large companies in other courts with even larger companies in Delaware and New York, and studying refiling (long-term success) rather than confirmation (short-term success), our study differed from the confirmation rate studies. But among the 98 cases in our study, measuring size six different ways—by assets, sales, or numbers of employees, each before and after bankruptcy—Joe and I found no relationship between size and propensity to fail in the five years after reorganization.[40] Contrary to the premise underlying the size argument, larger companies were not harder to reorganize successfully.

The claim that Delaware and New York cases were more complex than those in other courts was more difficult to investigate. Of the commentators who raised the issue, only Professor Skeel made any attempt to define "complex." "The firms that file for bankruptcy in Delaware," he said, "may have more complicated capital structures—such as more classes of debt and stock—than firms that take their cases elsewhere."[41] To investigate the claim, Joe and I counted the number of separate classes of debt and stock in each of the 98 reorganization plans.

The results were startling. Instead of the greater complexity of Delaware and New York plans on which Skeel had premised his argument, we found significantly less complexity. Delaware and New York reorganizations averaged 12.6 and 15.5 classes per plan, respectively, while other court reorganizations averaged 17.7 classes per plan.[42]

Professor Barry Adler of the NYU Law School would later argue that because proximity to the court was a more important advantage in complex cases, debtors took only the simpler cases to Delaware and New York.[43] Although that assertion is consistent with some of the evidence—for example, prepacks were simpler and prepacks went disproportionately to Delaware—Joe and I did not think it likely that the larger firms reorganizing in Delaware and New York had simpler capital structures than the smaller firms reorganizing in other courts. Instead, we concluded that the numbers of classes in plans of reorganization was probably not so much a measure of capital structure complexity as simply a measure of plan complexity. The professionals in other courts were drafting more complex plans, and more complex plans were more likely to succeed.[44] Even if the professionals in Delaware and New York were reorganizing more complex companies, they were not conducting more complex reorganizations.

In the follow-up study, we also investigated the possibility that the companies filing in Delaware and New York were in worse financial condition than those reorganizing elsewhere. In all, we tested eight different measures of company financial distress in the period immediately before bankruptcy. They included the companies' ratios of debts to assets (adjusted for industry and unadjusted), the companies' profits or losses during the one-year and five-year periods immediately prior to bankruptcy (including, as separate measures, operating profits or losses), and the companies' declines in profits or losses from the average of the five years before bankruptcy to the year before bankruptcy (including, as a separate measure, operating profits or losses). By none of these measures were the financial conditions of the firms filing in Delaware and New York significantly different from those of the firms filing in other courts. Finally, we looked for particular industries that had high failure rates and that might have been reorganizing disproportionately in Delaware and New York. We found none. If Delaware and New York were getting sicker or harder-to-reorganize companies, it was not showing up in any of these measures.

Nor did it appear from the data that sicker companies were harder to reorganize. That is, post-reorganization failure rates were not higher among the companies that had been sickest prior to bankruptcy. This finding may seem counterintuitive, but it makes perfectly good sense once one understands a little about the reorganization process. The financial condition of a company coming out of bankruptcy bears no necessary relationship to the financial condition of the company going in. Reorganization can change anything or everything about the company. For large public companies, bankruptcy reorganization is essentially surrender of the company to its creditors. The creditors own the stock of the emerging company and can cause the company to owe them as much or as little of the prepetition debt as they choose. Only when they choose an amount the company can't pay does refiling become likely. No good reason exists for a company to emerge with more debt than it can pay.

Lack of profitability is a bigger problem but still not one that necessarily takes any great business acumen to solve. Most large companies are engaged in several businesses, offering multiple products and services. Bankruptcy allows the company to keep what is good about its business and shed the rest. Most companies can be rescued simply by getting rid of the bad businesses and product lines while keeping the good ones. That is a substantial part of what happens in reorganization. As a result, companies on average shrink by about 20 percent to 25 percent during reorganization. Because the reorganizing business can jettison its problems, the size of those problems often does not matter. Even if the business is entirely bad and can't be fixed, the parties can avoid a later refiling or plan failure—and the accompanying losses—by liquidating the business in the first bankruptcy. Reorganizing businesses don't have to commit to any more than they can do. When they do, it is nearly always the result of miscalculation or control by someone with nothing to lose in any subsequent failure.

In summary, the Delaware- and New York–reorganizing companies were bigger, but bigger companies didn't fail more often after reorganization. The confirmed plans for Delaware- and New York–reorganizing companies were actually simpler than the plans of companies reorganizing in other courts. The Delaware- and New York–reorganizing companies were not sicker than those filing in other courts, and even if they had been, it wouldn't have justified higher refiling rates. The reorganizations of sicker companies weren't more likely to fail. In short, the causes of the high failure rates for Delaware- and New York–reorganizing companies were not in the companies. They were in the courts.

In a separate study conducted later, Joe and I tested the assertion made by Professors Rasmussen, Thomas, and Skeel that because Delaware was reorganizing firms faster, it was reorganizing them more cheaply. On the basis of actual fees and expenses approved by the courts in 48 cases, Joe and I found that despite Delaware's speed, the cost of reorganizing a company in Delaware was slightly higher than the cost of reorganizing it elsewhere.[45] (The difference was not statistically significant.) Delaware's cost advantage could not justify its higher refiling rates because Delaware had no cost advantage.

Why Were Delaware and New York Reorganizations Failing?

The companies choosing Delaware or New York reorganization were not different from the companies choosing other court reorganization at the time they went into bankruptcy. They were, however, different by the time they came out. The most important difference was that companies emerging from other courts had generally solved their profitability problems; companies emerging from Delaware or New York had not.

The follow-up study did not tell us what practices caused Delaware's high refiling rates, but it did offer some clues. First, Delaware processes cases faster than other jurisdictions; we found that speed was associated with failure. Prepacks were significantly more likely to fail than nonprepacks, and even controlling for whether the case was prepackaged, faster reorganizations were more likely to fail than slower ones. In practical terms, our regression model predicted that a firm whose bankruptcy lasted 100 days had a 44 percent chance of failing, a bankruptcy that lasted 200 days had a 31 percent chance of failing, and a bankruptcy that lasted 500 days had only an 18 percent chance of failing.[46] Delaware had high failure rates in part because it processed cases too quickly.

Second, Delaware's plans were significantly simpler than plans in other courts, and simpler plans were significantly more likely to fail than complex ones. That simplicity itself caused failure does not seem plausible. More likely, simplicity correlated with some other factor—such as a less-than-thorough negotiation between the debtor and its various classes of creditors—that was capable of causing failure.

From the data it appears that if the Delaware-reorganized companies had filed in other courts, many more of them would have survived. Court competition was not merely eroding the integrity of the courts, it was actually destroying companies.

Reaction to the Follow-up Study

In February 2002, Professor Robert K. Rasmussen convened a conference at the Vanderbilt Law School titled "Convergence on Delaware: Corporate Bankruptcy and Corporate Governance." I presented the follow-up study at that conference. Most of the leading bankruptcy academics in the United States were in attendance. They listened to my presentation and found no fault with the study. But when I spoke with individuals afterward, I found few convinced that Delaware was the problem.

The academics began with a firm conviction that markets work—particularly in big bankruptcies where sophisticated clients were represented by even more sophisticated professionals. The companies' choice of Delaware proved Delaware "efficient." If Delaware's outcomes were worse in some respect, they had to be better in some other even more important respect we had not yet discovered. Essentially, the academics were rejecting our empirical findings because they conflicted with their theories.

"It Changed since Then"

In listing the possible responses to social science empirical research earlier in this chapter, I left one out. Even a study that records human behavior perfectly becomes obsolete when that behavior changes. Because there are no limits on how quickly human behavior can change, any study of it can be met with a seat-of-the-pants rejoinder that "it changed since then."

A study of the causes of reorganization failure is particularly vulnerable to this defense because failure is not immediate. The refiling curve defined by Sara Kalin's data and depicted in figure 4 shows that bad reorganizations take about two to seven years to manifest in refilings or distressed mergers. To reach reliable conclusions, researchers must follow the companies for three to five years at a minimum.

Joe and I were able to release our five-year study within a few months after the last cohort of cases reached that age. That our findings were almost as up-to-date as possible did not, of course, exempt us from the "it changed since then" defense. By the time we released our study, five to 11 years had elapsed since the deeds that sowed the seeds of reorganization failure in those 98 companies. In the meantime, 58 more bankrupt companies had emerged and the large majority of them had not yet failed.

Defenders of Delaware and New York sometimes concede that those two courts had problems in the past, but they insist that the problems have been fixed. Near the end of a lengthy discussion I had with a prominent bankruptcy lawyer, the lawyer reluctantly conceded that the Delaware bankruptcy court confirmed bad plans in the period 1991–96. But the lawyer ended the interview by assuring me that the problem had been solved and so I was "just writing a history book." My response, of course, is that any book based on facts is, to that extent, necessarily just a history book.

The Bankruptcy Research Database (BRD) is my effort to deal with the argument that "it changed since then." I continuously update the BRD data (and make them available online). The BRD makes it possible to rerun studies as often as necessary to keep them up-to-date.

Table 7 shows the latest five-year refiling rates I could calculate in time for inclusion in this book. The first line of data in that table reproduces the five-year refiling rates reported earlier in this chapter for firms emerging during the years 1991 through 1996. The next four lines show the five-year refiling rates for firms emerging as

Courting Failure

public companies for each year from 1997 through 2000. The last line of that table combines the five-year refiling rates for firms emerging from 1997 through 2000. Comparison of the rates in the first and last lines of that table show that refiling rates have increased from the earlier period. (The increase will ultimately be greater than shown here because the firms emerging from bankruptcy in 1999 and 2000 had not yet had a full five years in which to refile when this book went to press.)

For Delaware, which already had high refiling rates, the increase was slight—from 42 percent to 46 percent. For New York and other courts, which had relatively low refiling rates in the earlier period, the increase was huge. New York's refiling rate went from 19 percent to 67 percent; the other courts' refiling rates went from 4 percent to 46 percent.

The difference in New York's refiling rates for the two periods is significant at the .107 level, which means there is about a 10.7 percent chance that so great a change would occur between the two periods even if refilings were distributed randomly among years. The difference in other courts' refiling rates for the two periods is significant at the .001 level, which means there is less than one chance in a thousand that so great a change would occur between the two periods if refilings were distributed randomly among years. The likelihood of the two changes occurring in tandem is far lower than the likelihood of each. *Something* must have caused these sudden, simultaneous changes at the end of 1996. Yet Congress made

TABLE 7. **Refiling Rates for Public Companies Emerging 1997–2000**

	Delaware			New York			Other Courts		
	Emerged	Refiled	%	Emerged	Refiled	%	Emerged	Refiled	%
1991–96	26	11	42	16	3	19	56	2	4
1997	6	2	33	3	2	67	4	2	67
1998	2	1	50	1	1	100	2	1	50
1999	8	5	63	2	1	50	2	0	0
2000	8	3	38	0			5	3	60
1997–2000	24	11	46	6	4	67	13	6	46

Source: Data from Lynn M. LoPucki's Bankruptcy Research Database.

no change in the bankruptcy laws during the relevant period and the courts handed down no major bankruptcy decisions.

From 1996 to 2001, initial bankruptcy filings by large, public companies increased sharply and steadily—from 17 to 97 (nearly six-fold). From 1997 to 2002, almost the same period, refilings increased sharply and steadily—from 1.6 percent of the companies that could have refiled in 1997 to 18.8 percent of the companies that could have refiled in 2002 (nearly twelve-fold). That near-coincidence might suggest that both increases were driven by general economic conditions, not court competition. But general economic conditions cannot explain either (1) why 78 percent of the increase in initial filings had occurred by the end of 2000, while the U.S. economy was still healthy, or (2) why Delaware's refiling rate would remain steady while the refiling rates for other courts increased sharply.

The similar movement of initial filing and refiling rates during this period seems more likely to have resulted from the effect of court competition on both rates. That is, the competition may have drawn companies into bankruptcy that would not otherwise have filed. For example, section 363 sale cases account for a substantial portion of the increase in initial filings. Some of the companies conducting those sales might not have filed at all but for the courts' increased willingness to approve 363 sales on short notice without adequate disclosure.

The refiling pattern shown in table 7 is consistent with court competition as the principal cause of high refiling rates. Delaware was an active competitor for cases from 1991 through 1996. During those years Delaware had high refiling rates. New York and other courts barely participated in the competition from 1991 through 1996. They had relatively low refiling rates during those years. The competition for big cases became the center of the bankruptcy world's attention in late 1996 and early 1997 with the coincidence of four major events. In June 1996, the National Bankruptcy Review Commission released its recommendation to end forum shopping. That year, Delaware obtained a near monopoly on big cases filings. In January 1997 the Federal Judicial Center released its bombshell study and Judge Farnan revoked the reference in Delaware. That quick succession of events focused the bankruptcy world's attention on the loss of cases to Delaware. That attention resulted in increased pressure on the other courts to adopt Delaware's methods in order to match Delaware's attractiveness.

Delaware's high refiling rates remained undiscovered until mid-2000. The other courts probably copied Delaware's practices thinking they would reproduce Delaware's success. Instead, they reproduced Delaware's failure. Beginning abruptly with firms emerging in 1997, refiling rates in the rest of the country jumped to roughly the same level as refiling rates in Delaware. As Delaware responded by adopting changes of its own, the competition intensified, transformed the bankruptcy system, and ultimately corrupted additional courts. The human interaction that produced those changes is the subject of the next chapter; the changes themselves are the subject of chapter 6.

5

The Competition Goes National

We are not lobbying to host a political convention or be the site for the Olympic Games. We are a federal court administering the laws of the United States as set out in the bankruptcy code.

—Miami bankruptcy judge Robert A. Mark (2000)

Without any discussion of interim fees, your court will have difficulty getting the big cases—in fact, you may make it impossible for big cases to file in your court.

—Pittsburgh bankruptcy judge Judith K. Fitzgerald (2003)

Through most of the 1980s, the other courts (i.e., all courts other than Delaware and New York) got about 70 percent of the big cases. That percentage dipped a little as Delaware began attracting cases and then from 1993 to 1995 plunged to under 40 percent. There it remained.

Not only was the Delaware court taking cases from other courts, the Delaware and New York lawyers were taking cases from the lawyers in the rest of the United States. The dispossessed lawyers' initial reaction was to cry foul. Many backed the National Bankruptcy Review Commission's condemnation of forum shopping, applauded the revocation of the reference in Delaware, and waited for Congress to rescue them.

As described in chapter 3, that rescue failed to materialize. Delaware senator Joseph Biden engineered the omission of venue reform from the omnibus bankruptcy bill introduced in Congress the following year, and by 1998, it was clear that bankruptcy venue reform was dead.

The Competition Heats Up

Although beaten in Washington, the other court lawyers were not ready to give up. In nearly every major city, the bankruptcy lawyers, individually or as a group, approached their local judges to ask for changes in the courts' practices to make the local court competitive with Delaware. For the reasons described in the introduction, the judges in many cities were willing to do whatever they could.

The bankruptcy bars of cities such as Dallas, Chicago, and Houston had been hurt the worst by the sudden migration of cases. Those cities are headquarters to many big companies and had substantial bankruptcy bars in part because their bankruptcy courts had hosted big cases in the past (see table 8). Even with the freedom given them under the 1978 venue statute, companies still had lots of reasons for filing in their local courts. Typically, their regular legal and financial advisers are in the companies' home cities. Their executives and other employees are integrated into the local communities, making local officials particularly sensitive to the loss of jobs,

TABLE 8. Corporate Headquarters

Major City Courts with the Most Bankrupt Company Headquarters (1980–2004)		Major City Courts with Few Bankrupt Company Headquarters (1980–2004)	
City	Number of Companies	City	Number of Companies
New York	46	Philadelpia	8
Dallas	37	Cleveland	8
Chicago	35	Baltimore	6
Houston	34	San Diego	6
Los Angeles	25	Pittsburgh	5
Boston	24	Washington, DC	3
Denver	20	New Orleans	3
Newark	17	Nashville	3
Detroit	17	Minneapolis	3
St. Louis	16	Seattle	3
Alexandria, VA	13	San Antonio, TX	1
Atlanta	13	Buffalo	1

Source: Data from Lynn M. LoPucki's Bankruptcy Research Database.

tax revenues, and business activity that might result from failure of a reorganization attempt. The home court is usually the most convenient for executives who may be required to participate personally in the bankruptcy case. Even though large public companies could file virtually anywhere they chose, over the past ten years 36 percent filed in the company's headquarters city. For the bankruptcy court of the company's home city, the case was its to lose.

Companies tend to have their homes in the largest cites, but as table 8 shows, the correlation between city size and numbers of bankrupt company headquarters is far from perfect. As more companies fled to Delaware and New York for their bankruptcies, the courts in the cities on the left side of table 8 tended to come under the heaviest pressure. While no empirical measure of these pressures exists, the pressures probably began to build as soon as the outflow of cases to Delaware became noticeable in early 1990s and accelerated once it became clear that Congress would not intervene.

Houston had been hit particularly hard by the competition. In 1999, Houston lawyers approached the Houston bankruptcy judges to complain about the city's losses to Delaware. The judges responded by requesting that the lawyers form a committee and formalize their recommendations for handling "complex" Chapter 11 cases.[1] ("Complexity" was merely a euphemism for big and lucrative; no court ever developed a method of determining complexity apart from company size.)

Eleven lawyers served on the Houston "Advisory Committee on Chapter 11 Issues."[2] When the committee reported, it asked the judges for several procedural changes in essentially two categories. First, the lawyers wanted quicker hearings, at more predictable times. Second, the lawyers wanted the local judges to award professional fees at rates comparable to those in Delaware and New York.

The judges issued new local rules providing for the designation of cases as "Complex Chapter 11 cases" and giving them certain priorities in scheduling. But the agenda was clearly much broader. Introducing the new rules at a January 26, 2000, bankruptcy bar luncheon, Houston bankruptcy judge William R. Greendyke told the assembled lawyers: "This is the sound bite. The war on fees is over."[3]

Houston was probably the first city to go through this process. But over the next two years, substantially the same thing occurred in Boston, Dallas, Chicago, Los Angeles, Minneapolis, Baltimore, Miami, and other cities. In each city, individual members of the local bankruptcy bar or an official delegation from the local bankruptcy bar association approached the local bankruptcy judges to express their dismay over the flight of local bankrupt companies to Delaware. In each city, the lawyers asked for the judges' help in dealing with the problem. In some—including Minneapolis and Chicago—the process included the preparation and submission of a written report. In some cities, judges actively participated in developing ideas for change. In Chicago, for example, the chief judge of the bankruptcy court convened a focus group that studied the "perceived loss of potential Chicago Chapter 11 Cases to Delaware."[4] In others they left development to the lawyers. But in nearly every city, the judges acknowledged problems and indicated their concern. In most cities, the judges' response included at least some changes to the local rules of court. In all or nearly all of the cities, the focus was expressly on the loss of cases to Delaware.

The rule changes differed from city to city. New York and Los Angeles committed by rule to match the Delaware practices that enabled companies with prepackaged cases to get in and out of bankruptcy in just over 30 days.[5] Courts that had not yet done so adopted the Delaware practice of paying fees at 30-day intervals rather than the customary interval of 120 days strongly suggested by section 331 of the Bankruptcy Code. (Section 331 provides that "any professional person . . . may apply to the court not more than once every 120 days . . . or more often if the court permits, for such compensation for services rendered. . . .") New York, Los Angeles, Houston, Dallas, Miami, Maryland, and Minnesota adopted new rules regarding first-day orders.

By October 2003, the process of organizing the bar and lobbying the judges to adopt megacase rules competitive with Delaware had been so routinized that an entire panel was devoted to the subject at the Annual Meeting of the National Conference of Bankruptcy Judges.[6]

The courts claimed they made these changes because each was the right thing to do. As one put it: "I don't see us as competing with any other court at all. What we're trying to do is be the best court we can."[7] The changes, they claimed, would smooth procedures, make fee practices fairer, and make bankruptcy more efficient.

The courts' claims lacked credibility because the Bankruptcy Code and Rules had remained essentially the same for nearly two decades. The courts would have us believe they coincidentally discovered these long-standing needs at the same time they faced a competitive challenge from Delaware. Were we really supposed to believe that the competition had nothing to do with these changes?

The courts that proceeded by local rule changes were limited in what they could expressly commit to do. Local rules can deal only with matters of procedure not already addressed by the national rules. The things Delaware was doing to attract cases—approving high professional fees and executive retention bonuses, releasing those professionals and executives from liability for wrongdoing, approving sales of businesses without following plan procedures, and the like—were nearly all contrary to the code and the national rules. Courts could not commit by local rule to match Delaware on these kinds of issues. But the rule changes courts could make stood as symbols of the courts' willingness to bend to the necessities of the marketplace on substantive issues as well. Their court, the lawyers could boast, had adopted complex case rules. Their court was willing to play the game.

In the five-year period from 1998 through 2002, the world of big-case bankruptcy experienced an unprecedented boom. The number of filings nationally went from 17 in 1997 to 97 in 2001. The number of new filings fell in 2002, but that year seven of the 13 largest filers in history chose bankruptcy courts: Worldcom, Conseco, Global Crossing, United Airlines, Adelphia Communications, NTL, and Kmart. As more and bigger companies filed, the world of big-case bankruptcy was like a lottery in which anybody with a

ticket could win. The local court's willingness to compete was the
bankruptcy professional's ticket.

Meanwhile, Back in Delaware . . .

The years 1998 and 1999 were good years in Delaware bankruptcy
practice. The increases in filings brought huge amounts of business
to Delaware, giving Delaware bankruptcy lawyers more work than
they could handle. Delaware firms expanded their bankruptcy
departments, and bankruptcy firms from outside Delaware opened
Delaware offices. In January 2000, the Los Angeles–based bankruptcy boutique Pachulski, Stang, Ziehl & Young announced that
it was opening a Delaware office and that Laura Davis Jones, the
highest profile bankruptcy lawyer in Delaware, would head it.
Later that year, Florida-based Zuckerman, Spaeder hired bankruptcy attorney Thomas G. Macauley away from Skadden Arps's
Delaware office to open its own Delaware office. Philadelphia-
based Buchanan, Ingersoll followed in 2001. Wilmington office
space was at a premium, and reservations at the luxurious duPont
Hotel two blocks from the bankruptcy court were hard to get.

In 2000, Delaware got 45 of the 79 cases filed nationally (57 percent). In those 45 cases alone, the Delaware bankruptcy court
would award over $700 million in professional fees and expenses.[8]
Considering the fees and expenses of parties to the bankruptcy case
not entitled to reimbursement through the court, the total professional fees and expenses in these 45 cases easily topped $1 billion.
To put these fees in perspective, were they distributed pro rata to
the residents of Delaware, each would be receiving $1,250 a year.

Of course, the money did not all stay in Delaware. Most of it
went to professionals based in other states, who traveled to
Delaware for hearings. But everyone involved knew that the longer
the big bankruptcy cases continued to go to Delaware, the larger
would be the percentages of fees sticking with Delaware professionals. In the early 1990s, lawyers from New York and other cities
brought the cases to Delaware. The young Delaware bankruptcy
lawyers such as Jim Patton; Laura Davis Jones; Thomas L. Ambro;

Gregg Galardi; William H. Sudell, Jr.; Mark D. Collins; and Anthony Clark served as local counsel. They sat in court, learned the ropes, and got paid for their time. But the lawyers from out of town were in charge of the cases and got nearly all the fees. In 1999, firms with offices in Delaware were lead counsel on some representations, but 76 percent of the fees awarded by the Delaware bankruptcy court were still going to out-of-state lawyers. In early 2003 Laura Davis Jones claimed that 75 percent of Pachulski, Stang's bankruptcy work in Delaware "was of the lead counsel variety."9 Jones's statistic probably exaggerated the rapidity of the shift of business to Delaware-based lawyers, but the shift was certainly occurring. If the Delaware court could continue to attract the cases, Delaware bankruptcy professionals would eventually dominate the field.

Delaware's biggest problem was a shortage of judges and courtrooms. Congress awarded Delaware its second permanent bankruptcy judge in 1993, a year when four large public companies filed in Delaware. In 2000, 11 times that many large public companies filed in Delaware, but the number of permanent judges had not changed. Delaware's tiny court was drowning in its own success.

In the early years of that success, the Judicial Conference of the United States had refused to authorize additional judges for Delaware. Bankruptcy judges are generally awarded on the basis of caseloads, and on that basis Delaware's entitlement to more judges had been clear. But the Judicial Conference had ignored Delaware's numbers, claiming that Delaware's need was temporary. By 1999, however, the Judicial Conference could no longer maintain that fiction. It recommended increasing the number of permanent judges in Delaware from two to three.10

The Judicial Conference appears to be deeply divided over the court competition. At its June 2001 meeting, the Judicial Conference Committee on the Administration of the Bankruptcy System (the "Bankruptcy Committee") approved a recommendation that would have required debtors to file in their local bankruptcy courts and ended the forum shopping.11 The Bankruptcy Committee placed the recommendation on the discussion calendar for the September 2001 meeting of the Judicial Conference. Then the Bank-ruptcy Committee mysteriously withdrew the recommendation without explanation. In 2002, the Judicial Conference recommended four additional bankruptcy judges for Delaware.[12] Through its Subcommittee on Venue-Related Matters, the Bank-ruptcy Committee then began working instead on a set of "best practices" with respect to the flurry of rule changes that was occurring. In June 2004, the subcommittee released the best practices report and recommended that the Bankruptcy Committee "reiter-ate its support for additional judicial resources in Delaware."[13]

The Judicial Conference's 2002 recommendation was to authorize a total of 36 new bankruptcy judgeships nationwide.[14] Knowing that senators and representatives from the areas slated to receive new judges would strongly support the authorizing legislation, congressional leaders decided to channel that support to a problem of their own. At the behest of banks and the consumer finance lobby, the congressional leaders were pushing an unpopular "omnibus" bankruptcy bill designed to make bankruptcy more difficult for consumer debtors. To increase support for the omnibus bill among reluctant rank and file members of Congress, congressional leaders were forcing any popular piece of legislation related to bankruptcy to be included in the omnibus bill. The judgeships bill was perhaps the most popular, so the congressional leaders included it. From 1999 to 2004, the omnibus bankruptcy bill continued to teeter on the edge of adoption, each time falling back. Delaware's new bankruptcy judges were held hostage to the omnibus bill, leaving the Delaware bankruptcy court to deal with the burgeoning caseload on its own.

Delaware used several strategies to cope with the problem. First, since Judge Farnan withdrew the reference effective February 1997, Delaware district judges had been handling some of the cases. Second, Delaware wrote to each of the more than 300 bankruptcy judges throughout the United States asking them to come to Delaware as "visiting judges." More than a half dozen responded by coming to Delaware to help out in their "spare" time. (The

Administrative Office of the U.S. Courts did not relieve the volunteers from any portion of their caseloads at home.) Third, the Delaware court began transferring some of its smaller megacases to other courts. Fourth, the Delaware court began assigning some of its megacases to judges from neighboring states who would do them as Delaware cases.[15] The Delaware court preferred such assignments to transfers because the assigned cases would continue to be counted as part of Delaware's caseload in computing the number of bankruptcy judgeships to which Delaware was entitled.

Even with these drastic measures in place, Delaware was losing ground. Debtors were having to wait longer to get hearings with the court, and the march of cases through the Delaware bankruptcy process was slowing. In 2001, for the first time since 1991, Delaware ended the year with more big bankruptcies pending than had been filed in the entire year. The slowing of Delaware's dockets began to show up in the exit statistics that same year (see table 9).

TABLE 9.   Filings, Backlog, and Days from Filing to Confirmation in Delaware

	Cases Filed during Year	Cases Pending Dec. 31	Length of Non-prepackaged (listed in confirmation year)			Length of Prepackaged (listed in confirmation year)		
			Mean, in Days	Median, in Days	Number of Cases	Mean, in Days	Median, in Days	Number of Cases
1990	2	2			0			0
1991	4	5	286	286	1			0
1992	6	5	399	448	3	37	36	3
1993	5	3	415	302	5	38	38	2
1994	4	1			0	38	36	6
1995	9	6	611	139	3			0
1996	13	9	257	203	5	66	67	4
1997	8	7	435	448	8	37	37	2
1998	13	13	263	248	5	53	53	2
1999	28	20	420	319	16	70	79	4
2000	45	42	280	170	18	43	37	3
2001	41	52	456	415	30			0
2002	25	36	433	469	32	286	46	3
2003	17	23	557	425	23	53	51	3

Source: Data from Lynn M. LoPucki's Bankruptcy Research Database.

Two, Three, Many Delawares

The clogging of the Delaware bankruptcy court in 2001 coincided
with the efforts of other bankruptcy courts to attract cases. New
York was the first to benefit. From 2000 to 2002, New York's market share rose from 6 percent to 26 percent. Delaware still attracted
a larger number of big cases in those years. But among the very
largest bankrupt companies—Enron, Worldcom, Global Crossing,
Adelphia, and NTL—New York had become the court of choice.

New York was not, however, the only court gaining market
share during this period. Through the decades of the 1980s and
1990s, the Chicago bankruptcy court had a total of only seven big
public company bankruptcies. In July 2000, Susan Pierson Sonderby, then the chief judge of Chicago's bankruptcy court, commissioned a focus group "to discuss why Chicago lawyers want to
travel to Delaware or New York, when we think we have an excel-
lent reputation."[16] The focus group reported back that the Chicago
court was doing a great job and merely suffered from "misperceptions." The court made some cosmetic rule changes, and in October 2000, the big cases began rolling in. In a period of 27 months,
Chicago got 14 big public company cases—twice as many as in the
preceding 20 years. They included some giants: Kmart, United Airlines, Conseco, National Steel, and Comdisco. Six of the 14—
including Kmart—were forum shops to Chicago by companies
headquartered elsewhere.

The explanation given by Daniel R. Murray, a bankruptcy
lawyer with Chicago's Jenner & Block, was typical.

> This is definitely not a coincidence. Large cases like Conseco,
> UAL, and Kmart don't just end up in any court by accident. . . .
> The number one reason for Chicago seeing these big Chapter 11
> cases is simple: Chicago is an attractive venue.
> For one thing, the courts in Chicago are readily available,
> with 10 bankruptcy judges at a time when many courts are suf-
> fering a judge shortage. . . . Hearings in Chicago move quickly
> and the judges are highly qualified. It is these factors primarily
> that have contributed to the shift of complex Chapter 11 cases
> from Delaware to Chicago.[17]

Murray's benign explanation, however, runs afoul of two nasty facts. First, even during Chicago's amazing 27-month run, as many large public companies were shopping out of Chicago as were shopping in (six). Chicago was merely holding its own. Second, Chicago's run ended in December 2002, without any change in the factors Murray cites in his explanation. Not a single big bankrupt shopped into Chicago in 2003 or the first half of 2004. Of the three Chicago companies filing bankruptcy during that period, two shopped out.[18]

Attracting big bankruptcy cases takes more than good judges in ample supply. The lawyers and executives who choose venues for large public companies—the case placers—are hard-nosed businesspeople. They know they have something valuable to offer: tens or hundreds of millions of dollars of business for local bankruptcy practitioners. They expect something in return: advantages their bankruptcy courts at home would not give them. They know they cannot get a binding commitment. The placement of a megabankruptcy case is a transaction that must be done on trust. But among repeat players, trust is possible even without honor.

The case placers place their trust along with their case. The court chosen is one they believe will reciprocate. If a court does not reciprocate, neither the lawyers nor the executives can do much about it in that case. But future lawyers and executives can take their cases elsewhere. The Delaware bankruptcy community understands this; Delaware was in the trust business long before the first big bankruptcy case arrived. In comparison, the Chicago bankruptcy community was naive.

In 2003, the Chicago bankruptcy court failed to deliver on two matters of trust in two very high profile cases. First, the executives of Conseco came to Chicago expecting releases from personal liability for their own wrongdoing. Some creditors objected to the releases,[19] but Conseco bought the objectors' approval by increasing the amounts the objectors' class would receive under the plan.[20] In other courts, the resulting lack of objection would have guaranteed confirmation. But Chicago's U.S. trustee pursued the objections the creditors had dropped, and Chicago bankruptcy judge

Carol Doyle refused to confirm the plan while the releases remained in it.[21] The U.S. trustee and the judge were doing the right thing, but it wasn't the competitive thing. Shortly after filing the Conseco case in December 2002, debtor's counsel James Sprayregan had said he expected Conseco to be out of bankruptcy no later than by the end of June.[22] Judge Doyle did not confirm the plan until September.

Chicago's second failure was the reversal on appeal of the critical vendor order in the city's most prominent case, Kmart.[23] (Critical vendor orders are discussed in more detail in the next chapter.) The Chicago court's reluctance to approve critical vendor orders had been cited in the Chicago focus group report as one of the reasons debtors preferred Delaware to Chicago.

Susan Pierson Sonderby—the Chicago judge who had commissioned the Chicago focus group report—was the judge on the Kmart case. The critical vendor order she entered was a whopper. It authorized a $300 million slush fund from which Kmart could immediately begin paying prepetition debts owing to "critical vendors" selected by Kmart's top managers.[24] (The money would come out of the entitlements of other, less fortunate unsecured creditors who were not selected for special treatment.)

But on appeal, the Chicago District Court reversed the bankruptcy court's decision, saying that *all* critical vendor payments violated the Bankruptcy Code and strongly implying that the bankruptcy court should order return of the money.[25] Kmart appealed to the Seventh Circuit Court of Appeals. While the appeal remained pending, Judge Sonderby refused to order the critical vendors to return Kmart's money. But the matter was already beyond her control. In February 2004, the Seventh Circuit agreed with the district court that the Kmart critical vendor order had been improper.[26] Kmart had trusted the Chicago bankruptcy system, and the Chicago bankruptcy system had not come through. To use the lawyers' favorite code word, Chicago lacked "predictability."

Chicago may or may not survive these failures. Pressure will continue for the Chicago judges to keep trying. The judges who made the decisions in Conseco and Kmart have likely already felt the heat from Chicago boosters. Maybe next time they will give in. Maybe not. (District Judge Grady has life tenure.) But if the Chicago judges do not give in, other judges in other cities will. The cases will go there, Chicago bankruptcy practice will wither, and the corruption of the bankruptcy courts will continue unabated.

6

Corruption

My client was assured that court approval was
merely a rubber-stamp process.

—Attorney M. Blake Cleary, Young, Conaway, Stargatt & Taylor,
explaining to Delaware bankruptcy judge Mary Walrath why his client
had relied on a sale of assets not yet approved by the court

To understand how competition is corrupting the U.S. bank-ruptcy courts, begin by distinguishing court competition from mere forum shopping. Courts inevitably differ in ways that advantage one litigant over another. A court may interpret a law differently or favor a particular kind of litigant or case. One court may process cases faster than others or be geographically more convenient. For centuries, lawyers have maneuvered their cases into the courts most advantageous to themselves or their clients. Forum shopping can yield benefits to shoppers without courts changing what they are doing—or even realizing that the shopping is occurring.

By contrast, court competition is an active, deliberate response by the court to forum shopping. When courts compete, they change what they are doing to make themselves more attractive to forum shoppers. If more than one court competes, the process becomes reiterative. Court A offers to do X for shoppers; court B offers to do X plus Y. Court C—or court A—can then offer to do even more. The court that offers forum shoppers the most may be the only one that gets cases in the end, but all of the judges who compete are corrupted along the way. Their actions are "corrupt" in that they are dictated not by an attempt to apply the law to the facts of the case but by the need to remain competitive.

The beneficiaries of competition are the case placers—the debtor's executives, professionals, and DIP lenders. Because the case placers decide which court gets the case, they are the people to whom competing courts pitch their services. The interests of the case placers will sometimes be congruent with those of the company and sometime sharply at odds with them. For example, the case placers may want to minimize the company's problems in order to shift blame away from the company's current management. If the company emerges from bankruptcy and fails a few years later, the failure will appear to be that of a later management.

Serving the case placers usually requires serving the case placers' contractual allies. For example, if the case placers make a prepetition deal with an unsecured creditors' committee or prospective purchaser of the company, a competing court will require the case placers to honor it. The reason is that the case placers need binding deals with creditors' committees and purchasers to achieve the case placers' own goals. If the relevant court allowed case placers to dishonor such deals, case placers couldn't make them in the first place. If a particular court would not honor such a deal, the case placers, creditors' committees, and purchasers would avoid that court by including as part of the deal a commitment to take the deal to a court that will enforce it.

Defenders of court competition frequently seize on examples of courts enforcing such prepetition agreements as proof that the competing courts are serving the interests of both debtors and creditors. But this kind of protection is not available to those whose only relationship to the debtor is as a creditor. In the period immediately prior to bankruptcy, creditors lack sufficient leverage over the case placers to control the choice of a court. Even if a particular court disregarded the creditors' interests, similarly situated creditors in the next case could do nothing about it. The leverage that enables some creditors to benefit from court competition comes not from their status as creditors but from other sources such as their status as future lenders, suppliers, or purchasers.

To ally with the case placers often requires that the future lenders, suppliers, or purchasers offer benefits directly to the case placers. For example, a DIP lender that seeks the debtor's consent to a plan beneficial to itself may need to permit ineffective management to remain in place. A prospective purchaser of the company who seeks the case placer's support for the purchase may need to signal to the current managers that the purchaser will hire them as managers of the purchased company and give them stock in the purchased company. The court will be slow to interfere with such self-dealing because it needs the support of the case placers to maintain its flow of new cases.

Bankruptcy court competition brought quick, fundamental change to the bankruptcy system. Without policy debate or legislation, cases got faster, compensation for professionals and managers increased, and laws and procedures designed to protect small stakeholders were increasingly ignored. The movements in these directions have not been relentless. Sometimes they proceeded by fits and starts. Embarrassed by public criticism, courts sometimes took steps to rein in the most egregious of their practices. Some waver so much it is difficult to say whether they are even in the competition. But once a new practice that benefits case placers is introduced, competition assures its acceptance. The only way for the system to reject the new practice is for every court to reject it. If even a single court breaks ranks, that court tends to get the cases, and the practice becomes dominant.

The most damaging changes competition brought were these.

1. The courts lost control over professional fees.
2. Failed managers tightened their grips on their jobs and companies.
3. Corporate debtors had more difficulty recovering money taken by failed managers.
4. Failed managers began paying themselves huge retention bonuses.
5. The courts began rubber-stamping prepackaged plans.
6. So-called critical vendors began grabbing the shares of other unsecured creditors.
7. Managers began selling their companies at inadequate prices for personal benefit instead of reorganizing them.

In each of these respects, practices changed quickly throughout the United States. In each, the change occurred after 1990, the year in which Delaware initiated the competition. In none were the changes prompted by legislation, judicial decision, or policy debate. In all, the direction of change favored the case placers. The remainder of this chapter explains why each of these seven changes is corruption rather than mere evolution.

Professional Fee Practices

Competition ordinarily holds prices down. Customers seek the supplier who will charge the lowest price for a given level of quality. To attract customers, suppliers compete by lowering the prices their customers must pay. Bankruptcy court competition works precisely the opposite way. To attract companies needing reorganization, courts compete by raising the amounts of the professional fees the courts will approve, thus raising the client-companies' costs for reorganization.

Three factors contribute to make this upside-down competition work. Most important, the professionals themselves usually dominate the company's choice of a bankruptcy court. When they choose among the bankruptcy courts, all most executives know about those courts is what their lawyers and investment bankers have told them. That means lawyers can steer clients away from courts that won't approve high fees toward courts that will. Second, total professional fees are small in relation to the amounts of money at risk—about 1 to 2 percent of the debtor's total assets.[1] A bad result in reorganization can cost 20 to 40 percent of the debtor's total assets.[2] Third, the top executives who hire bankruptcy professionals are spending other people's money. The executives' primary concern may not be how their companies will fare in bankruptcy but how they themselves will. Overcompensating the company's lawyers may engender a feeling of obligation on the part of the lawyers to the executives themselves, and so the executives are happy to do it.

This competitive inversion may at first seem both bizarre and unfamiliar. But the inversion is closely analogous to a common kind of corruption—the bribing of corporate purchasing agents. Just as a supplier of hammers or toilet seats might bribe a customer's purchasing agent to buy at the supplier's high price instead of at a competitor's lower price, so the competing bankruptcy courts offer high fees to bribe the lawyers to bring them cases.

Numerous bankruptcy lawyers have assured me in interviews that they do not let their own fee considerations determine what bankruptcy court they recommend. But many of the very same lawyers acknowledge that courts that don't pay the "going rates" don't get cases. Other lawyers make no attempt to hide the relationship between their own fees and the courts they recommend. In a recent *National Law Journal* interview, for example, leading bankruptcy lawyer Stephen H. Case of New York's Davis Polk & Wardwell "readily admitted steering his clients to venues that will pay his going rate, but added that he explains to clients that his partners will not allow him to work for less."[3]

The evidence that fee practices affect the placement of cases is overwhelming. In our study of forum shopping by large companies in the 1980s, Bill Whitford and I conducted more than 120 interviews with lawyers involved in the cases. On the basis of those interviews, we concluded that other courts' reluctance to approve fees at New York rates was a principal reason for the forum shopping to New York.[4] In 2001, Professor Marcus Cole—an ardent defender of Delaware and court competition—interviewed 30 lawyers regarding the reasons for forum shopping. A majority acknowledged that fees influenced the forum shopping decision and that the direction of influence was to move cases toward the courts paying higher rather than lower fees.[5] The Conference on Large Chapter 11 Cases convened by the Judicial Conference's Venue Subcommittee discussed the "appointment and payment of attorneys and professionals" as one of seven "possible venue drivers."[6]

Most important, the judges themselves understand the role that fees play in the decision to file. When judges throughout the country sought to mollify their local lawyers about the Delaware threat, they almost invariably mentioned their own fee practices. In introducing the new complex court rules intended to make Houston competitive with Delaware, Houston bankruptcy judge William R.

Greendyke reassured the gathered lawyers that "the war on fees is over."[7] In explaining how she countered the "misperceptions" that sent Chicago cases to Delaware, Chicago chief bankruptcy judge Susan Pierson Sonderby told the *Wall Street Journal* that "she began spreading the word to attorneys that if they showed they deserved their pay . . . the [Chicago] judges would accept their fees."[8] In an article published in the local bankruptcy bar newsletter explaining why he would *not* change Miami court practices in an effort to compete with Delaware, Chief Judge Robert A. Mark paused to reassure the lawyers that "I will not suffer from 'sticker shock' when I see large numbers in fee applications or when I am presented with applications to retain consultants or investment bankers which provide for large retainers and non-hourly based fee arrangements."[9] In the wave of local rule changes prompted by lawyer concerns about the loss of cases to Delaware, the New York,[10] Los Angeles,[11] Chicago,[12] Dallas,[13] and Maryland[14] courts all copied the Delaware practice of paying fees at 30-day intervals instead of the 120-day intervals that had been standard practice for a decade. And when the panel of lawyers and judges that would discuss "issues that affect Chapter 11 forum choice" at the National Conference of Bankruptcy Judges' 2003 Annual Meeting settled on the five issues most worthy of discussion, "[professional] retention and compensation orders" appeared second on the list.[15]

From early on, bankruptcy judges took essentially two approaches to controlling fees. One was to review fee applications to determine whether each of the charges was "reasonable and necessary." As discussed in chapter 1, that approach is hopeless. No mechanisms exist by which judges can evaluate each of the thousands of charges that may comprise a single application. The other approach was to impose bright-line limits on the lawyers' hourly billing rates—referred to as "fee caps"—and control the aggregate number of hours based on the judge's sense of the case. For example, a judge might announce that he rarely approved fees in excess of $300 an hour. This method was somewhat arbitrary, but it was sufficiently effective that lawyers avoided the courts using it.

As the competition heated up, the fee caps came off. Judge after judge announced that he or she had seen the error of fee caps and would cease to impose them. Courts continued to go through the motions of fee control, sometimes even appointing fee examiners or fee committees. But the bottom line is that the courts are approving nearly all of the fees for which the professionals apply. In a study of professional fees awarded in 48 large public company bankruptcies concluded from 1998 to June 2002, Joseph Doherty and I found that the judges approved almost 98 percent of the amounts for which the professionals applied. The Delaware court approved more than 99 percent.[16] The bankruptcy courts are operating virtually on an honor system. In a new study just completed as this book went to press, Joseph Doherty and I found that professional fees in large public company bankruptices increased by 47 percent from 1998 to 2003.

Helping Failed Managers Keep Their Jobs

In most of the world's bankruptcy systems, a creditor representative takes control of the debtor company upon the filing of a case. In the United States, the debtor's management ordinarily retains control. That the system should operate this way is somewhat surprising. Experts are in near-universal agreement that bad management is the leading cause of business bankruptcy. In many cases, leaving debtor's management in control means leaving the very people who caused the debtor's failure in control. The United States' "debtor-in-possession" system exists nevertheless because bankruptcy lawyers convinced Congress that if managers lost their jobs too frequently or too easily in bankruptcy, managers would not bring their companies into bankruptcy until it was too late to save them.

U.S. bankruptcy law gives the judge the power to appoint a creditor representative—a trustee—to take control of the debtor company in cases of gross mismanagement, fraud, or similar cause. Even before the onset of court competition, that power was exercised only in extreme cases.[17]

Despite the rarity of trustees, Whitford and I found that the bankruptcy system of the 1980s dealt surprisingly well with the management problem. Through a combination of pressures from creditors, stockholders, suppliers, and others, prepetition managers were almost invariably ousted from control by the end of the reorganization case. In our study of the 43 largest reorganizations of the early part of that decade, we identified the CEO in office at the time the company's financial problems came to light (the "tainted" CEO). In only two of those reorganizations (5 percent) did the tainted CEO manage to remain in office through confirmation of the plan.[18] (Interestingly, the two cases in which tainted CEOs survived in office were in Delaware and New York. In the rest of the country, every tainted CEO was swept from office.) In some cases, the CEOs resigned, in some they were forced from office by the board or the creditors, in some the company failed, and in some the CEOs negotiated their exit. But one way or another, the problem was solved. Other research on management turnover in bankruptcy during that era made similar findings.[19]

In the 1990s—the era of court competition—the dynamic was different. Studying the 98 companies that emerged from reorganization from 1991 to 1996, Doherty and I found that tainted CEOs—and CEOs in general—were significantly more likely to remain in office through the bankruptcy case than were managers in the 1980s.[20] Other researchers have recently made similar findings. The trend for bankrupt companies was particularly surprising because it was the opposite of that for large public companies generally. From the 1980s to the 1990s, the jobs of top managers of big companies grew less secure in the economy as a whole,[21]—the same period in which the jobs of top managers of big bankrupt companies grew more secure.

A study of cases in the early 1980s found that management turnover was significantly higher in companies reorganizing in bankruptcy than in similarly distressed companies reorganizing outside bankruptcy.[22] The bankruptcy process was removing failed managers who otherwise would have remained in place. By 2001, the bankruptcy process was no longer doing so. Turnover was no higher in companies reorganizing in bankruptcy than in companies reorganizing outside bankruptcy.[23]

The inability to force out bad managers in the era of court competition was actually hurting the companies. Examining data from cases in the 1990s, Doherty and I found that when a member of the prepetition management team remained as CEO through the crucial stages of the bankruptcy case, the company was more likely to fail in the five years after it emerged. Although the statistical relationship was weak, firms that "cleaned house" by hiring a new CEO from outside the company before proposing their plan of reorganization were more likely to succeed.[24]

Helping Corporate Thieves Keep the Money

In 2001, a corporate scandal of unprecedented magnitude struck the American economy. It began with the collapse of Enron in late 2001. Within eight months, three other corrupt corporate giants had followed Enron into bankruptcy: Worldcom, Global Crossing, and Adelphia. Each had the same problem: fraudulent managers who had cooked the books and looted the companies.

The bankruptcy remedy for corporate fraud is the appointment of a trustee to replace the suspect management. Bankruptcy Code § 1104 provides that "the court *shall* order the appointment of a trustee for cause, including fraud, dishonesty, incompetence, or gross mismanagement of the affairs of the debtor by current management, either before or after the commencement of the case" (emphasis added). That language certainly seemed to apply to these four cases. But the New York bankruptcy court—which got all four cases—appointed a trustee in none of them.

Appointment of a trustee is a drastic remedy. A trustee replaces the board of directors as the corporation's ultimate decision maker. Typically, the trustee will retain some members of former management for those members' company-specific knowledge, but it is the trustee who is in charge. Bankruptcy courts have always been reluctant to appoint trustees in situations where the business will continue to operate. But before the era of court competition, operating trustees were appointed in circumstances less extreme than these four cases.[25]

These four cases were among the biggest, boldest frauds in history. The *Wall Street Journal* reported that the shredding of documents in the Enron case continued even after the shredding had been exposed in the national media and the bankruptcy case had been filed.[26] If the appointment of a trustee for fraud and gross mismanagement was not warranted in these cases, it would never be warranted. In the introduction I discussed how New York bankruptcy judge Arthur J. Gonzalez avoided appointing a trustee in the Enron case. What remains to be told is how that failure to appoint a trustee altered the dynamics of the Enron case.

Except for a six-month period in which Jeffrey Skilling was CEO, Kenneth Lay was the CEO and chairman of the board of directors of Enron from the founding of the company until he resigned under public pressure on January 23, 2002. Lay's successor was bankruptcy turnaround manager Stephen F. Cooper. Cooper was a respected outsider, and his hiring was regarded as a transparent effort on the part of Enron's board and creditors' committee to avoid the appointment of a trustee.[27] That effort succeeded.

On January 24—the day after Lay's resignation—the *Wall Street Journal* had the Cooper story by press time.[28] Considering that Enron's management must have arranged Cooper's candidacy and vetted him before setting the appointment with the board reported in the *Journal,* it is a reasonable inference that Ken Lay at least participated in choosing Cooper.

The creditors who sought the appointment of a trustee asked Cooper if he would accept the role of a neutral trustee, along with the responsibility to investigate the fraud. He refused. On the day his appointment was announced, Cooper said that he planned to "spend little to zero of my time" on what happened in the past at Enron. "It's literally of no interest to me."[29] In other words, he wasn't going after Ken Lay or the other members of Enron's deposed management who together had taken hundreds of millions from the company in its last two years and left it mortally wounded.

Nor was the board. The 17 directors in office before the Enron scandal broke in 2001 were Ken Lay's friends and cronies. Like

Lay, the directors had participated in the board meetings at which the transactions with offshore entities that would later lead to indictments had been approved. According to the Senate Permanent Subcommittee on Investigations, the directors had "witnessed numerous indications of questionable practices by Enron management over several years, but chose to ignore them" "knowingly allowed Enron to engage in high risk accounting practices," "exercised inadequate oversight," "knowingly allowed Enron to conduct billions of dollars in off-the-books activity to make its financial condition appear better than it was," and "failed to halt [compensation] abuse by Kenneth Lay."[30]

Because the court had not appointed a trustee, the board remained in control of Enron—and Cooper. Board members who had approved the offshore transactions in 1999 and 2000 and a $60 million golden parachute for Ken Lay in 2001—and were found by the congressional subcommittee to have knowingly engaged in substantial wrongdoing—remained a substantial majority on the board until Cooper proposed and won acceptance of his plan to liquidate Enron.[31] Then Lay's appointees elected their own successors, who, not surprisingly, didn't go after their benefactors either.[32]

Hiring Cooper under these conditions split Enron's obligation to pursue its fraudulent managers three ways. Cooper and the board controlled Enron, its employees, attorneys, and store of documents. The court appointed an examiner to investigate the fraud but gave the examiner no authority to sue anyone. The court authorized the creditors' committee to bring suits on a case-by-case basis. The effect of this three-way division of authority was to bureaucratize and ultimately cripple the effort to hold Enron's corrupt executives civilly and criminally accountable.

In addition to the awkward triumvirate, criminal prosecutors, the Securities and Exchange Commission, and class action plaintiffs' lawyers were also after Enron's fallen executives. But each worked under limitations that prevented them from being as effective as an Enron trustee might have been.

Prosecutors have little power to require defendants to give them information, yet they must be ready to prove their case beyond a reasonable doubt before they file it. Ken Lay was not indicted until three years after the scandal broke.

Shareholders could and did file class actions to recover their losses from the officers and directors legally responsible. But shareholder class actions are a cumbersome and disfavored means of proceeding against corrupt executives[33] and often end in small settlements principally benefiting the lawyers. The federal Multi-District Litigation Panel moved the Enron shareholder fraud actions to the U.S. district court in Houston, where, years after the initial filing, the numerous parties were still squabbling over how they would organize their investigation.[34] In the meantime, the Enron examiner was seeking authority to destroy some of the documents the class action lawyers were seeking because the examiner had promised confidentiality to the sources.[35] Ironically, some of the consolidated cases were "derivative,"[36] meaning that the plaintiffs were suing in the name of Enron because Enron refused to bring the case.[37] That meant the shareholder faced every barrier to recovery Enron faced and, in addition, the barriers Congress had placed in the way of derivative actions.

The recently defanged Securities and Exchange Commission took no action against Lay or Skilling. That left only the conflicted creditors' committee to pursue the cases against Enron's crooked executives. Had the New York bankruptcy court instead treated Enron as the fraud case it was and appointed a trustee, the trustee probably would have concluded that at least five matters required immediate attention.

1. *The unauthorized repurchase case against Kenneth and Linda Lay.* In the year prior to bankruptcy, Kenneth and Linda Lay sold about $74 million of Enron stock to Enron. The Enron examiner concluded that these sales are "voidable at the election of Enron. Upon such event . . . Enron would return to Lay 2,131,282 shares of Enron common stock, and Lay would be liable to repay loans in the amount of $94,267,163."[38] A trustee would have elected to avoid those transactions, but Enron's management did not. That

forced the unsecured creditors' committee to sue on a fraudulent transfer theory,[39] which may be considerably more difficult to win.

2. *The mismanagement case against Kenneth Lay and Jeffrey Skilling*. The Enron examiner found that

> Acting in their capacities as directors, Lay, Skilling and the Outside Directors authorized Enron to enter into the Rhythms hedge and three of the Raptors hedges, none of which had a rational business purpose. . . . There is evidence that Lay, Skilling and the Outside Directors were aware of facts demonstrating this lack of rational business purpose. . . .
>
> Both Lay and Skilling failed to respond to indications of potential problems related to the use of SPE transactions. In addition, Skilling failed to respond to red flags regarding the SPE transactions that Enron entered into with LJM1 and LJM2. By failing to respond to such red flags, Lay and Skilling were at least negligent and, therefore, breached their fiduciary duties as officers.[40]

The SPE (special purpose entity) transactions were entered into to conceal Enron's true financial condition from investors. They injured Enron by postponing reorganization efforts until those efforts were too late.[41] That meant Enron had the right to recover its damages from Lay and Skilling. A trustee would certainly have sued. Neither Enron nor its creditors' committee has done so.

3. *The house builders*. As the possibility Enron would sue its corrupt executives loomed, three of the prime suspects—Jeffrey Skilling, Andrew Fastow, and Michael Kopper—began building new homes in River Oaks, "the neighborhood where the rich live."[42] What the executives were doing was stashing the loot in a place from which even judgment creditors couldn't get it back. Each of the houses cost millions of dollars. Under Texas law, if the executives completed their homes and moved into them, the homes would be "homesteads" and exempt from the claims of their creditors—including Enron. Because the mansions were exempt, the executives would be entitled to keep them even if creditors could prove that the executives sank their money into the mansions for

the purpose of defrauding the creditors.[43] The only way to stop the executives would have been for Enron to make its claim against the three and persuade a court to enter an injunction against the making of the fraudulent transfer. Even though television news programs repeatedly showed the progress of construction on those mansions, Enron didn't even try. At about the same time, Scott Sullivan, the CFO of Worldcom, who had been charged with securities fraud for cooking Worldcom's books, was building a $22 million mansion in Florida. Florida is probably the only other state besides Texas where the law permits a debtor to fraudulently invest ill-gotten gains in a homestead to beat his or her creditors.[44] Worldcom's management, which, like Enron's, was operating under the protection of the New York bankruptcy court without a trustee, also took no action.

4. *The eve-of-bankruptcy bonus case.* About a month before bankruptcy, Enron paid $53 million in deferred compensation to executives.[45] The examiner eventually concluded that these payments were likely avoidable as preferences.[46] Then, less than a week before bankruptcy, Enron paid bonuses totaling $73 million to about 500 key executives, traders, and other employees. Eventually, the Enron employee committee sued to recover the deferred compensation payments, and the Enron creditors' committee sued to recover 292 of the bonuses.[47] The belated lawsuits were predictably ineffectual in recovering the money. Bonus recipients still working for Enron paid back most of the money they owed,[48] but predictably, those no longer working for Enron did not. Recipients who had been allowed to keep the money for a year or two had adjusted their personal finances accordingly, and Enron no longer had the leverage that came from being their employer. As of December 2003, only about $7 million had been recovered for the estate from recipients no longer employed by Enron.[49]

Had the court appointed a trustee in the early days of the bankruptcy case, the demand for return of the illegal payments would have been made before the recipients had met the condition that they remain in Enron's employ for 90 days.[50] Employees who quit instead of repaying would have breached the condition, making their liability for return of the money clear. Much more of the money would have been recovered.

5. *The case against the banks for their participation in the SPE transactions.* The examiner found there was sufficient evidence to proceed against Citigroup/Citibank and JP Morgan Chase & Co.[51] The two banks were, however, prominent members of the committee that was supposed to sue them—the creditors' committee. In September 2003—nearly two years after Enron filed bankruptcy—Enron itself finally brought the action.

Enron and the other parties who wished to sue on Enron's behalf had only two years in which to file their cases or be barred by the statute of limitations.[52] Because the case was handled so awkwardly, nearly six months had passed before the examiner was even appointed.[53] The effect was to rush the investigation.[54] The examiner worked quickly but was still completing his report when the deadline expired. That left parties who discovered their causes of action through the examiner's work little or no time in which to digest the 4,500-page report, retain counsel, and prepare their lawsuits for filing.[55] Cases and issues may have been lost in the shuffle. The appointment of a trustee would have avoided the awkward sharing and sequencing of the investigation and litigation, but court competition had precluded that solution.

Retention Bonuses

Bankruptcy courts commonly review the compensation of incumbent managers for reasonableness. During the 1980s, the issue was usually whether the managers' compensation should be cut. The idea that a bankrupt company should pay its failed managers a bonus to stay with the company had not yet occurred to anyone. After all, those managers had no place else to go. In a study of managers who departed from bankrupt New York Stock Exchange– or American Stock Exchange–listed companies from 1979 to 1984, Professor Stuart Gilson of the Harvard Business School found that none landed another job as the top executive of a New York Stock Exchange– or American Stock Exchange–listed company.[56] Gilson concluded that "top managers leave the labor market in large numbers following their departure from financially-distressed firms."[57]

In the 1980s employers often paid "retention bonuses" to types of employees who were in short supply, such as nurses or pilots. They also paid retention bonuses to employees whose jobs would be terminated at some fixed date in the future—the date of a plant closing or merger—but whose services were needed in the meantime. The bonuses were typically a few thousand dollars per employee.

Beginning in the 1990s some companies also paid retention bonuses to managers working on short-term assignments. For example, a company that sold its entire business might offer a retention bonus to its top managers to keep working until the sale closed. Or a company in financial distress might fire its managers, hire new ones to turn the company around, and pay the new ones retention bonuses to stay with the company until the turnaround was complete.

As executive compensation skyrocketed in the 1990s, the retention bonus idea was quickly put to abuse. Entrenched managers who had caused the downfall of their companies decided that not only should their companies retain them, the companies should pay them "retention bonuses" to stay. Sometimes those managers had sufficient power within their companies to win board approval.

That left the bankruptcy courts as the last line of defense. But bankruptcy courts that were competing for cases were not up to the task—even in cases where the managers had already failed in the jobs they held and had no employment prospects elsewhere. The Kmart case illustrates the nature and extent of the problem.

Kmart hired Charles C. Conaway as CEO in May 2000. Conaway agreed to a salary of $1.4 million a year, an annual bonus of $1.75 million, other benefits worth an additional $447,000, and a onetime signing bonus of $6.3 million.[58] It was a lot of money, but to Charles Conaway's mind, it must not have been enough. Over his 22 months at Kmart, Conaway renegotiated his contract three times, extracting about $26 million in total personal compensation. Some was in the form of retention bonuses and loans.

The extra money was not to reward successful performance. A few months after Kmart hired Conaway, Kmart reported its first quarterly loss. From there, Kmart's performance grew progressively worse. By the end of 2000, Kmart's losses for the year totaled $268 million. The following year, 2001, Kmart lost $2.4 billion. The Conaway team covered up a portion of the 2001 loss by booking $420 million in phantom revenues in the first half of that year.

In December 2001, Conaway persuaded Kmart's board to make $28.5 million in "retention loans" to 22 top executives (Conaway not included). If the managers stayed with the company, the company would later forgive the loans without repayment. The purpose was to induce Kmart's top managers to remain with the firm through its bankruptcy reorganization. The problem with that rationale was that Kmart's top managers were not turnaround experts brought in to clean up someone else's mess. They were the people who made the mess. Kmart would eventually come to its senses and sue to get the money back.[59] But by then it would be too late.

On January 22, 2002, less than two months after making the retention loans, Michigan-based Kmart filed for bankruptcy in Chicago. In early March, Kmart's board forced Conaway out of office. Instead of suing him for the mismanagement that landed Kmart in bankruptcy, the board—under the leadership of its new chairman, James B. Adamson—approved a $4.5 million severance package for Conaway and proposed to forgive a $5 million retention loan Conaway had received as part of his May 2001 renegotiation. As is usual in such transactions, Kmart sought the approval of the bankruptcy court. The Conaway-Adamson grab put Chief Bankruptcy Judge Susan Pierson Sonderby in a difficult position. In an article published later that same year, the *Wall Street Journal* described Sonderby as having led "a decade-long mission to keep major cases in her city."[60] Conaway had helped make that mission a success by bringing one of the largest debtors in history to Sonderby's court. (With a workforce of 225,000, Kmart had more

employees than any company that had ever filed bankruptcy anywhere.) Approval of the severance pay and loan forgiveness would
be the first and last thing Conaway would seek from Sonderby in
return. In the eyes of future CEOs in search of an accommodating
bankruptcy court, Sonderby's ruling on Conaway's pay would be
the measure of how the Chicago court responded to CEOs who
brought the court cases. Yet Sonderby's signature on an order giving $9.5 million to the fired executive who led the company into
bankruptcy would have been embarrassing. Sonderby finessed the
issue by announcing orally in court that the payments did not
require her approval.[61] Conaway got the $4.5 million and didn't
have to repay the $5 million he had borrowed.

Within two months after Kmart filed bankruptcy, 16 of the 22
executives that received the $28.5 million to stay had left—taking
Kmart's money with them. Kmart demanded the money back, but
only three of the executives paid.[62] If the retention loans had not
been a fraud, they had at least been a monumental stupidity.

To replace Conaway as CEO, the board chose one of the archi-
tects of the retention loan program, the Kmart board's own chairman, James B. Adamson. The board touted Adamson as an experienced turnaround manager. The record didn't support it.

Adamson had been successful at Burger King in the early 1990s.
He rose to CEO in just two years and held that position for two
more years. In 1995, Adamson left Burger King to take the top job
at Denny's, which he held for six years. At Denny's however,
Adamson clearly failed. Two-and-a-half years after Adamson took
over, the company filed bankruptcy. Denny's discharged $1 billion
in debt, but even that wasn't enough to turn the company around.
Denny's unbroken string of annual losses continued for the rest of
Adamson's tenure in office. In January 2001, at the age of 54,
Adamson "retired"—a corporate euphemism for unemployment.
But in April 2002, the Kmart board—headed by Adamson—chose
Adamson as Kmart's new CEO. A month later, a major portion of
Denny's that Adamson had supposedly "turned around"—the
Carrows and Coco's restaurants—slipped quietly back into bank-

ruptcy. In 2004, Denny's—which had never recovered from the Adamson era—itself appeared close to refiling.[63]

Adamson had landed his spot on the Kmart board in 1996, on the heels of his success at Burger King. When he lost his job at Denny's, he stayed on the Kmart board, rising to chairman under Conaway. When Adamson became chairman of Kmart's board—four days before the company filed bankruptcy—Kmart set his director's fee at $1 million per year.[64] That was about seven times what successful companies of Kmart's size paid directors annually.[65] In addition, Adamson was paid an "inducement fee" of $2.5 million and promised a $4 million bonus if Kmart emerged from bankruptcy by July 31, 2003. Kmart also agreed to pay Adamson's taxes on all these amounts. Last, to assure that Adamson would get his money even if Kmart failed, Kmart established a $10 million bank letter of credit in Adamson's favor.[66] Even by the lax standards of corporate America, it was an astonishing grab. And it was just the prelude.

Two months later, with Kmart in bankruptcy, Adamson took over as CEO. His new compensation contract in that position provided for a salary of $1.5 million a year and an annual bonus of $1.9 million.[67] It specifically provided that he could keep the $2.5 million inducement fee he had just received for becoming chairman and promised him an additional $5.9 million on termination of his employment—even if he was fired.[68] Adamson's contract also provided for continuation of what the company called "certain reasonable travel and housing benefits as were originally provided under his contract as Chairman of the Board." *Fortune Magazine* described those benefits as "weekly private plane service between his residences in Detroit, New York, and Florida, a car and driver in Michigan and New York, and temporary accommodations at the swanky Townsend Hotel near Kmart headquarters. A standard room there costs $320 a night."[69] The deal was expressly subject to court approval.[70]

One of Adamson's first moves as CEO was to seek court approval of another retention bonus plan. On April 23, 2002, Judge Sonderby approved the first three tiers of Kmart's Corporate Annual Performance Plan—the tiers that gave money to 45 top executives. That day, she decided that Kmart's compensation contract with Adamson did not require her approval. The contract was binding without it.[71] Nine months later, with Kmart still mired in bankruptcy, Kmart's board fired Adamson and paid him $3.6 million in settlement.[72] The last five remaining executives who had shared in the December 2001 retention loans Adamson had approved left along with him.

In the early 1990s, retention bonuses for top managers were rare. The numbers increased in the late 1990s and then exploded in 2001. Late that year, the *Wall Street Journal* cited pay-to-stay bonuses in Chapter 11 cases as "an increasingly popular trend" and highlighted four cases in which such bonuses doubled or tripled CEOs' pay during Chapter 11.[73] Some of the retention bonuses were necessary to induce managers from outside the company to accept jobs and stick with them through the bankruptcy. But others were paid to managers who were responsible for the company's problems and had no other job prospects. The competing bankruptcy courts approved them all. (The Salt Lake City bankruptcy court initially rejected a retention plan proposed by Geneva Steel but approved the company's second try.)[74]

Apologists for the companies and the courts defended retention bonuses with the argument that the companies needed continuity and institutional memory in a time when organizational instability was already high. But the data indicated otherwise. Companies that brought in a new management team for the reorganization fared better than those that did not. A court not hobbled by its own need to attract cases could simply order the former managers to furnish information the new managers needed.[75]

Locked in competition for big cases, the bankruptcy courts were in no position to resist firms' requests for authority to pay retention bonuses. The same executives who sought the bonuses brought the cases. The bonuses would be one of the first issues on each court's agenda when a case was filed. Bankruptcy judges could not fail to realize that if they interfered with the top executives' retention bonuses, future CEOs would take their business elsewhere.

Rubber-Stamping Prepackaged Cases

Generally speaking, a bankruptcy reorganization case consists of three steps. First, the debtor discloses its financial condition, future prospects, and reorganization plan to its creditors and stockholders. Second, the creditors and stockholders vote on the plan. Third, if the court is satisfied that the plan has been properly proposed and accepted, the court confirms it. Confirmation makes the plan binding on the debtor and all of its creditors and shareholders—including those who voted against it or did not vote at all. Ordinarily, all these events occur while the debtor is in bankruptcy, a period that averages about one year.

The same three steps occur in a prepackaged bankruptcy case. The difference is that the first two steps—plan proposal and voting—occur before the debtor files the bankruptcy case. The debtor arrives in court with a "package" of plan, disclosure statement, and cast ballots already in hand. The purpose of the bankruptcy filing is to impose the plan on the creditors and shareholders who did not vote for it. The confirmation order does that.

In each case, the court enters two key orders. The first is an order approving the debtor's disclosure statement as providing adequate information for voting on the plan. The second is the confirmation order. The Bankruptcy Code requires that the debtor give a minimum of 25 days notice to creditors of the hearing on each of these two matters. In designing the procedure, the drafters of the Bankruptcy Code assumed that the court would enter an order approving the disclosure statement before the court set a hearing on confirmation of the plan. Under that assumption, a prepackaged case would take a minimum of about 60 days from filing to confirmation.

Shortly after the Bankruptcy Code became effective in 1979, Palo Alto attorney Lincoln A. Brooks realized that the two 25-day notice periods could run simultaneously. That is, the court could hold both hearings on the same day without necessarily violating any provision of the code. Based on this realization Brooks began doing some prepackaged bankruptcies for small and midsized companies in about 30 days.

Despite the fact that language of the code permitted these 30-day prepacks, the reorganization process did not fit comfortably into that period. When a debtor files bankruptcy, the United States Trustee appoints an official creditors' committee to represent the creditors as a group. The members of that committee have fiduciary duties to act in the creditors' interests.[76] The committee can hire professionals to represent it and charge their fees to the debtor. The committee is the eyes, ears, and voice of the unsecured creditors. But the time required for the United States Trustee to appoint the creditors' committee, the committee to organize and select professionals to represent it, and the professionals to familiarize themselves with the case alone is about 30 days. A 30-day prepackaged case may be over by the time a committee is ready to participate.

That is not the only problem with trying to squeeze a bankruptcy reorganization into 30 days. The rules require the debtor to file schedules of debts and assets and a statement of the company's financial affairs within 15 days after the filing of the case. The courts are permitted to extend that period and do so in large cases. Thus, in a 30-day prepackaged case, the debtor will furnish these documents when it is already too late for them to be of much use. The Bankruptcy Code also requires that the debtor appear at a meeting of creditors held 20 to 40 days after the filing of the petition and submit to examination under oath. In a 30-day prepack, the meeting would occur only a few days before the confirmation hearing—or even after it. Either way, the meeting could not serve its purpose of enabling the representatives of creditors and shareholders to prepare for participation in the case. The bankruptcy reorganization process simply can't work in 30-day cases.

Only a single large public company filed a prepackaged case before 1990. For tax reasons, Crystal Oil was rushing to complete its reorganization in 1986. Despite its hurry, Crystal Oil proceeded traditionally, obtaining approval of the disclosure statement before seeking confirmation of the plan.

The first attempt to combine the hearings on disclosure and

confirmation in a big prepackaged case occurred in Dallas, Texas, at the end of 1990. Judge Harold Abramson set the disclosure and confirmation hearings for Southland Corporation (now 7-Eleven Stores) for December 14, 1990, 50 days after the filing of the case.[77] The United States Trustee appointed the prebankruptcy bond-holder's committee as the official creditors' committee over the objection of creditors who opposed the plan. The dissidents formed their own, unofficial committee and objected to confirma-tion. (Their "unofficial" status meant that they were paying their own attorneys' fees while the debtor was paying the fees of their opponents.) The grounds for their objections were that the disclo-sure statement was confusing, the creditors were given only eight days in which to vote, errors were made in the tabulation of the votes, and the tabulation of votes ignored the numbers of bond-holders whose bonds were held in the names of trustee banks, counting only a single vote by the bank.[78] Judge Abramson agreed with the objectors and ordered that a new vote be held. Before the new vote was held, the parties settled on a plan that gave more value to the dissidents.

Judge Abramson confirmed the amended plan on February 21, 1991, just 120 days after the case was filed. Although the case took longer than expected, Southland's reorganization was a success for the company. Southland was profitable immediately after confirmation. Thirteen years later, the firm has changed its name to 7-Eleven and continues to thrive.

In the view of Southland's case placers, however, Judge Abram-son had shown himself to be "unpredictable" by failing to confirm the plan presented to him. Abramson was tagged as a toxic judge. Sixty big public companies have filed prepacks since Southland, including three companies headquartered in Dallas. None have chosen the Dallas bankruptcy court.

JPS Textile's prepackaged case, filed in New York in February 1991, was the mirror image of Southland. JPS Textile's case went smoothly, and the court confirmed JPS's plan in just 42 days. For the company, disaster ensued. After it emerged from bankruptcy,

JPS Textile's operations lost money for five years in a row. The company fell back into bankruptcy in 1997. But by confirming the plan without incident on the debtor's schedule, the New York bankruptcy court had proven itself trustworthy. Five of the 59 big public companies that have filed prepacks since JPS Textile have filed them in New York. Four of the five were—like JPS—forum shops by companies based elsewhere. Together, the two cases illustrate the incentives competition provides for bankruptcy courts to serve the case placers' interests—even when those interests are squarely in conflict with the interests of the debtor and its creditors and shareholders.

Delaware, with a prepack refiling rate even higher than that of New York, is the most popular venue for prepackaged cases. The reasons are subtle. Prepacks do not go to Delaware because other courts refuse to confirm them. Every large public company prepack filed in any U.S. bankruptcy court since prepacks were authorized by law in 1979 has been confirmed. Nor do they go there for speed. The median time to confirmation for prepacks in Delaware is 44 days—exactly the median time for prepacks in other courts (i.e., all courts other than Delaware and New York) and shorter than the 59.5-day median time in New York. Even excluding Delaware's Glenoit prepack, which fell apart and lasted 773 days, the average time to confirmation in a prepack is only two days shorter in Delaware than in other courts. Nor does the Delaware bankruptcy court exercise any great skill or sophistication. The court does little except sign the orders approving the disclosure statement and confirming the plan. The difference must be that—despite the statistics—the case placers put greater trust in the Delaware court.

In the earliest prepacks, the parties sought to comply with the procedural requirements of bankruptcy law. They hurried the filing of documents, the organization of committees, and the holding of meetings of creditors. But in a system where the courts always approved the plan anyway, the hurried compliance did little or nothing for creditors and shareholders. Little by little, in the early 1990s the parties and the competing courts stopped trying to comply with the law. United States Trustees began reporting that they

TABLE 10. Delaware Dominates the 30-Day Prepack

	Delaware	Days	New York	Days	Other Courts	Days
1986					Crystal Oil	91
1990					Southland	120
1991			JPS Textile	42	Trump Taj Mahal	43
					Edgell	31
1992	SPI Holding	42	West Point	87	Hadson	46
	Charter Medical	36			Gaylord Container	35
	Memorex Telex	32			Trump Plaza	52
					Mayflower Group	45
					Trump's Castle	57
1993	USG Corp.	37	Petrolane	35	Great American	32
	Restaurant Enterprises	45			Live Entertainment	43
	Cherokee	39			Calton	58
	Thermadyne	47			Ladish	46
1994	Kash N' Karry	33				
	Memorex Telex	31				
	Resorts International	32				
	Westmoreland Coal	38				
1995					Americold	41
					TWA	35
					Mortgage & Realty	35
1996	Heilman Brewing	84				
	Morrison Knudsen	62				
	Bibb Co.	71				
	Ithaca Industries	45				
1997	Koll Real Estate	36	JPS Textile Group	39		
	Consolidated Hydro	38				
1998	CAI Wireless	62			Grand Union	42
	Farm Fresh	44				
1999	Goss Graphics	83				
	Trism	84				
	Wilshire Financial	40				
	Zenith Electronics	74				
2000	Pathmark Stores	57				
	Tokheim	37				
	DecisionOne	36				
	Glenoit	773				
2001						
2002	Globix	39	APW Ltd.	77	Orius	59
	Leiner Health	46	ViaSystems	105		
2003	Aurora Foods, Inc.	71				
	Redback Networks	49				
	Neenah Foundry	51				
	Chart Industries	58				
2004	Tower Records	36				

Source: Data from Lynn M. LoPucki's Bankruptcy Research Database.

Note: Cases are listed in year of filing.

were "unable to form committees" even though unofficial committees (whose fees were being paid by the big bondholders) filed
appearances in many of the cases. Courts began excusing the filing
of schedules and statements of affairs. The New York bankruptcy
court adopted General Order 2002, providing for the cancellation
of the meeting of creditors if it had not been held by the time the
plan was confirmed—a rule that is flatly illegal because it contra-
dicts section 341 of the Bankruptcy Code. A general order adopted
in Los Angeles in 2002 cut straight to the chase, declaring that "a
hearing on confirmation of a [prepackaged] plan . . . shall be scheduled, if practicable, no more than 30 days after [filing of the
case]."[79] By 2002, almost all pretense of deliberation had disappeared from prepackaged cases. The bankruptcy courts had
become mere rubber stamps.

No one argues that the procedures followed in 30-day prepacks
comply with a literal reading of the code or afford a fair opportunity for creditors, shareholders, and other affected parties to participate in the case. The procedures don't. Instead, defenders of the
30-day prepack argue that such participation is unnecessary
because the parties voluntarily fixed the terms of reorganization
before the debtor filed the case. That defense, however, fails the
test of logic. The purpose of the bankruptcy procedure is to determine *whether* the parties voluntarily fixed the terms of reorganization before the debtor filed the case. Until the court determines that
the disclosure statement is adequate and the votes fairly counted, it
is too soon to draw any conclusions about what the creditors
wanted. Bankruptcy law requires that the determination be made
by an adversary process. The purpose is to protect the typically
large majority of creditors who voted against the plan, voted for
the plan without attempting to understand it, or did not participate
in the voting at all.

Thirty-day prepacks appeal to case placers because they provide
no opportunity for opposition to form. For the debtor companies,
however, the results have generally been bad. Prepackaged cases
have been significantly more likely to fail than nonprepackaged

cases,[80] and the little evidence available suggests that the failures of prepackaged cases are more costly than the failures of non-prepackaged cases.[81]

"Critical" Vendors

From the moment a debtor files bankruptcy, its creditors are pro-hibited by the "automatic stay" from making any further effort to collect their debts. The stay will continue in effect until the end of the case, when the court confirms the reorganization plan. For debtors, the stay provides welcome relief. They can use their rev-enues to pay current operating expenses and make improvements in the business instead of applying them to the payment of past debts.

When the plan is finally confirmed, whatever is available for unsecured creditors is divided pro rata among them. That is, each general unsecured creditor receives the same proportion of the debt owing to it, whether that is two cents on the dollar, 47 cents on the dollar, or 100 cents of the dollar. Achieving this equality among similarly situated creditors in distribution has historically been considered one of the most important policies of bankruptcy law. It reduces the incentives for wasteful, strategic activity designed merely to shift recoveries among creditors.

Critical vendor payments threaten the policy of equality. A crit-ical vendor is a supplier the debtor cannot replace or can replace only at great expense. Consider the example of a reorganizing debtor that manufactures an appliance from purchased parts, some of which are made by Motorola. To continue in business after filing the bankruptcy case, this debtor may need to buy more parts from Motorola. If so, Motorola is, for this debtor, a critical vendor.

What if Motorola refuses to sell more parts to the debtor until the debtor pays in full the debt owing for parts Motorola sold the debtor before bankruptcy? Before the bankruptcy courts were cor-rupted by court competition, all pretty much shared the same view. Payment of a prepetition debt, even to a critical vendor, violated the Bankruptcy Code because it enabled some unsecured creditors to recover a greater portion of the debts owing to them than others.[82] Courts rarely approved them.

How, then, could this hypothetical business survive? If the Motorola case had arisen during the 1980s, the bankruptcy court would likely have persuaded Motorola to change its mind about refusing to sell to the debtor. Suppliers have an absolute right to refuse to deal with a debtor in bankruptcy. But suppliers do not have the right to condition their refusal on payment of their prepetition debt. Any act to collect a prepetition debt—including a simple request for payment—violates the automatic stay. At a supplier's first suggestion that the debtor should pay its prepetition debt, the 1980s courts threatened to hold the supplier in contempt of court.[83] Because the courts took this hard line, few critical vendors made the suggestion. And because the courts firmly took the position that debtors could not make critical vendor payments, suppliers could gain nothing by seeking them. With the possibility of prepetition debt repayment off the table and most debtors paying cash for postpetition deliveries anyway, few vendors demanded special treatment.

Maintaining this hard line against critical vendor payments required effort and risk on the part of reorganizing debtors. The debtors had to confront overreaching suppliers, perhaps take legal action against them, and run the risk—however small—that some suppliers would ultimately refuse to deal even under the threat of contempt. For any particular debtor, the path of least resistance was to give in to the demands of its critical vendors, pay them with other creditors' money, and leave the line-holding duties to others. For that reason, managers preferred courts that would permit critical vendor payments.

In the mid-1990s, the Delaware bankruptcy court began routinely authorizing critical vendor payments. In the early cases, approval was usually for the payment of a single critical vendor or a short list. But as creditors realized that money was available, more and more decided that their principles did not allow them to continue doing business with debtors who had not paid them in full. Critical vendor payments made were like blood in the water, driving suppliers into a feeding frenzy and driving cases into Delaware. As the number of demands for critical vendor payments increased, the lists of critical vendors got longer. Eventually, the increasing cash demands became a significant burden on the reorganization process. By that time, however, it was too late for managers to put a stop to them. The process had acquired a life of its own. To make their assertions that they would not sell without payment of prepetition debt credible, some critical vendors—Motorola was an example—had irretrievably committed to that position. Such policies assured that the first reorganizing debtors to resist the feeding sharks would be torn to shreds. To avoid being those first, debtors flocked to the safety of the courts most likely to approve their critical vendor orders. By the late 1990s, the competing bankruptcy courts were all following Delaware in approving long lists of "critical" vendors. The size of the payments often reached tens of millions of dollars and sometimes hundreds of millions of dollars. In cases where debtors requested it, some courts authorized slush funds for the payment of critical vendors not yet identified. The debtors' managers could decide later which vendors would get the money. As prominent practitioner Tom Salerno put it, critical vendor payments had "gone from an extraordinary remedy to something that is simply done as a matter of course in almost all cases."[84]

The critical vendor payment problem came to a head in the Kmart case. Chicago bankruptcy judge Susan Pierson Sonderby authorized Kmart to use $200 million to $300 million of cash—cash that otherwise could have been used to make improvements in the business—to pay prepetition debts to supposedly critical suppliers instead. The 2,300 suppliers who received those payments recovered 100 cents on the dollar of their prepetition debts. The 43,000 unsecured creditors who were not included on the list of critical vendors received only about ten cents on the dollar of their prepetition debts, and they got their money more than 15 months later.[85] A nonvendor creditor of Kmart appealed Judge Sonderby's order to the Chicago district court. In April 2003, that court reversed the order, saying that the Bankruptcy Code does not authorize critical vendor payments in any circumstances. The debtor appealed the district court's decision to the Seventh Circuit Court of Appeals.

Determined to remain in the competition for cases, Judge Sonderby refused to order the recipients of the critical vendor payments to return the money pending the outcome of the appeal. In February 2004, the Seventh Circuit Court of Appeals sided with the district court against Judge Sonderby. In the opinion, Judge Frank Easterbrook wrote that the doctrine of necessity—the doctrine used to justify critical vendor payments—"is just a fancy name for a power to depart from the Code."[86] The court stopped short of saying that preferential payments to prepetition suppliers were always improper, but it went far enough to seriously impair the Chicago court's ability to attract future cases.

In addition to the threat critical vendor orders pose to the policy of equality of distribution, economy of bankruptcy administration, and the survival of debtor companies, they also provide managers with a new—and abusable—source of power. Minneapolis lawyer Bill Kampf tells the story of his client Riscomp Industries, a small janitorial firm that was reorganizing in bankruptcy in late 2002. Riscomp had the contract to clean the United Airlines terminal at the Los Angeles airport. From reading the newspapers, Riscomp's CEO knew that United was preparing to file bankruptcy. Riscomp needed the United work, but it wouldn't do them any good if they weren't paid for it. Riscomp discussed the problem with United's managers. The two agreed that Riscomp would do the work and United would put Riscomp on its critical vendor list. Riscomp performed, and when United filed bankruptcy, it owned Riscomp $300,000. Ignoring its promise, United omitted Riscomp from its critical vendor list.

Riscomp had no legal remedy. United's prepetition promise—even if made fraudulently—is merely a prepetition debt dischargeable in bankruptcy. United didn't pay Riscomp, and as a result, Riscomp's business failed. Kampf reports rumors that United also duped other creditors with the promise of critical vendor treatment.

By 2003, bankruptcy lawyers and judges were acknowledging

that the bankruptcy courts had grown too lax in granting critical vendor orders. The problem was how to stop. As one court put it in a memorandum opinion: "[B]ecause payment of prepetition claims outside of a plan has become commonplace in some jurisdictions, the court recognizes that a vendor might condition future dealings with Debtors on payment of its prepetition claim, whether or not payment of that claim could be justified . . . ."[87] What the court should have added was that the problem resulted from bankruptcy court competition.

Section 363 Sale Practices

The filing of a bankruptcy reorganization case gives managers tremendous power. They remain in office and control the company, the case, and the flow of information. Increasingly, neither shareholders nor creditors can oust them. The plan process is an important limit on their power. To complete the bankruptcy, the managers must make extensive disclosures to shareholders and creditors and persuade requisite majorities that confirmation of the plan is in the shareholders' and creditors' interests.

The power of managers is particularly problematic when managers try to sell the company. The managers may arrange a sale to themselves or their allies or to a buyer who will continue the managers' employment on generous terms. Partly for this reason, the appellate courts have held that management can sell the business during bankruptcy only through the plan process—unless there are sound business reasons why they need to deviate from that process.[88]

The alternative to sale through the plan process is sale under section 363 of the Bankruptcy Code. That section authorizes trustees to sell property of the estate—a routine, uncontroversial part of every Chapter 7 case. Other sections of the Bankruptcy Code provide that section 363 applies in Chapter 11 cases and that debtors-in-possession have the rights of trustees. The result is to set up section 363 as an alternative procedure for selling an entire business without the plan process safeguards for creditors and shareholders.

The drafters of section 363 probably thought in terms of sales of particular assets, not entire businesses.[89] But the text of the section contains no such limitation. Absent court competition, that would not have been a problem. The courts would have imposed reasonable restrictions on the use of section 363 to sell entire businesses.

As the courts apply section 363, a debtor that proposes to sell its entire business may disclose the proposal only to the unsecured creditors' committee and the court. The disclosure may consist of nothing but a ten-page summary of the terms of sale. Management need not make the extensive disclosures of the debtor's financial condition, reasons for sale, alternatives to sale, and ulterior motives for sale that would be required as part of the plan process. Nor does management need to tell the creditors what their recoveries will be if the sale goes through. The courts generally require that the debtor afford others who wish to bid for the company an opportunity to do so, but the dissemination of information to bidders and the bidding itself are largely secret processes, accessible only to the professionals representing official committees—and to them only grudgingly. Creditors and shareholders not on official committees may be unable to discover even the nature of the assets being sold. The sale of a company worth billions of dollars may be concluded in less than two months—less than the time most people take to sell their homes.

During the 1980s, few large public company debtors had "sound business reasons" to sell their entire businesses outside the plan process. By the end of that decade, only three large public companies had done so. These few exceptions were emergencies in which there was not sufficient time to comply with the plan process.

Table 11 lists all cases since 1979 in which the bankruptcy courts allowed managers to bypass the plan process to sell large public companies under section 363. The number of such cases increased rapidly in the late 1990s and then exploded in 2000.

Delaware did not invent the quick section 363 sale, but table 11 shows that Delaware perfected it. If a "quick sale" is defined as one that takes place within 130 days of the filing—a time short enough to suggest that the debtor had sale in mind when it chose the

court—Delaware conducted all eight of the quick section 363 sales
from 1992 through 2000. Companies filed in other courts, encoun-
tered adversities, and eventually ended up selling their businesses
under section 363. But companies came to Delaware with section
363 sales already in mind. Many of them—like Trans World Airlines—first contracted to sell the business and only then filed bankruptcy to obtain a sale approval order.

In late 2000 and 2001—following the spread of competition from
Delaware to New York and other courts—other courts began wel-
coming managers who brought their companies into bankruptcy
only to sell them. Since January 1 of 2001, 11 of 21 quick section 363
sales (52 percent) were conducted in courts other than Delaware.
Numerous courts were allowing debtors to sell their entire companies without complying with the requirements of the plan process.

The order approving a bankruptcy sale binds everyone with an
interest in the case and prevents them from later challenging the
sale. No appeal from the order is permitted; the order is final when
entered. If corrupt managers and purchasers can get their sale past
the bankruptcy court, they are home free. Bankruptcy sale orders
are so appealing to buyers and sellers that companies that would
otherwise conduct their sales outside bankruptcy sometimes file
bankruptcy cases to get them.

Managers seeking to deliver a company to themselves or their
accomplices at a bargain price tend to announce their intention to
sell only at the last minute and then seek to conclude the sale as
quickly as possible. That minimizes the opportunity for discovery
of the true identities of the buyers or the emergence of other bidders for the company. The case of Derby Cycle Corporation, manufacturer of Raleigh and Diamondback bikes, illustrates.

Alan Finden-Crofts founded Derby in the late 1980s and sold it
in January 1999. The new owners quickly got the company into
financial difficulty. Two years later, they invited Finden-Crofts to
return as a turnaround manager. He became CEO in January 2001
and brought in several of his associates as top managers.[90]

Five months later, on June 3, 2001, Finden-Crofts announced
that he and a group of managers proposed to buy the company—

TABLE 11. Section 363 Sales of the Entire Company, 1980–2003

	Court	Date of 363 Sale	Date of Filing	Days from Filing to 363 Sale
McLouth Steel Corporation	Detroit	11/15/82	12/8/81	342
Air Florida System Inc.	Miami	9/15/84	7/3/84	74
Frontier Holdings Inc.	Denver	10/17/86	8/28/86	50
Daisy Systems Corporation	Denver	1/3/91	5/30/90	218
Telesphere Communications Inc.	Chicago	10/25/91	8/19/91	67
Days Inns of America Inc.	**Wilmington**	**1/9/92**	**9/27/91**	**104**
FoxMeyer Health Corporation	**Wilmington**	**11/15/96**	**8/27/96**	**80**
Plaid Clothing Group Inc.	New York	11/22/96	7/17/95	494
Mid-American Waste Systems, Inc.	**Wilmington**	**3/11/97**	**1/21/97**	**49**
Ernst Home Center, Inc.	**Wilmington**	**3/14/97**	**7/12/96**	**245**
Best Products Company, Inc.	Richmond	5/29/97	9/24/96	247
McCrory Corporation	New York	7/31/97	2/26/92	1,982
Molten Metal Technology, Inc.	Boston	11/24/98	12/3/97	356
Caldor Corporation	New York	2/11/99	9/18/95	1,242
Thorn Apple Valley, Inc.	Detroit	8/26/99	3/5/99	174
Renaissance Cosmetics, Inc.	**Wilmington**	**9/10/99**	**6/2/99**	**100**
Hechinger Company	**Wilmington**	**2/15/00**	**6/11/99**	**249**
Costilla Energy, Inc.	Midland-Odessa	6/9/00	9/3/99	280
Cambridge Industries, Inc., of DE	**Wilmington**	**6/23/00**	**5/10/00**	**44**
System Software Associates, Inc.	**Wilmington**	**7/10/00**	**5/3/00**	**68**
Stone & Webster, Inc.	**Wilmington**	**7/14/00**	**6/2/00**	**42**
New American Healthcare Corporation	Nashville	9/14/00	4/19/00	148
GST Telecommunications, Inc.	**Wilmington**	**9/21/00**	**5/17/00**	**127**
Flooring America, Inc.	Atlanta	11/27/00	6/15/00	165
Bradlees Inc. (2000)	New York	2/6/01	12/26/00	42
Drypers Corporation	Houston	3/1/01	10/10/00	142
Grand Union Company	Newark	3/5/01	10/3/00	153
Trans World Airlines, Inc.	**Wilmington**	**3/12/01**	**1/10/01**	**61**
NorthPoint Communications Group	San Francisco	3/23/01	1/16/01	66
Orbcomm Global, LP	**Wilmington**	**4/23/01**	**9/15/00**	**220**
U.S.A. Floral Products, Inc.	**Wilmington**	**5/1/01**	**4/2/01**	**29**
Vlasic Foods International, Inc.	**Wilmington**	**5/31/01**	**1/29/01**	**122**
Einstein Noah Bagel Corporation	Phoenix	6/11/01	4/27/00	410
Payless Cashways, Inc.	Kansas City, MO	9/19/01	6/4/01	107
Derby Cycle Corporation	**Wilmington**	**10/2/01**	**8/20/01**	**43**

Company	City			
Winstar Communications, Inc.	Wilmington	12/19/01	4/18/01	245
ABC-NACO, Inc.	Chicago	1/11/02	10/18/01	85
Network Plus Corporation	Wilmington	3/15/02	2/5/02	38
International Fibercom Inc.	Phoenix	4/16/02	2/13/02	62
IT Group, Inc. (The)	Wilmington	4/25/02	1/16/02	99
Casual Male Corporation	New York	5/7/02	5/18/01	354
U.S. Aggregates, Inc.	Reno	5/23/02	3/11/02	73
e.spire Communications, Inc.	Wilmington	3/22/01	6/4/02	439
Kellstrom Industries, Inc.	Wilmington	6/10/02	2/20/02	110
Polaroid Corporation	Wilmington	7/3/02	10/12/01	264
Coho Energy, Inc.	Dallas	8/15/02	2/6/02	190
Republic Technologies International	Akron	9/1/02	4/2/01	517
Phar-Mor, Inc.	Youngstown	9/1/02	9/24/01	342
Velocita Corporation	Newark	11/7/02	5/30/02	161
Budget Group Inc.	Wilmington	11/8/02	7/29/02	102
Iridium LLC (and six subsidiaries)	New York	11/20/02	8/13/99	1,195
RSL Communications, Ltd.	New York	12/9/02	3/19/01	630
Asia Global Crossing, Ltd.	New York	1/29/03	11/17/02	73
Clarent Corporation	San Francisco	2/4/03	12/16/02	50
Genuity Inc.	New York	2/4/03	11/27/02	69
DTI Holdings, Inc./Digital Teleport	St. Louis	2/13/03	12/31/01	409
Graham-Field Health Products, Inc.	Wilmington	4/14/03	12/27/99	1,204
National Steel Corporation	Chicago	4/21/03	3/6/02	411
Bethlehem Steel Corporation	New York	4/23/03	10/15/01	555
Carbide Graphite Group, Inc.	Pittsburgh	9/21/02	7/24/03	671
Read-Rite Corporation	Oakland	6/17/03	7/24/03	37
ANC Rental Corporation	Wilmington	11/13/01	8/6/03	631
Wherehouse Entertainment, Inc.	Wilmington	1/21/03	9/29/03	252
Pillowtex Corporation	Wilmington	10/7/03	7/30/03	69
AT&T Latin America Corporation	Miami	4/11/03	11/4/03	207
Globalstar LP	Wilmington	2/15/02	11/21/03	644
Republic Engineered Products Holdings, Inc.	Akron	10/6/03	12/16/03	71
Rouge Industries, Inc.	Wilmington	10/23/03	12/22/03	60

Source: Data from Lynn M. LoPucki's Bankruptcy Research Database.
Note: Delaware court cases are shown in bold.

not including its European subsidiary, Gazelle—for a purchase price that ultimately turned out to be about $40 million.[91] From the moment of that announcement, everything was suddenly urgent. According to Derby's attorneys, "in mid-July, 2001, after extensive marketing by Lazard, the Debtor, in consultation with the Bondholders' Committee, decided to sell" Gazelle, and "the Gazelle Sale closed on July 19, 2001"[92] for a purchase price of about $120 million. (The money went to pay Gazelle creditors.)[93] "Without Gazelle's revenues," the attorneys continued, "the Debtors' business is not viable on a stand-alone basis" and so "must be sold as soon as possible or liquidated."[94] On August 20, 2001, the debtor signed a contract to sell all of Derby's assets to the Finden-Crofts group for about $40 million and filed for bankruptcy in Delaware. The following day, the debtor's attorneys filed a statement with the court stating that "debtor needs to consummate this sale no later than September 28, 2001" and that "unless there is a sale by September 28, there is not likely to be a business to sell."[95] The attorneys explained that "[t]he major bike trade shows start on September 30, 2001. It is vital to the ongoing business that a buyer be selected prior to these shows, so that orders can be secured by the buyer for the following season."[96]

The court set September 26 as the last day for the submission of competing offers. The court did not meet Derby's deadline for approving the sale, but luckily, there still was a business to sell when the court approved the sale on October 2, 2001. The sale was completed on October 29, 2001.[97] Derby's estate received $23 million of the $40 million purchase price. The buyer paid the remaining $17 million by assuming secured debt.

Based solely on the record, Derby's sale looks suspicious. The Finden-Crofts management took nearly eight months to put Derby into bankruptcy and then insisted that the court approve a sale to themselves in just five weeks. If it took Finden-Crofts—the former owner of Derby—five months to evaluate the company from the inside and prepare a bid, how were competing bidders supposed to do it from the outside in five weeks? The trade shows and the approaching Christmas selling season were the "emergency" used to justify the hurried schedule, but that emergency could hardly have come as a surprise to anyone. As the United States Trustee put it in an objection to the sale:

> [T]he rushed nature of this sale appears to be a creation of the Buyer's own doing, who, it can be assumed, as Chief Executive Officer of the Debtor, played some role in the decision to delay the filing of Chapter 11 until shortly before these events. Indeed, it is arguable that the Buyer's actions caused the quickly deteriorating conditions that Debtor now alleges require a quick sale.[98]

No proof exists that Derby Cycle was worth more than the $40 million Finden-Crofts paid. Two well-known investment banking firms—Lazard Frères on behalf of the debtor and Jefferies & Company, Inc., on behalf of the creditors' committee—had supposedly shopped the company and found no one else interested.[99] But Lazard was hired by Derby, and Finden-Crofts was in control of Derby, so in failing to find another interested buyer, Lazard was telling its client what the client wanted to hear. Jefferies's final fee application—which lists all of the services performed on behalf of the committee during the case—makes no mention of any attempts to discover or interest additional buyers.[100] As soon as the debtor signed the sale agreement, it sought court approval of bidding procedures that contained a "no-shop" provision—that is, a provision restricting the debtor's efforts to interest additional bidders in the property during the open bidding period that the bankruptcy court would require.[101]

The Polaroid case provides another illustration of the problem of conflict of interest in section 363 sales. Shortly after Polaroid filed for reorganization in Delaware on October 12, 2001, the company entered into a contract to sell its Identification Systems Division unit to the manager in charge of it for $32 million. The sale required court approval after a public opportunity to bid. Insisting that the sale was urgent, Polaroid sought to limit the opportunity for outside bidding to the extent it could.[102] Polaroid's investment bankers, Dresdner, Kleinwort, Wasserstein, said they had shopped the Identification Systems Division thoroughly and $32 million was the best offer they could get. But when Polaroid tried to get Judge Walsh to approve the sale for $32 million, several would-be bidders appeared in court to protest that they hadn't been solicited, that they had encountered difficulty in getting bid packages from Dresdner, Kleinwort, Wasserstein, and that Polaroid was trying to push the sale through without giving them time to prepare their bids.[103] Judge Walsh extended the bidding period by 10 days, and competitive bidding pushed the price to $60 million.[104] Later, an Identification Systems executive said that in shopping the company, Dresdner, Kleinwort, Wasserstein, had been asking $75 million to $125 million, an excessive asking price that had discouraged bidding.[105] It appears that bidders who came forward on their own thwarted Polaroid management's attempt to sell Polaroid's Identification Systems Division to one of their colleagues at a bargain basement price.

Most section 363 sales of big companies are not to the managers themselves. But preliminary results from an empirical study I am conducting indicate that the debtor's managers get some kind of publicly announced payoff—in the form of employment or consulting contracts—from the buyer in a substantial proportion of all entire-business 363 sales. These payoffs are facilitated by a custom that has arisen for the buyers in section 363 sales to hire the debtors' managers and reward them with stock totaling in value as much as 5 percent to 10 percent of the entire company.[106] The custom amounts, in effect, to a standing bribe offer for managers to arrange sweetheart deals on the sales of their companies. The incumbent managers don't have to get the buyer's agreement in advance to pay the bribe; they can do the deal on the basis of trust. The custom played a key role in the controversial sale of the remainder of Polaroid.

On its petition, Polaroid claimed assets of $1.8 billion and liabilities of $948 million. Dresdner, Kleinwort, Wasserstein and Pirella had begun shopping the entire company even before the bankruptcy filing. Wasserstein contacted some 170 possible purchasers.[107] About 60 of them signed the confidentiality agreements required before a prospective purchaser could get information about Polaroid.[108] Only two, however, expressed serious interest in bidding, and only one actually bid.

Six months into the case, on April 18, 2002, Polaroid petitioned to sell its assets to that sole bidder. OEP Imaging was a newly incorporated firm set up by venture capitalists at Bank One Equity. The identity of its owners has never been publicly disclosed. OEP's bid was $265 million. The purchaser would take the assets subject to about $200 million in debt, which meant the deal implicitly valued Polaroid's assets at about $465 million. Following the customary procedure for section 363 sales, the Delaware court required that Polaroid offer prospective purchasers one last opportunity to outbid OEP. On May 10, the court fixed procedures for competitive bidding, and Polaroid conducted an auction on June 26 in the offices of Polaroid's attorneys, Skadden, Arps. At the auction, OEP's bid was again the only one presented.

The creditors' committee opposed the sale to OEP because they considered the price to be grossly inadequate. Polaroid had valued its assets at $1.8 billion on the petition it filed in October 2001. Two months later, Polaroid filed schedules that listed each of its assets and placed values on most. The values listed totaled $715 million, even though no values were listed for many of Polaroid's most valuable assets. The unvalued assets included Polaroid's more than 1,000 patents, 2,000 trademarks, and 24,000 art objects and the stock of about two dozen foreign subsidiaries. The foreign subsidiaries continued to operate, were not in bankruptcy, and owned—among other things—about $100 million of the $948 million in debt owed by the bankruptcy estate. Taken as a whole, the schedules suggested that Polaroid's assets might be worth the full $1.8 billion previously estimated. Now, just four months later, Polaroid's managers were trying to sell Polaroid for $465 million.

That price did not reflect the entire extent of the bargain. More than $200 million of Polaroid's assets were cash. After various credits OEP would receive at closing, OEP would pay $225 million in cash for Polaroid. Thus, on paying $225 million in cash OEP would own a company that had $200 million in cash. In effect,

OEP was buying Polaroid for $25 million in cash and the assumption of $200 million in secured debt.

The unsecured creditors' committee vehemently objected to the sale and by threatening to try to reorganize the company themselves eventually managed to force a settlement. The deal was that Polaroid would sell to OEP on OEP's terms and Polaroid's unsecured creditors would get 35 percent of the stock of OEP.

The day after the auction and settlement, Delaware bankruptcy judge Peter J. Walsh heard testimony regarding the sale, overruled the objections of Polaroid's stockholders and retirees, and approved the sale. From the first public announcement of intent to sell Polaroid to the entry of a binding, unappealable order approving the sale, the sale process took only 70 days.

The sale hearing transcript shows Judge Walsh to have been completely uninterested in any evidence that might have been presented as to the true value of Polaroid's assets. As Judge Walsh put it:

> [T]he principal conflict here is between those persons and entities who preach and believe that there must be some valuation done which would demonstrate that this enterprise is [not] worth more than what is being proposed by the proposed transaction. . . . I have never accepted the proposition that the court should be guided by valuation when a sale transaction, and in many of these cases, including this one, an appropriately shopped sale transaction, is the alternative. And even in this case where the disparity is dramatic, to say the least, I think the fundamental proposition, which this court has fought for a lot of years, is that a transaction appropriately conducted is the better test of value . . . . I favor the market test approach and that was done in this case.[109]

To put Judge Walsh's argument another way, because Dresdner, Kleinwort, Wasserstein found no buyer willing to pay more than $465 million for a $1.9 billion company with $200 million in cash, Judge Walsh concluded that Polaroid's noncash assets were worth no more than $265 million.

Walsh's logic was faulty. The sale arranged by Dresdner, Kleinwort, Wasserstein, obviously wasn't for the full market value of the company. By settling with the creditors' committee for 65 percent of Polaroid, but paying the same price it had bid for 100 percent, OEP acknowledged that it would have bid about 50 percent more than the $465 it actually bid. How much more it would have bid is anyone's guess.

Companies can and do sell for market prices when a motivated buyer appears, and the company has the right and ability to refuse to sell until the deal is right. But the market for large public companies is thin. At any given time there may or may not be someone willing to pay a fair price. A traditional justification for bankruptcy reorganization is that reorganization enables the company to keep going on its own until a buyer willing to pay a fair price comes along.

Instead, Polaroid's top managers insisted that Polaroid was "a melting ice cube" that could not reorganize. Testifying at the sale hearing in mid-2002, William L. Flaherty, Polaroid's CFO, said that Polaroid's sales for 2002 were down 25 to 30 percent from the previous year and would continue to decline at about that rate through 2004.[110] Along with that assessment, Flaherty opined that Polaroid was projecting operating losses "in every quarter of 2002." Repeating Flaherty's testimony regarding sales and his characterization of Polaroid as a "melting ice cube," Judge Walsh concluded that "it is inconceivable to me that anybody could put together a plan which would produce any value whatsoever for the equity interests in this corporation."[111]

The Polaroid sale closed on July 31, 2002, just over a month after Flaherty pronounced Polaroid a melting ice cube. The following day, Flaherty and Neal Goldman—the two executives who performed the function of CEO for Polaroid in its final days—went to work for OEP in the same capacity. Miraculously, the ice cube immediately stopped melting. As shown in table 12, Polaroid's sales increased and its losses shifted to profits as of the day the sale closed.

Nor did the 25 percent to 30 percent annual decline in sales and the continuing operating losses Flaherty predicted in his June 27 testimony[112] occur. A year after approval of the sale, a merger and acquisition specialist consulted by the *Boston Globe* estimated that, based on earnings alone, OEP could sell Polaroid for $500 to $900 million.[113] At the top of that range Polaroid's stockholders would have been in the money. (Recall that $100 million of Polaroid's $948 million in debt was owed to Polaroid's foreign subsidiaries. Polaroid's real debt was only $848 million.)

Suspicions focused on Goldman and Flaherty. Polaroid had paid them generously for their loyalty during the bankruptcy case. Goldman's base salary at bankruptcy was $375,000; Flaherty's was $390,000. As the only employees in "Tier One" of Polaroid's retention bonus plan, each received a retention bonus of 62.5 percent of his annual salary and an additional 62.5 percent of his annual salary in severance pay on termination of his employment—75 per-

TABLE 12.   Polaroid's Profits and Losses

	Net Sales	Operating Profit (loss)	Net Profit (loss)
1991	2,070.6	246.6	683.7
1992	2,152.3	213.8	99.0
1993	2,244.9	141.4	(51.3)
1994	2,312.5	200.3	117.2
1995	2,236.9	(157.8)	(140.2)
1996	2,275.2	51.8	(41.1)
1997	2,146.4	(159.1)	(126.7)
1998	1,845.9	(49.0)	(51.0)
1999	1,978.6	107.6	8.7
2000	1,855.6	109.1	37.7
2001 Q1	330.8	(118.0)	(90.9)
2001 Q2	333.5	(51.8)	(109.9)
2001 Q3	Not disclosed		
2001 Q4	189.4	(76.2)	(112.3)
2002 Q1	158.8	(20.8)	(20.3)
2002 Q2 (4 months)	224.2	(32.4)	(183.1)
Polaroid sale closes			
2002 Q3 (2 months)	152.6	1.8	0.2
2002 Q4	211.3	22.8	14.5
2003 Q 1	183.0	22.9	16.2
2003 Q2	195.8	29.7	16.5

Source: Compiled by the author from Polaroid financial statements.

cent more than any other Polaroid employee. In the year before the sale, Polaroid paid Goldman a total of more than $844,000 and Flaherty a total of more than $878,000.

OEP claims that Goldman and Flaherty went to work for it at salaries of $165,000 and received annual bonuses of $107,250.[114] Goldman and Flaherty testified that OEP did not discuss continued employment with them at all until after the auction[115] and made no commitment to give them an equity share until months after they began work.[116] Nevertheless, a year after closing each owned stock in OEP probably worth $3 million to $4 million.[117] The evidence indicates that even before the auction, OEP planned to give 10 percent of its stock to its new managers.[118] Financial statements issued by OEP a year later showed management as owning 9.7 percent of its stock, Goldman and Flaherty's 2.6 percent included. In addition, Stanley P. Roth, an influential member of the creditors' committee, also showed up on the other side of the fence as a director of OEP owning 42,440 shares.[119] OEP's disclosure does not explain how he got those shares.

The fact that no other bidder stepped forward even though Polaroid was being sold at a bargain price can be easily explained, even without assuming any wrongdoing. OEP had a deal under which it could not lose. If, as turned out to be the case, OEP was the only bidder at the sale, it could buy Polaroid cheaply and make a lot of money. If someone had outbid OEP, Polaroid had agreed to pay OEP a $5 million "termination payment."[120] (The Delaware bankruptcy court routinely approved such payments and had done so in Polaroid.) The second bidder—the one that did not materialize—would have neither of those advantages. With two bidders at the sale, the likely result was that bidding would have continued until the price reached an amount approximating the true value of Polaroid. If so, the second bidder—the one that never materialized—would have been in a situation in which it could not win. If it won the bidding, it would have paid the full value of what it bought; if it lost the bid it would have spent millions of dollars for which it would not have been compensated. An auction with two bidders might have yielded the full market value of Polaroid. But that is probably the very reason no second bidder was willing to come forward. Far from the panacea Judge Walsh thinks they are, auctions work only in limited circumstances. Polaroid was not one of those circumstances, and the professionals conducting the sale must have been aware of that.

Outside observers—including the *Wall Street Journal*,[121] the *Boston Globe*,[122] *CFO Magazine*,[123] Congressman William D. Delahunt,[124] and Polaroid's stockholders and retirees—all indicated suspicions about the bankruptcy and sale of Polaroid. But because the court allowed Polaroid to use section 363 instead of requiring it to follow plan formalities, the facts that fueled the Polaroid scandal were hidden until after the sale became final. The facts I report here ultimately came to light only because OEP's investors decided to cash in on their newly acquired wealth by selling Polaroid to the public and so had to make public disclosures under the securities laws. Even when this information came out, the response was muted by the realization that whatever might be found after the sale, nothing meaningful could be done about it. Sales under section 363 are final even if accomplished through fraud.

The Ideology That Facilitates Corruption

This chapter described seven bankruptcy court practices that have been corrupted by court competition. There are numerous others. The bankruptcy courts have relaxed their standards for professionals' conflicts of interest. They allow managers and professionals to insert into plans of reorganization provisions releasing themselves from liability for their own negligence or wrongdoing, including, in some cases, even gross negligence. These are just a few of many competition-driven changes have transformed the landscape of American bankruptcy over the period since 1990.

The changes are not yet complete because the interests of the case placers have not yet triumphed completely. There is still more that courts can offer. Some judges have had second thoughts about concessions they have made in order to attract cases, and they have reversed course. But such reversals accomplish nothing. The cases go elsewhere, and the practices continue. Unless Congress intervenes, the process will continue until the managers and the professionals have complete control over case outcomes.

The actions competition forced them to take have made many of the judges uncomfortable. Some alleviate their discomfort by embracing a promarket ideology that assures them that in yielding to the competitive pressure they are doing the right thing. The nature and effect of that ideology are the subject of chapter 9. One of the ideology's teachings is that judges should not interfere with solutions "generated in the marketplace." That exemption could apply to virtually anything on which the major parties to a case are in agreement. Thus the judges approve the parties' reorganization plans, section 363 sales, retention bonuses, fee agreements, and first-day orders as the infallible products of the market's invisible hand. The judges' newfound belief in markets enables many of the judges to do what they have to do to compete for cases: yield their power to those who place the cases.

In relying solely on markets to solve the problems of bankrupt companies, the judges forget that bankruptcy was invented to deal with the illiquidity of failing business. Failing businesses are difficult to sell because the market for such businesses is thin, the records of such businesses are often in disarray, the businesses' circumstances are often changing rapidly, and the businesses lack the working capital needed to continue operations during the negotiations. Bankruptcy addresses the problem of liquidity by protecting a business from its creditors and giving it an alternative to distress sale—reorganization using the assets it already has. That reorganization alternative acts as a sort of competing bid, giving the debtor the leverage to negotiate a fair sale price when only a single outsider is bidding. When managers give up the reorganization alternative—as the managers did in Derby Cycle and Polaroid—they put their company at the mercy of that single outside bidder.

7

The Competition Goes Global

We used to make TVs and export them. Now, the
thing we do better than anyone else is bankruptcy.

—New York bankruptcy lawyer Conor Reilly (2003)

[T]he "reputation" of Chapter 11 as an unfair and
inefficient process seems to be gaining momentum,
particularly among foreign creditors.

— Freshfields Bruckhaus Derringer (a leading
bankruptcy law firm in London) (2003)

Forum shopping within the United States is tame in comparison
with what goes on internationally. The law governing forum shopping domestically is highly permissive and often ignored, but it
exists. If a court does not follow that law, the injured party may be
able to appeal. If the U.S. bankruptcy system breaks down, there
exists a government with the power to fix it.

Internationally, no law, appeals, or government exists. With few
exceptions, the countries of the world have been unable to agree on
bankruptcy treaties or conventions. The United States is not party
to even a single one. (In 1979, U.S. and Canadian negotiators
reached agreement on a treaty between them, but that treaty was
never ratified because the parties could not agree on the venue
question.)[1] In fact, except for treaties among a few small groups of
countries with similar bankruptcy laws[2] and a new, uncertain
bankruptcy regulation in the European Union,[3] no international
treaties regulating bankruptcy exist worldwide. Companies are
free to file their bankruptcies in the courts of any nation that will

have them, have those courts adjudicate their cases, and then make of those adjudications elsewhere whatever the companies can.

Selling Bankruptcy Reorganizations to the World

The bankruptcy courts of the United States are by far the most popular destination for international forum shoppers. Leading American bankruptcy professionals claim it is because Chapter 11 of the United States Bankruptcy Code is the best, most efficient bankruptcy law in the world.[4]

The actual explanation is much simpler. The U.S. bankruptcy system offers the companies' lawyers and managers—the people who pick the courts—the best deal. In a U.S. bankruptcy, the company's managers will be allowed to remain in control of the company. They can decide whether to sell the firm as a going business, liquidate it, or restructure its debt and remain in business. As we saw in earlier chapters, their control over the company and the proceedings enables them to minimize investigation of their own wrongdoing, pay themselves handsomely, and cover their own tracks. In most other nations, the managers of the firm are ousted upon the filing of the bankruptcy case and replaced by creditors' representatives.

U.S. bankruptcy offers other advantages. In the United States all creditor collection effort is stayed during the bankruptcy case. In many other nations, secured creditors can continue to enforce their debts against the collateral during the bankruptcy case, giving them life-or-death power over the firm. In the United States, managers have the option of reorganizing the firm. In many other nations, the bankruptcy law provides only for liquidation, making reorganization possible only with the acquiescence of nearly all creditors.

The U.S. bankruptcy system also has three other features that appeal to international forum shoppers. First, the competing bankruptcy courts in the United States welcome foreign debtors, including debtors with absolutely no business presence in the United States. Second, U.S. law—as shaped by the competing courts—is "extraterritorial." That is, it purports to apply throughout the entire world. Third, most major foreign creditors must obey those extraterritorial orders because they have business interests in the United States that render them vulnerable to enforcement here.

Welcome to America

U.S. law authorizes bankruptcy filing in the United States by any debtor with "property" in the United States. U.S. bankruptcy courts have claimed jurisdiction over bankruptcy cases on the basis of as little as a few hundred dollars in a U.S. bank account—even when the debtor has no other U.S. contacts.[5] This lax jurisdictional rule allows U.S. courts to attract filings by foreign firms. Foreign firms opting for U.S. bankruptcy have included several international shipping companies,[6] a Norwegian oil field services company,[7] the Colombian national airline (Avianca),[8] one of Brazil's leading cable television providers,[9] a Colombian firm engaged in oil and gas exploration and development there,[10] one of the largest owners and operators of hotels in the Carribean,[11] and a European ferry operator.[12]

In a recently published opinion, the Delaware bankruptcy court explored the limits on foreign debtors seeking to have their bankruptcy cases decided by U.S. courts.[13] The subject of that opinion was Global Ocean Carriers, a group of 15 corporations engaged in international shipping ("the Global group"). All 15 Global group corporations filed Chapter 11 cases in Delaware in February 2000.[14]

To anyone without legal training, the corporations of the Global group appeared to have very little connection with the United States. The group's headquarters, books, and records were all in Athens, Greece. The group's parent corporation was Liberian, and only one of the 14 subsidiaries was incorporated in the United States. Ships owned by the subsidiary corporations sometimes visited U.S. ports, but none was in a U.S. port at the time the corporations filed their bankruptcies. Global's stock had traded on the American Stock Exchange, but the stock had been delisted prior to the bankruptcy filing. Some Global creditors were in the United States.

Because all 15 Global group members guaranteed payment of bonds issued by Global, all 15 needed bankruptcy discharges. Thus, each of the 15 had to meet the requirements for filing bankruptcy in the United States separately. But evidence presented to the court showed that, except for the bankruptcy filing and the location of some of the bondholders in the United States, most of the 15 corporations had no links whatsoever to the United States.

The Delaware bankruptcy court began from the accepted premise that having "property" in the United States qualified a foreign corporation to file bankruptcy in the United States. That property, the court said, could be "a dollar, a dime, or a peppercorn."[15] The court acknowledged that most of the corporations in the Global group did not have a dollar, a dime, or a peppercorn in the United States. But the Delaware court nevertheless managed to find that each had property in the United States.

In the cases of large public companies, bankruptcy lawyers do much of their work on credit. When the debtor is foreign, however, the lawyers routinely require that the debtor pay a substantial portion of the fees—referred to as a "retainer"—in advance. One of the corporations in the Global group had paid such a retainer for representation of the entire group. That, the court pointed out, meant that all 15 corporations had property in the United States—their right to the lawyer's representation.

The court's decision makes it virtually impossible for any corporation to fail to meet the jurisdictional requirements for filing in Delaware. As soon as any corporation pays a Delaware lawyer to file the corporation's bankruptcy, the corporation has property (the right to the services) in Delaware and so is qualified to file there. Everyone who pays to file in Delaware, qualifies to file in Delaware.

At the conclusion of the case, the Delaware bankruptcy court entered a confirmation order that discharged the Global group's debts worldwide; canceled the common stock and promissory notes of the company; and authorized the distribution of new common stock, notes, and cash.[16] Thus a court of a country with virtually no contacts with the debtors prior to the filing of the case presumed to alter the debtors' financial relationships worldwide.

Extraterritoriality by Intimidation

Ordinarily, the laws made by a country apply only within the country.[17] If a statute of the United States says "no person shall spit on the sidewalk" it means no person shall spit on the sidewalk in the United States. Other countries control their own sidewalks.

The United States Bankruptcy Code gives the bankruptcy court in which a case is filed jurisdiction over "all [of the debtor's] property, wherever located and by whomever held."[18] The U.S. bankruptcy courts have interpreted this language to give them jurisdiction over property not just anywhere in the United States but anywhere in the world.[19] In fairness to the courts, the legislative history indicates that was Congress's intent.[20] The first court decision to that effect came in 1986. In deciding the *U.S. Lines* case, a New York bankruptcy judge simply assumed that the automatic stay provided by the U.S. Bankruptcy Code applied to prohibit foreign creditors from seizing the debtor's ships in Hong Kong and Singapore.[21]

Ten years later, New York bankruptcy judge Burton R. Lifland—the judge who had been the principal destination for domestic forum shopping in the early 1980s—took the concept of the extraterritorial stay yet a step further. In what would become a pivotal decision in international court competition, Judge Lifland held that once a debtor filed a bankruptcy case in the United States, any attempt by creditors to file a bankruptcy case against the same debtor in another country violated the automatic stay.[22]

The debtor in that case was Joseph Nakash, the chairman of the board and a cofounder of Jordache Enterprises. Jordache, based in New York, is a major producer of jeans and other clothing. Nakash had been a member of the board of directors of North American Bank, Limited, an Israeli banking institution that was declared insolvent.[23] The bank's Israeli receiver sued Nakash in

Israel for breach of his fiduciary duties to the Israeli bank and obtained a judgment in the amount of $160 million. When the receiver attached some of Nakash's property in the United States,[24] Nakash responded by filing for bankruptcy in the New York bankruptcy court. The Israeli receiver—an Israeli government official— then filed a bankruptcy case against Nakash in Israel. Judge Lifland held that receiver's filing violated the U.S. automatic stay.[25]

The principle Judge Lifland sought to establish in his ruling was not the one you might expect: that bankruptcies should take place in the country where the debtor has the strongest ties. Instead, Judge Lifland chose to say nothing in his ruling about Nakash's U.S. ties. The opinion makes no reference to Jordache, gives no clue as to Nakash's nationality or place of residence, and does not say whether the Israeli bank Nakash helped to manage was in the United States or Israel. Because Judge Lifland omitted these facts, his opinion stands for the proposition that once a bankruptcy case is filed by or against any debtor in the United States, the automatic stay bars the filing of a competing bankruptcy elsewhere—including a filing in the debtor's home country.

Nakash has been a great marketing tool for U.S. bankruptcy lawyers trying to convince foreign debtors to file in the United States. The lawyers could rightly tell foreign debtors that if they filed in the United States, the case would probably stick despite the foreign debtor's lack of U.S. contacts. Upon filing in the United States, the U.S. automatic stay would bar the debtor's creditors from filing a bankruptcy case against the debtor in the debtor's home country. The creditors could request of the U.S. court that it lift the stay so that the creditors could file their case in the debtor's home country, but making such a request is expensive and time consuming. By the time the creditor could evaluate the situation, retain counsel, and get its request before the U.S. court, the case would have grown roots in the United States. A creditors' committee would have been appointed, the main parties would have U.S. lawyers, plan negotiations would have begun, and a plan might even be on the table. Those facts might provide all the justification the U.S. court would need to keep the case permanently.

A more recent case, *In re Cenargo*,[26] shows the degree to which U.S. courts have been willing to use their contempt power to defend their jurisdiction over companies located entirely outside the United States. Cenargo is a group of companies, mostly incorporated in England, that operates ferries between England and various British Isles and European destinations. Although Cenargo had no operations in the United States, it filed for reorganization in the New York bankruptcy court on January 14, 2003. When a major creditor of Cenargo filed a bankruptcy case against Cenargo in London, Judge Robert Drain of the New York bankruptcy court found that the creditor violated the U.S. stay and began the process of assessing money damages against the creditor.[27] Judge Drain aborted his efforts only when he realized that the creditor had no assets in the United States and so was beyond the reach of his enforcement powers.

Cases like *Nakash* and *Cenargo* cast doubt on the common assertion that the steady procession of foreign firms to U.S. bankruptcy courts proves the superiority of U.S. bankruptcy law. When a debtor files in the United States, the creditors are put to a choice. They can acquiesce and move directly to the substantive issues, or they can spend time and money and incur risk fighting over venue. The mere fact that so many cases go forward in the United States without active opposition does more to prove the effectiveness of U.S. intimidation than the superiority of Chapter 11.

Stays to Go

Companies need not intend to reorganize in the United States to benefit from filing a reorganization case in the United States. To analogize to the restaurant business, the U.S. bankruptcy courts are also in the business of selling stays à la carte for consumption off the premises. Consider, for example, the case of Maruko, Inc. Maruko was a Japanese firm headquartered in Tokyo when it filed for bankruptcy reorganization in the Tokyo District Court in 1991. At the time, Maruko owned a major resort development on the Gold Coast of Australia. A Japanese bank held a mortgage against the resort and sought to foreclose.[28] The filing of the Japanese bankruptcy did not stay the Australian foreclosure because Japanese bankruptcy law was not at that time extraterritorial. Japanese law expressly provided that it did not apply outside Japan.[29] Maruko could not obtain a stay from an Australian court because the Australian law in force at the time did not provide for stays of real estate foreclosures. Maruko nevertheless obtained a stay of the Australian foreclosure proceeding by filing a bankruptcy reorganization case in the United States.

To understand how that could happen requires a digression. Recall that U.S. law is extraterritorial. That is, the United States insists that U.S. law applies to people and events in other countries (though not to foreign courts). The courts of other countries have no obligation to give U.S. law the extraterritorial effect the United States claims. Some, like the English court that decided *U.S. Lines,* are even offended by the United States' extraterritorial claims.

But, even if no other country recognized or enforced the U.S. extraterritorial stay, that would not necessarily prevent the U.S. extraterritorial stay from being effective worldwide. Consider, for example, the *U.S. Lines* case. U.S. Lines was a U.S.-based shipping company that operated throughout the world. In November 1986, it filed bankruptcy in the United States. In December, GAC Marine, a foreign creditor of U.S. Lines, sued U.S. Lines in the courts of Hong Kong and Singapore and won orders seizing U.S. Lines ships in those two countries. U.S. Lines did not contest the seizures in Hong Kong or Singapore. Instead, it asked the New York bankruptcy court to hold GAC Marine in contempt of court for violating the U.S. automatic stay. Based on his assumption that the U.S. stay applied in Hong Kong and Singapore, New York bankruptcy judge Howard Buschman held GAC Marine in contempt of court [30] and began fining GAC Marine $5,000 a day.[31] GAC Marine could not ignore the accumulating fines because it operated in the United States through a small, two-person office in New Jersey.[32] The U.S. court might have had a U.S. marshall seize GAC Marine's property at the New Jersey office to satisfy the fines. For GAC Marine to continue in business in the United States, GAC Marine had to abide by the U.S. court's interpretation of the automatic stay, including the U.S. claim that its stay was extraterritorial.

In *Maruko,* matters did not go that far. Apparently fearing enforcement of the U.S. extraterritorial stay against its assets in the United States, the Japanese bank did not continue with the Australian foreclosure.[33] Thus, by filing an additional bankruptcy in the United States, the Japanese company stayed an Australian mortgage foreclosure.

This same strategy is frequently used to export the U.S. stay to Canada. Canadian bankruptcy law does not automatically stay foreclosures.[34] The omission is a policy deliberately adopted by the Canadian government in order to encourage secured lending. But Canadian debtors have figured out that they can get automatic extraterritorial U.S. stays of Canadian foreclosure proceedings by filing parallel bankruptcy cases in the United States. The result has been a series of U.S. bankruptcies filed by large Canadian firms, some of whom have little U.S. presence. The Canadian courts may or may not enforce the extraterritorial U.S. stay with respect to any given firm, but even if the Canadian courts don't enforce it, Canadian creditors who have assets or operations in the United States will be vulnerable to enforcement of the U.S. stay by the U.S. courts. To the U.S. bankruptcy courts that compete for big cases, Canadian firms shopping for stays are welcome customers.

Cenargo, the English debtor discussed earlier in this chapter, found the limits of the extraterritorial stay strategy. Cenargo filed in the United States in the belief that its major secured creditor and principal antagonist, Lombard, would consider itself bound by the U.S. stay. Cenargo's belief was based on its understanding that Lombard had assets in the United States that the New York bankruptcy court could go against to enforce the stay.[35] That belief turned out to have been erroneous.[36] When Lombard filed for administration of Cenargo in the English court, it boldly admitted that its actions were in violation of the U.S. stay.[37] Unconcerned, the English court opened proceedings. Beaten at its own game, the New York court complained that Lombard should have applied to it for a lifting of the stay and the New York court would have granted it.[38] But Lombard hadn't applied, and, in the end, there was nothing the New York court could do about it.

Reaction

To date, the international competition for big cases has been one sided. The U.S. bankruptcy courts have been competing, and bankruptcy courts in the rest of the world have been letting them win. Cenargo is one of the first signs of real resistance. The English court ousted the Cenargo managers put in place by the American court and replaced them with the English court's own administrators. It did so without even contacting the New York court, humiliating that court to an extent unusual in international relations. The English court had that power because Cenargo's assets and managers were in England, where the English court could enforce but the New York court could not.

With no control over Cenargo's assets, the New York court could not even assure that the lawyers who worked in the New York case would be paid.[39] In a final show of bravado after Lombard filed against Cenargo in England, the New York court enjoined Lombard and its representatives from proceeding further in the English court.[40] Then the New York court began backpedaling as fast as it could. It acquiesced in a settlement under which the case would go forward only in England with the English administrators in control. The New York court dismissed the U.S. stay litigation without receiving any quid pro quo from the English court. As a fig leaf to cover the New Yorkers' embarrassment, Lombard agreed not to terminate the English reorganization effort as long as the administrators reasonably believed that the company could be reorganized on a basis that permitted Lombard to be paid in full.[41] The English court completed the reorganization, with apparent success, December 19, 2003.[42]

By ignoring the U.S. stay—and refusing to punish the English lawyers who flaunted their violation of it—the English court served notice that it would resist the taking of obviously English cases. Post-*Cenargo,* the risks to foreign companies and their U.S.

lawyers of filing in the United States are clear. As a result, the number of such filings probably will decline.[43] *Cenargo* will not, however, eliminate the preference of case placers for U.S. reorganization. Foreign and multinational debtors will continue to file in the United States in situations where they believe they can get away with it.

One effect of the migration of cases to the United States has been to put pressure on other nations to change their bankruptcy laws to more closely resemble those of the United States. England recently implemented changes in its bankruptcy system designed to reduce the power of a firm's major lenders and make it easier to "rescue" firms. Many believe these changes were made to stem the outflow of cases from the United Kingdom to the United States. As one prominent U.S. bankruptcy practitioner, Keith Shapiro, warned early in the reform process: "The UK must change its insolvency laws or lose the big cross-border restructurings."[44]

Thus, the downward spiral of international competition has already begun. That competition differs from the U.S. domestic competition in being a competition among lawmakers as well as courts. (I will have more to say about that later in this chapter.) As with its domestic counterpart, the structure of the international competition is not one that will reward the courts or countries that reorganize firms most efficiently. The structure is one that will reward those who best cater to the interests of case placers.

Bankruptcy Havens

Besides the United States, the other big winners from international forum shopping have been the offshore havens, most notably Bermuda and the Cayman Islands. Recent filings in Bermuda include Global Crossing, FLAG Telecom, Loral Aerospace, Trenwick, and Premier Cruise Lines. Recent filings in the Cayman Islands include Fruit of the Loom, InverWorld, National Warranty Insurance, and subsidiaries of Parmalat. Satellite telephone giant ICO Global Communications filed cases in Bermuda and the Cayman Islands.

Most of these cases are "parallel proceedings"—cases filed simultaneously in the haven country and another country. In parallel proceedings, the two courts typically confirm precisely the same plan of reorganization.

The purposes of these haven bankruptcies are often difficult to discern. That is in part because offshore havens are highly secretive. Only local lawyers can obtain access to court files, which means that the only information available regarding haven cases is what the parties choose to release. Even the existence of a haven court file is secret, meaning that if the debtor and its creditors kept their mouths shut, a debtor could go through bankruptcy reorganization in Bermuda or the Cayman Islands without the public ever knowing.

One can, however, draw some inferences about what can or cannot be happening in haven bankruptcies from the circumstances. Bermuda is a small island 890 miles off the coast of North Carolina with a total population of 65,000. Hamilton, Bermuda's business district, has modern, well-manicured three- and four-story office buildings. Those buildings house the international headquarters of many large, well-known multinational corporations, including Tyco and Global Crossing.[45] The headquarters are not, however, real. The "headquarters" often consist of two or three rooms, and the employees who work in them—if any—have little or no authority. One reporter recounted going to Global Crossing's "international headquarters" in Bermuda in the middle of a business-day afternoon and being unable to get anyone to come to the door.[46]

In fact, the large majority of companies incorporated in Bermuda have no employees on the island. Their offices are what traditionally were known as "brass plate headquarters"—a brass plate on the outside of a building, probably alongside dozens of other similar plates for other companies. Inside one could expect to find a single agent authorized to represent all of the companies but in very limited ways. Because most corporate havens no longer require a sign, the brass plates have mostly disappeared. The newer term is *file drawer offices.* Some 13,000 companies are incorporated in Bermuda, but only about 400 actually do business there.[47]

The Cayman Islands are three small islands—two of them nearly deserted—located about 150 miles south of Cuba in the Carribean. The total population of the islands is about 25,000. Georgetown, the Cayman Islands' only city, looks like a rural county seat in the United States. Judging from the exteriors of the buildings, there are no offices in the city where Wall Street lawyers would be willing to work.

From these circumstances, I draw two conclusions about the nature of bankruptcy practice in the haven countries. First, secrecy is essential. What happens there could not stand the light of day. Second, the business activity of a haven does not occur in the haven country. People outside the haven—on Wall Street, on Miami's Brickell Avenue, or in London—invent the schemes and put together the transactions. The haven is a rubber stamp, generating elegantly signed and sealed documents and bank transfers that can be traced back to the haven and no further.

What haven bankruptcy courts seem to be selling is the recognition their orders will receive elsewhere. Their orders receive that recognition because the companies the havens reorganize are incorporated in the havens and much of the world regards a multinational corporation as located at its place of incorporation. Apparently, little actually happens in a haven bankruptcy. The debtors' lawyers file bankruptcy cases in both the haven and a real court—such as Delaware or New York—and the lawyers then prepare a protocol that gives control to the real court. The case actually proceeds in the real court. After the real court confirms the reorganization plan, the plan is submitted to and rubber-stamped by the haven court.

Rarely is the purpose of a haven filing to make the plan effective in the haven country. The debtor typically has neither assets nor debts in the haven, making effectiveness in the haven country of no practical importance. The purpose of a haven filing seems to be to legitimize the parallel case—in this example, the one in Delaware or New York—and thus to improve the chances for recognition of the U.S.-generated plan in third countries.

Those not already familiar with the strange world of multinational bankruptcy might find it odd that a haven with no link to the multinational company except incorporation and no stake in the outcome of the bankruptcy case could confer legitimacy on the bankruptcy courts of the United States. But throughout most of the world, a debtor corporation's country of incorporation is considered an appropriate venue—if not *the* appropriate venue—for the corporation's bankruptcy case. In *U.S. Lines,* for example, the English court stated the rule to be that "[t]he authority of a liquidator appointed under the law of the place of incorporation is recognised in England."[48]

Some U.S. courts follow much the same approach. For example, National Warranty Insurance insured "manufacturers, administrators, and automobile dealerships" in the United States against automobile warranty claims.[49] When National Warranty failed, it caused the failure of at least two automobile warranty service retailers,[50] "invalidating as many as 1 million auto warranty policies" in the United States.[51]

National Warranty's principal place of business was in Lincoln, Nebraska,[52] and the company apparently did business only in the United States. National Warranty was, however, incorporated in the Cayman Islands. The company transferred its remaining reserves ($24 million) to the Cayman Islands and filed bankruptcy there.[53] When U.S. policyholders attempted to sue National Warranty in the United States, a U.S. bankruptcy appeals court composed of three judges from midwestern states stayed the policyholders' lawsuits in deference to the Cayman Islands bankruptcy. The Cayman Islands were an appropriate venue, the court said, because National Warranty was incorporated there.[54] The court of appeals affirmed that ruling, so the U.S. policyholders will have to file claims in the Cayman Islands and will get only what the Cayman Islands court gives them.[55]

Whatever explains the choice of so many companies to file bankruptcy cases in these two havens, it is not the presence of sophisticated bankruptcy laws, judges, or lawyers. Neither country has specialized bankruptcy courts or judges with international reputations. Immigration laws and restrictions on admission to practice law prevent practitioners with expertise developed elsewhere from practicing in Bermuda or the Cayman Islands.[56] Neither country has even a modern law governing bankruptcy reorganization. In the Cayman Islands, for example, liquidation cases proceed under the winding up provisions of companies laws initially copied from the English Companies Law of 1948. The only authorization for reorganizations is a few short paragraphs of the companies law that say the court can order meetings of creditors and bind dissenters to a compromise of debts agreed to by a majority in number and 75 percent in amount of creditors in each class.[57]

The ICO Global Communications case illustrates one of the ways that a bankruptcy haven can help a forum-shopping multinational. In 1995, a 47-member consortium invested $1.5 billion in ICO to establish a worldwide satellite telephone network.[58] In 1999, four years after its founding, ICO was shopping for the right bankruptcy court.

ICO was based in England. The company had over 200 of its 240 employees there, working under the direction of ICO's newly hired CEO and turnaround manager, Richard Greco. ICO did not, however, want to file bankruptcy in England. Under English law, the court would have appointed administrators to take control of the company, ousting Greco and ICO's top managers. ICO preferred U.S. rules, under which the managers would remain in control. But the ICO group had little presence in the United States—apparently just 30 employees working for a fifth-level subsidiary.[59] Of course, that presence was enough to satisfy a U.S. court and obtain confirmation of a plan of reorganization. The issue was whether the English courts would recognize and give effect to the plan.

The ICO group's main operations were carried on by the 200 employees working in England.[60] Those employees worked for the parent corporation's direct subsidiary, ICO Limited, a U.K. corporation.[61] They included ICO's top managers.[62] But ICO's parent corporation, ICO Global Communications (Holdings) Limited, was incorporated in Bermuda. Another direct subsidiary, ICO Global Communications (Operations) Limited, was incorporated in the Cayman Islands.[63] The latter corporation had few or no employees but did hold a number of the ICO group's contracts.[64]

ICO filed six bankruptcy cases. The parent company filed in Bermuda.[65] The Cayman Islands subsidiary filed in the Cayman Islands.[66] Those two corporations, the Delaware subsidiary, and a Netherlands Antilles subsidiary filed in Delaware.[67] The English subsidiary that was the heart of the business, ICO Limited, didn't file at all. Without expressly saying so, the plan effectively reorganized the entire company.

Without the havens' involvement, the Delaware court's claim for English recognition of the reorganization would have been weak. The United States was not ICO's home country by any of the three tests commonly applied: incorporation, headquarters, or principal assets. Acting alone, the Delaware court had no business reorganizing an English company. But acting together with the courts of ICO's countries of incorporation, the Delaware court had a plausible claim to legitimacy.

The Delaware-Bermuda protocol permitted Greco to remain in office in England and run the firm while the bankruptcy was pending. No case had been filed in England, and so there was no English court to say otherwise. The plan was forged in the Delaware bankruptcy court, confirmed by that court, and sent along to the havens for rubber-stamping. (Chris Mallon, a lawyer representing ICO in the proceedings, described the rubber-stamping more gracefully, applauding "the flexibility the Cayman and Bermudan courts have shown. They have ceded their right to control how a company should be run in the Cayman Islands or Bermuda to another country, in the interests of creditors globally.")[68] Once the plan was confirmed by the haven courts, it was entitled to recognition in England and other countries.

The effect of these complex arrangements was to make it possible to reorganize an English firm in Delaware, pursuant to U.S. law, and obtain recognition of the proceedings in England. Alternatively, the havens might have enabled ICO to reorganize in any other nation whose courts would take its case.

Commodore International's 1994 bankruptcy illustrates how havens can sometimes share in or take control of major bankruptcies. Through the 1980s and into the early 1990s, Commodore was a leading manufacturer of personal computers worldwide. The firm was clearly American, incorporated in the United States with its headquarters and manufacturing facilities in West Chester, Pennsylvania. But Commodore was more successful in selling its products in Canada and Europe than in the United States and soon was drawing the largest portion of its income from outside the United States. In an attempt to reduce U.S. taxes on its worldwide income, Commodore reincorporated in the Bahamas in the mid-1970s and set up a nominal headquarters there.[69] Irving Gould, a 20 percent shareholder and the chairman of Commodore's board, spent part of each year in the Bahamas. Commodore International listed a Bahamian address along with its West Chester address on the annual report the firm filed with the U.S. Securities and Exchange Commission early in 1994. But Commodore's Bahamian facilities, whatever they were, were not even large enough to merit disclosure among the firm's 17 "principal facilities" listed in the report.[70] Commodore's president continued to work from the firm's New York offices, and the U.S. Internal Revenue Service challenged the Bahamas headquarters as bogus.[71]

When Commodore fell into financial difficulties in 1993, the company shattered. Many of the Commodore subsidiaries were forced into liquidation proceedings in the countries where they operated.[72] The parent companies of the Commodore group—both of which were incorporated in the Bahamas—filed liquidation proceedings there on April 29, 1994. Five days later, creditors filed involuntary bankruptcy cases against those same entities and their U.S. subsidiary in New York. The involuntary cases were resolved by the American creditors' committee and the Bahamian liquidators entering into an agreement (protocol) by which the cases would proceed in both countries under joint control.[73] Commodore's assets were sold pursuant to the protocol. After years of squabbling over the proceeds, the parties ultimately reached a compromise on their distribution.[74]

The Commodore case shows that when a debtor's assets are spread among several countries, a bankruptcy haven in which the debtor has virtually no physical presence can become a major player. With management favoring the haven and no other country with a sufficient portion of the firm to give it a credible claim to being the firm's center of gravity, the haven may dominate by default. By negotiating protocols with the courts of the countries where the multinational's assets and operations are located, a haven court could even take effective control of a worldwide bankruptcy process.

The Difference International Makes

Forum shopping is a greater threat to the international bankruptcy system than to the U.S. domestic bankruptcy system for several reasons. Perhaps the most important is that the stakes are usually higher in an international forum shop. Both kinds of shopping give litigants a choice among bankruptcy courts. But a choice among U.S. bankruptcy courts is a choice among courts bound to apply the same laws and procedures and whose decisions can be appealed to a unified system of appellate courts. A choice among the courts of different countries is a choice among courts that may apply entirely different laws and procedures and answer to entirely separate appellate court systems.

The two most important differences among countries' bankruptcy laws are the remedies countries offer bankrupt firms and the relative priorities they assign to types of creditors. Three major differences in remedies have already been discussed. First, U.S. law permits the debtor's management to remain in control during bankruptcy, while the law of most other countries ousts management in favor of a court- or creditor-appointed official. Second, some countries' laws provide for reorganization, while others require liquidation—sale of the debtor's assets to the highest bidder. Third, the law of some countries stays the collection efforts of secured creditors during bankruptcy, while the law of others allows them to seize the debtor's assets even while the debtor is in bankruptcy. In a country of the latter sort, debtors are essentially at the mercy of their secured creditors.

The relative priorities of creditors also differ from country to country. "Priority" is an entitlement to be paid in full before lower priority creditors get any payment at all. Bankruptcy priority rules are complex. The laws of the United States, for example, recognize literally thousands of types of creditors who may be entitled to different priorities.

To illustrate the magnitude of the international differences, U.S. bankruptcy law gives first priority to secured creditors against the collateral specified in their agreements with their debtors. "Secured creditors" include mortgage lenders and banks with setoff rights, as well as creditors with "security interests" in goods, such as equipment or inventory, and intangible property, such as accounts receivable, contract rights, or intellectual property rights. The term *secured creditors* also encompasses hundreds of different kinds of creditors—from garage mechanics to taxing authorities to suppliers of building materials—who have been granted "statutory lien" priority by the laws of their states in particular types of property.[75] In many U.S. bankruptcy cases, secured creditors are entitled to everything the debtor has, leaving nothing for distribution to anyone else.

U.S. law gives second priority—after all priorities of secured creditors in their respective collateral—to administrative expenses in the bankruptcy case.[76] This category includes the lawyers and financial advisers who charge multinational companies millions and sometimes tens of millions of dollars for their work on a bankruptcy case. Among the types of priorities considered here, U.S. law gives third place to employees for wages and benefits but limits this priority to $4,650 per employee.[77] Unsecured taxes owing to the United States or the various states have a lower priority.[78]

By contrast, Mexican law generally gives first priority to employees for wages and benefits, without dollar limit.[79] Second

priority goes to various administrative expenses and the third to
taxes,[80] leaving most secured creditors in no better than fourth
position.[81] Bahamian law puts secured creditors behind all three of
those classes and also behind the claims of injured workmen.[82]
Creditors that are considered secured under U.S. law might be considered unsecured under Mexican or Bahamian law. As Professor
Jay L. Westbrook, a leading international bankruptcy scholar, put
it: "[T]here is no doubt that national insolvency laws differ greatly,
especially as to priority in distribution, and that these differences
will continue to exist for some time."[83]

Regardless of whether the debtor is a domestic company, a
purely foreign company, or a multinational company, the bankruptcy court that gets the case will apply its own (domestic) regime
of remedies and priorities. The reasons are mostly practical. A case
can follow only a single set of procedures, and the court is already
familiar with its own. Either the court allows management to
remain in control or replaces management with a court-appointed
representative. The court cannot provide one of these remedies to
some creditors in a case and the other remedy to other creditors in
the same case. Priorities are similarly indivisible. The assets of a
debtor constitute a fixed pool, and priorities in that pool are relative. To give priority to one creditor is necessarily to take priority
from some other.

Courts have difficulty determining and applying the laws of
their own countries; a requirement that they determine and apply
the laws of some other country would be overwhelming. Courts
can and do make some accommodations to foreign law at the mar-
gins, but generally speaking, the bankruptcy court that gets the
case will apply its own laws, procedures, and priorities.

It follows that when a debtor chooses among courts of different
countries, it is choosing the remedies that will be available to it and
the relative priorities of its creditors. The Lernout & Hauspie
Speech Products N.V. bankruptcy illustrates the potential for last-
minute forum shopping to alter creditors' long-standing entitle-
ments. Lernout & Hauspie was incorporated in Belgium and had
its headquarters there.[84] In May 2000, the company bought Dicta-

phone Corporation from Stonington Partners[85] for about $510 million.[86] The price was paid almost entirely in Lernout & Hauspie stock. About 40 percent of the stock was restricted such that Stonington Partners could not sell it for two years.[87]

Six months later, Lernout & Hauspie admitted it had been cooking its books for the preceding two and a half years,[88] and the company filed parallel bankruptcy proceedings in Delaware and Belgium.[89] Lernout & Hauspie's stock was worthless, including, of course, the stock Stonington Partners held. Stonington Partners filed claims for its $500 million loss in both bankruptcies.

In Belgium, the claims of defrauded stockholders rank equally with the claims of general unsecured creditors.[90] The claims of Lernout & Hauspie's defrauded stockholders were so large they "dwarf[ed]" the claims of other unsecured creditors.[91] Thus if Belgian law governed, the stock fraud claimants would receive the large bulk of the distribution to unsecured creditors.[92] The Belgian court ruled that they should.[93]

In the United States, stock fraud claims are subordinate to general unsecured creditors.[94] If U.S. law governed, the holders of the stock fraud claims would receive nothing. The U.S. court ruled that the stock fraud claimants should receive nothing.[95]

Had it chosen to do so, Lernout & Hauspie probably could have determined Stonington Partners' fate by its choice of court. If the Lernout & Hauspie bankruptcy had gone forward only in Belgium, Belgian law would have governed the distribution; if it had gone forward only in the United States, U.S. law would have governed the distribution. Because Lernout & Hauspie went forward in both courts, and those courts made inconsistent rulings, Stonington Partners' fate will be decided by the interaction between the courts.

Lernout & Hauspie's headquarters were in Belgium, and the firm was incorporated there.[96] The Delaware bankruptcy court nevertheless sought to impose its resolution of the stock fraud claim dispute on the Belgian court. To accomplish that, the Delaware court used a familiar technique: It enjoined Stonington from further prosecuting its claim in the Belgian court.[97] Stonington appealed the bankruptcy court's injunction to the Third Circuit

Court of Appeals. The court of appeals reversed the bankruptcy court's decision and strongly suggested that the bankruptcy court attempt to negotiate a protocol with the Belgian bankruptcy court.[98] More than a year after that decision, no protocol has been negotiated, and the issue remains unresolved.

Why the International Bankruptcy System Hasn't Yet Collapsed

The discussion thus far has shown that international forum shopping is easy to do and, if successful, can yield huge gains. Readers might wonder why bankrupt companies don't routinely shop the world's bazaar for bankruptcy laws that enable them to best their creditors, ultimately leading to a complete system collapse. The answer is not that the creditors will stop them by contesting venue. Alert, motivated creditors—like Lombard and Stonington—will counter the shops in some cases. But even when they do, the usual result is merely compromise, leaving the case placers better off for their effort.

A large part of the answer is that bankruptcy court decisions are effective only in countries that choose to recognize and enforce them. To illustrate, assume that the New York bankruptcy court had confirmed Cenargo's reorganization plan without objection from any court or creditor, the plan gave Cenargo additional time in which to pay Lombard, but Lombard refused to abide by the plan and instead sued Cenargo in England. Cenargo would have raised the New York court's ruling in defense, and the English court would then have had to decide whether to "recognize" that ruling. If the English court concluded that Cenargo should not have reorganized in the United States, the English court could refuse to recognize the New York court's decision and instead rule that Lombard could foreclose. At that point, the orders of the two courts would be in direct conflict. Which would prevail?

The answer is that each court would prevail with respect to enforcement against people and assets in its own country. U.S. courts control what happens within the borders of the United

States; English courts control what happens within the borders of England. The most fundamental principle of international relations—known as "territoriality"—is that each country has the exclusive right to use force within its own borders. English law enforcement officers can seize and sell assets located in England, and those officers take their instructions exclusively from English courts. To enforce a U.S. court ruling in England, one must first persuade an English court to adopt the ruling as its own and order the enforcement.

So, to complete the illustration, the English court's ruling would determine the disposition of Cenargo's English assets, and the New York court's ruling would determine the disposition of Cenargo's U.S. assets. In other words, a debtor can reorganize in any jurisdiction it chooses, but that reorganization will be effective only in countries where the courts later recognize it.

U.S. law requires both state and federal courts within the United States to recognize and enforce decisions of any U.S. bankruptcy court. No laws or treaties require foreign courts to recognize or enforce decisions of U.S. bankruptcy courts. If the U.S. bankruptcy court seems to have overreached in taking the case, a foreign court may simply refuse to recognize or enforce the U.S. court's decisions. The need for recognition thus limits what case placers can gain from international shopping and what the bankruptcy courts of a country can gain from competing. Thus, this after-the-fact, case-by-case need for recognition is the linchpin that holds the international bankruptcy system together.

The next chapter examines a movement called "universalism" that seeks to precommit the countries of the world to recognize and enforce each other's bankruptcy decisions. If the universalists succeed, they will eliminate the need for after-the-fact, case-by-case recognition and thus remove the linchpin.

8

Global and Out of Control?

"Forum shopping" for the most favorable place
to go bust seems set to flourish.

—International bankruptcy commentator John Willcox (2003)

The potential for economic harm from international forum shopping is greater than the potential for harm from domestic shopping. By choosing a different city's court within the United States the domestic shopper can gain only a different interpretation or application of the same U.S. Bankruptcy Code and Rules of Procedure. But by choosing a different country's court, an international shopper can access an entirely different set of remedies and priorities.

That potential for greater harm is held in check by the need for international recognition and enforcement of bankruptcy orders. When competing courts overreach internationally—by attempting to apply their own laws to people and events in other countries— courts of those other countries can nullify the attempt by refusing to recognize or enforce the overreaching courts' orders.

The need for foreign recognition limits what courts can offer case placers and thus moderates the competition. Competing courts tend to act more reasonably in multinational bankruptcy cases, and the potential for harm goes largely unrealized.

Unfortunately, many of the world's leading bankruptcy professionals—lawyers, judges, and academics—are trying to eliminate the recognition requirement. If they succeed, they will unleash the international system's full potential for harm. Most of these professionals are well-meaning, good-hearted idealists, working for what they see as an improvement in the system. A few are schemers, seeking to advance themselves or their local bankruptcy courts. Under the banner of "universalism," the professionals seek to give a single court effective worldwide jurisdiction over each multinational company's bankruptcy case. Alone, that would be an improvement in the system. But to put a single court in control of a case requires some method for selecting that court. So far the universalists have proposed no method that is likely to work. If they are allowed to implement their current proposal, it will trigger an international bankruptcy court competition far more destructive than the domestic competition in the United States.

To illustrate how universalism is supposed to work, assume hypothetically that Daimler-Benz, a multinational company based in Germany, properly filed for bankruptcy in Germany. The German court would administer Daimler-Benz's assets—not just in Germany but in the United States and other countries. In accord with the general understanding that a court of one country is not competent to administer a case according to the laws and procedures of another,[1] the German court would administer the U.S. assets according to German laws and procedures. German law would control, for example, the priorities and remedies of Daimler-Benz's American employees and customers. The courts of the United States would be required to recognize orders of the German court—whether they agreed with those orders or not—and assist in enforcing them.

If, in a universalist system, Daimler-Benz could instead file in the United States, U.S. law would determine the remedies available to the company and the priorities of the company's creditors, employees, and customers throughout the world. The company's choice of the United States over Germany would provide windfall priorities to some creditors while depriving others of priorities for which they bargained and paid.

Universalists and their opponents agree that a system that allowed multinational companies a last-minute choice of law would not be viable. Parties who deal with a multinational company—particularly one already in financial difficulty—need to know what rules will govern in the event of bankruptcy.

To prevent multinational companies from changing their remedies and their creditors' priorities by the companies' last-minute venue choices, universalist laws and treaties require that each multinational case proceed in the debtor's "home country." The image of a single court—that of the debtor's home country—fairly and in good faith coordinating the worldwide reorganization of a sprawling multinational is appealing. That appeal probably explains why so many bankruptcy professionals have accepted the home country standard so uncritically. Universalist proposals incorporating it have been adopted by the European Union, the United Nations Commission on International Trade Law (UNCITRAL), and the prestigious American Law Institute, and implementation is already well under way.

In thinking that the home country standard will be sufficient to control international forum shopping, the universalists have underestimated the incentives for such shopping, the strategic nature of international bankruptcy practice, and the pressures on courts and countries to each win at least a share of the world's multibillion-dollar bankruptcy industry for themselves. The home country standard has four fatal flaws that in combination will permit almost unbridled forum shopping and encourage court competition. First, many of the largest multinational companies do not have home countries in any meaningful sense. When they file for bankruptcy, these companies each will be able to choose among the courts of two or more countries. Second, even multinational companies that do have clear, unmistakable home countries can, and already do, change them. Third, as the U.S. experience has shown, with billions of dollars of business at stake for bankruptcy professionals, competing courts cannot be counted on to determine fairly and in good faith whether they are the home court of multinationals that choose to file with them. Each will be biased in favor of its own jurisdiction. Finally, if international forum shopping and competition do—as I expect they will—run out of control, mechanisms for fixing the problem do not exist. International institutions are not strong enough to impose a solution.

In a universalist system, case placers would be free to choose the bankruptcy systems that gave them and their companies the greatest advantage over other parties to the bankruptcy cases. The case placers could choose countries whose laws left even corrupt managers in control, barred criminal prosecutions of top managers during bankruptcy cases, lowered the priorities of hostile creditors while raising the priorities of friendly ones, or provided benefits we cannot yet even imagine. If no countries yet have such laws, aspiring bankruptcy havens will enact them.

Of course, major creditors such as banks and insurance companies would anticipate their borrowers' desire to forum shop in the event of bankruptcy and insist on contract provisions to protect themselves. Those contract provisions probably would not, however, prohibit forum shopping. Prohibiting forum shopping would protect everyone, including less sophisticated creditors, customers, landlords, employees, taxing authorities, suppliers, and others. The major creditors and their borrowers could gain more from a contract that permitted forum shopping, exploited the less sophisticated stakeholders, and split the benefits of that exploitation among the major creditors and their borrowers. When billions of dollars are at stake, there are no free riders.

Universalism's Progress

The universalist dream is more than a century old. In an article published in the *Harvard Law Review* in 1888, Professor John Lowell wrote of international bankruptcy:

> It is obvious that, in the present state of commerce and of communication, it would be better in nine cases out of ten that all settlements of insolvent debtors with their creditors should be made in a single proceeding, and generally at a single place; better for the creditors, who would thus share alike, and better for the debtor, because all his creditors would be equally bound by his discharge. . . . It is not so easy to see how this result is to be reached in actual practice.[2]

In the sixty years that followed, universalists continued to push for an international bankruptcy regime in which the decisions of bankruptcy courts in one jurisdiction would receive automatic recognition in others. In Europe, their efforts resulted in several bilateral treaties in which adjacent countries with similar bankruptcy systems agreed to recognize each other's bankruptcy proceedings.[3] In Latin America, 15 nations ratified the Bustamante Code of Private International Law, which provided for a mostly universalist bankruptcy regime among those countries.[4] But by 1948, the leading international bankruptcy scholar concluded that the push toward universalism had failed.

> Progress has been made only by negotiation between specific countries. The reason is not difficult to ascertain. A treaty-type fitting neighbor-states with a similar bankruptcy legislation, for example, cannot possibly be acceptable to countries which may be distant from each other and have entirely different legal systems. . . . [C]onclusion of a multilateral convention appears impracticable at the present time for many reasons, particularly because of the great diversity of national laws . . . .[5]

The universalists did not give up. In the five decades that followed, they negotiated convention after convention. All failed to obtain ratification. In nearly every case, the sticking point was the provision that would determine which country's courts got the cases. The earliest in this succession of failures was the Model Treaty on Bankruptcy negotiated at the Hague Conference in 1925.[6] That convention would have given jurisdiction over bankruptcy cases to a court of the country "where the statutory registered seat" of the corporation was located—essentially the country of incorporation.[7] It was not ratified by even a single country.[8]

In the mid-1980s, the International Bar Association drafted the Model International Insolvency Cooperation Act (MIICA) for adoption by individual countries. The law provided that the adopting country would recognize foreign bankruptcy proceedings in the "principal forum." When all countries had adopted the act, the result would be a worldwide universalist system. The act—which failed to specify where the "principal forum" would be[9]—was never adopted in any country.[10]

Beginning in the 1970s,[11] European Community and later European Union negotiators proposed a series of Europe-only universalist bankruptcy conventions. A prominent early draft—the 1982 Common Market Draft—would have given jurisdiction to the country in which "the centre of administration of the debtor" was located. With typical British understatement, Professor Ian Fletcher, a leading commentator on international bankruptcy, found it "necessary to voice some apprehension that the correct identification of the location of a debtor's 'centre of administration' . . . may not in all cases be so straightforward as to produce total unanimity amongst the courts concerned." That uncertainty, Fletcher wrote, "could well give rise to 'positive' conflicts of jurisdiction which . . . could prove virtually irresolvable in practice."[12]

After the failure of the 1982 draft, later European convention drafts typically proposed to give jurisdiction to the court where the debtor had the "centre of its main interests." When UNCITRAL decided to propose a model law based on MIICA, its negotiators settled on the same standard. The "centre of its main interests" was at least as vague as the standard Fletcher had criticized. Universalists liked it because the vagueness enabled them to reach agreement. That did not, however, stop numerous commentators from pointing out that the "centre of [the debtor's] main interests" standard begged the question of which country should have the case and thus threatened to generate conflict rather than cooperation.[13]

Universalism in the United States

As of this writing, the U.S. government is not yet a party to any universalist treaty or convention and has adopted no universalist law. U.S. negotiators did settle on a universalist bankruptcy treaty with Canada in 1979. That treaty gave jurisdiction to the country in which the debtor had the majority of its assets. The treaty was not ratified because of "disagreements about the proper choice-of-country rule."[14]

Unable to win adoption of a universalist law or convention, the universalists asserted that section 304 of the U.S. Bankruptcy Code, which had been adopted in 1978, was such a law. Section 304 authorized the bankruptcy courts of the United States to turn over

control of U.S. assets to foreign bankruptcy courts. But the statute
added:

> (C) In determining whether to grant [such] relief . . . the court
> shall be guided by what will best assure an economical and expe-
> ditious administration of such estate, consistent with—
> (4) distribution of proceeds of such estate substantially in
> accordance with the order prescribed by [U.S. bankruptcy law].

Read literally, section 304 clearly limits authority to surrender U.S.
assets to situations in which the foreign court will distribute them
in substantially the same way a U.S. court would. But the universalists, many of whom were themselves bankruptcy judges, chose
not to read section 304 as written. Instead, they claimed that section 304 authorized turnover of assets to foreign courts that would
distribute the assets substantially differently, as long as the foreign
country had a bankruptcy law "of the same sort generally as [the
United States]."[15] Universalist judges, including Judge Burton R.
Lifland, began surrendering U.S. assets for distribution by foreign
bankruptcy courts,[16] and universalist commentators, including
Professor Jay L. Westbrook, cheered them on.[17] The effect was to
sporadically implement universalism in the United States, at the
expense of the particular U.S. creditors whose assets were surrendered.

In 2001, the United States Court of Appeals for the Second Circuit dealt the universalists a major setback. In *In re Treco*,[18] Merid-
ian International Bank, Limited (MIBL), filed bankruptcy in the
Bahamas. At the time, MIBL had $600,000 on deposit in the Bank
of New York. The Bank of New York had a security interest in
those funds securing a debt owing from MIBL to the Bank of New
York in an amount exceeding $4 million. U.S. law gives secured
creditors first priority, and so if the money remained in the United
States, the Bank of New York would be entitled to it. If the money
were surrendered to the Bahamian court, the Bahamian court
would use it to pay administrative expenses in the bankruptcy
case—essentially, the fees of the Bahamian court-appointed liquidators. Bahamian law gives administrative expenses priority over

secured creditors. If the money went to the Bahamas, it was unlikely any of it was coming back. The Bahamian court had collected $10 million of MIBL assets and paid out nearly $8 million of it in administrative expenses.[19] The case was a perfect illustration of the dangers of international forum shopping and court competition.

The New York bankruptcy court ordered the Bank of New York to surrender the funds to the Bahamian court. The district court affirmed that decision on appeal. The court of appeals reversed the decision, giving the money to the Bank of New York. The court cited universalist scholars with seeming approval and disparaged territoriality as "grab law." In the end, however, it came down squarely against the universalists' interpretation of section 304. The issue, the court held, was not whether the foreign law was sufficiently similar to the U.S. law but whether the money surrendered in this case would be distributed in substantially the same way. The universalists sought to spin the decision their own way,[20] but few were buying it.

Universalism Comes in the Back Door

After more than a century of failure, the universalists suddenly won three major victories. In 1997, UNCITRAL promulgated the Model Law on Cross-Border Insolvency, which incorporates the universalists' home country concept.[21] That law has so far been adopted by only a few countries, including none of major commericial importance. But U.S. congressional leaders have already made the decision to adopt it in the United States. Since 1998, it has been included in the omnibus bankruptcy bill that has nearly been enacted several times. The UNCITRAL model law is also near adoption in England.

The second universalist victory came in 2000, when the European Union adopted the Regulation on Insolvency, which also incorporates the home country concept.[22] The EU regulation became effective in 2002. The third victory came in 2002 with the promulgation by the American Law Institute of a universalist set of principles, "Principles of Cooperation in Transnational Insolvency Cases among the Members of the North American Free Trade Association." These principles are not themselves law, but they are recommendations to judges made by the largest and most prestigious law reform organization in the United States.

Both the EU regulation and the model law require recognition of a multinational company bankruptcy filed in a court of the company's home country.[23] Each law specifically authorizes local courts to sacrifice the rights of local creditors under local laws to the commands of home country courts.[24] Both laws are clear endorsements of universalist principles. Neither makes any attempt to explain where the "centre of [a debtor's] main interests" is located.

The EU regulation is the more clearly universalist of the two. Once the court of an EU country determines for itself that it is the debtor's home country and declares its own case the "main proceeding," the courts of other EU countries are obligated to recognize it as such. Theoretically, it would still be possible for local creditors to file a "secondary proceeding" in another country. But the secondary proceeding could only liquidate the debtor's assets in that country; it could not reorganize them. In addition, at the request of the liquidator in the main proceeding, the local court would be obligated to put the secondary proceeding on hold.[25] That could leave creditors filing secondary proceedings stranded between courts for months or years. As a practical matter, universalism is now the law in the European Union.

Despite the provision of the UNCITRAL model law requiring recognition of a main proceeding filed in another country, the U.S. promoters of the law claim it is not universalist.[26] In the law's defense, they point to provisions that would permit a parallel proceeding in the United States even after a foreign main proceeding has been recognized. But that parallel proceeding, the universalists acknowledge, would have to be brought as an "involuntary" bankruptcy.[27] What the defenders fail to mention is that involuntary bankruptcies are highly disfavored in U.S. law and notoriously difficult to initiate. The filer of an involuntary case must meet technical requirements[28] and risk liability for damages if the filer does not succeed—including a possible award of punitive damages.[29]

Any doubts about whether adoption of the UNCITRAL model law would commit the United States to a universalist position in international bankruptcy have been rendered moot by the promulgation of the Principles of Cooperation in Transnational Insolvency Cases among the Members of the North American Free Trade Association, adopted by the American Law Institute in 2002 (the ALI principles). Professor Westbrook, a principal drafter of the principles, describes the crucial provisions as follows.

> General Principle V urges that the courts of the NAFTA [North American Free Trade Agreement] countries determine distributions from a universalist perspective to the maximum extent permitted by their respective laws. Thus, for example, the ALI Principles expressly contemplate the possibility of dismissing one or more full insolvency proceedings, so that a reorganization (rescue) plan can be adopted in the main proceeding.[30]

In other words, even if U.S. creditors succeed in initiating an involuntary parallel proceeding, the ALI principles direct the court to dismiss it. Although the ALI principles were developed in the context of NAFTA, the ALI also recommends their application "to cooperate with proceedings in non-NAFTA jurisdictions."[31] Together, the UNCITRAL model law and the ALI principles will commit the United States to international bankruptcy universalism to substantially the same extent that adoption of the EU regulation committed the Europeans.

Once that commitment is in place, forum-shopping multinationals, acting in concert with DIP lenders if necessary, will choose among the courts that are plausibly their home country courts. The chosen courts will, of course, be competitive ones. Those courts will hold quick hearings, declare themselves to be the home country courts, open the proceedings, and declare those proceedings to be main. The proceedings will then be entitled to recognition in other countries. The case placer's opponents will not participate. At this stage, they probably will not yet know that the case has been filed. If this sounds far fetched, consider this description by a leading English bankruptcy law firm describing the English system as it currently operates under the EU regulation.

> First, the hearing to open administration proceedings [in England] is generally unopposed, largely as very few people need to be notified in advance. . . . At the hearing, the debtor will address the court as to where its [centre of main interests] is located. While the debtor should put "points against" as well as "points for," it is always easier to win a match if the other team does not show up. . . . [A] judge is unlikely to second guess the company—especially if no one is arguing the contrary. Importantly, once administration proceedings are opened in [England], that decision can only be challenged in the [English] court itself.[32]

Other commentators agree that the venue decision of the first court to open proceedings is binding on other courts.[33] This is not a peculiarity of the EU system but, rather, a general principle by which courts have long operated.[34] Someone must decide who gets the case. Giving that power to the first court is hardly an ideal solution, but with no international government to take control, it is probably the best of a lot of bad alternatives.

As soon as that first case is filed, the parties will begin putting the infrastructure of a universalist bankruptcy regime in place. The court will appoint a representative, and that representative will file ancillary cases in the courts of other countries. Committees will organize at the site of the main proceeding, parties from all over the world will hire professionals to represent them at the site of the main proceeding, the court will enter first-day orders, and new lenders will rely on those orders by supplying the debtor with new working capital. The case will grow roots where it was filed, making challenges to that venue virtually impossible to win. At the conclusion of the case, the court's decision will be entitled to automatic recognition in other countries.[35]

Forum Shopping in a Universalist System

All the case placer need do to forum shop in a universalist system is make a plausible argument that the chosen court is at the "centre of [the debtor's] main interests."[36] The chosen court will do the rest, pondering the issues and then solemnly concluding that the debtor is indeed correct.

The plausible argument can be based on the presence in the chosen country of any of these four attributes: (1) incorporation (registered office), (2) headquarters, (3) administrative employees and operations, and (4) assets. Each of these attributes has, at various times and places, been considered the most appropriate basis on which to fix the location of a multinational company.

1. *Incorporation.* Bankruptcies filed in the country of incorporation are routinely recognized and deferred to in much of the world today. When companies such as Tyco, Global Crossing, and Fruit of the Loom "move" offshore to defeat U.S. taxation, what they in fact do is incorporate offshore. When a court refers to a company as a "Delaware corporation" or a "Bahamian corporation," what the court means is that the company is incorporated in Delaware or the Bahamas.

Both the UNCITRAL model law and the EU regulation state that "the debtor's registered office . . . is presumed to be the centre of the debtor's main interests." In this context, "registered office" simply means the country of incorporation; no real office is involved. The center of a corporation's main interests is presumed to be in the country of its incorporation.

If incorporation is the debtor's only contact with the forum country, the argument may not be plausible. The presumption is rebuttable. It logically follows that in the weakest case, the presumption can be rebutted. That weakest case is the one in which incorporation is the only contact. The first case to interpret this provision of the EU regulation was that of BRAC Rent-A-Car International, Inc., a former subsidiary of the Budget Rent A Car group. The London High Court of Justice was faced with these facts.

> [The debtor] is incorporated in Delaware and has its registered address in the United States. However, that is not an address from which it trades, and it has never traded in the U.S. Its oper-

ations are conducted almost entirely in the UK. . . . It has no employees in the US, and all its employees work in England . . . apart from a small number in a branch office in Switzerland. [BRAC] is . . . in Chapter 11 administration in the US.[37]

The English court reached the only plausible conclusion. The center of BRAC's main interests was in England. But add even a little trading in the United States, and the Delaware bankruptcy court might easily claim the case.

2. *Headquarters.* In defending the "centre of main interests" test, Professor Jay L. Westbrook, the leading American universalist, analogizes it to the "principal place of business" test used for various purposes in the United States.

> [T]he principal place of business standard in one formulation or another is commonplace throughout American law—state and federal—and is found elsewhere as well. That sort of standard has produced some litigation, but I am unaware of any widely held view that it is so imprecise as to be impractical or to maim any important legal objective.[38]

The case law to which Westbrook refers, however, holds that a company's principal place of business is at its headquarters, as opposed to the place where it has the bulk of its assets or operations. A court could easily hold isolated corporate headquarters to be the center of a corporation's main interests. Westbrook himself as much as endorsed this interpretation when he wrote that England was the "center of gravity" of Maxwell Communications, even though the great bulk of Maxwell's assets and operations was in the United States.[39]

3. *Administrative employees and operations.* The failure of Bank of Commerce and Credit International (BCCI) was one of the major financial scandals of the twentieth century. BCCI was founded by Saudis, incorporated in Luxembourg, and operated in numerous countries through subsidiaries. For most of BCCI's existence, its headquarters were in London along with most of its central administration. Before BCCI filed for bankruptcy, the firm

moved its headquarters, including nearly all of its top managers, to Saudi Arabia. (The firm's top executives apparently felt they would be more comfortable dealing with the world's criminal courts from their home country.) BCCI's central administrative operations remained in London. BCCI filed for bankruptcy in Luxembourg, and the Luxembourg proceeding was recognized as a main proceeding throughout the world. (Some countries, including both the United States and England, recognized the Luxembourg proceeding but did not fully cooperate with it. Both the United States and England kept some BCCI assets for their local creditors.)

At the time it filed for bankruptcy, BCCI had neither its headquarters nor its registered office in England. But if a firm identical to BCCI were to file in England today—away from its place of incorporation, its headquarters, and the bulk of its assets—an English court's decision that England was the firm's home country would be more than plausible. The location of the central bureaucracy that holds a far-flung firm together is arguably the most substantial presence that a firm can have in a country.

The Delaware bankruptcy court seems to have proceeded on that basis in the Lernout & Hauspie case, discussed in chapter 7. Lernout & Hauspie's headquarters were in Belgium, and the firm was incorporated there. After the firm filed parallel proceedings in Delaware and Belgium the Delaware court sought to take control of the main issue in the case: the priority of Stonington Partners' stock fraud claim. None of the three American courts that reviewed the case even suggested that the U.S. court should defer to the Belgian court simply because Lernout & Hauspie was both headquartered and incorporated in Belgium.[40] Instead, the U.S. Third Circuit Court of Appeals pressured the Delaware bankruptcy court to negotiate with the Belgian bankruptcy court, an approach that begs the home country question.[41]

4. *Assets*. Some large public companies consist principally of hard, tangible assets. An oil exploration company may own hundreds of millions of dollars worth of properties. Those properties may or may not be producing, and even if they are producing, the production may be managed by others. The assets may actually be

the company. The same might be true of a shipping company, such as Global Ocean Carriers (discussed in chap. 7), that owns ocean-going vessels. A court where the assets of such a company were located could plausibly hold its country to be the home country, even if the place of incorporation, headquarters, and central operations were elsewhere.

In fixing so vague a standard for venue, the universalists undoubtedly imagined courts proceeding in good faith to determine the best application of the standard to the facts of the particular case. But in a world where a single big bankruptcy case can bring more than a billion dollars in fees to the bankruptcy professionals of a locale, such imaginings are naive.

Is the Home Country That of the Corporation or the Group?

Nearly all multinational companies are corporate groups, not single corporations. The largest are often composed of hundreds of corporations. For example, General Motors is a group consisting of over 500 corporations.[42] Some of those corporations operate independent businesses, others are integral parts of the group's main automobile manufacturing businesses, and the rest are somewhere in between.

In deciding whether the members of these groups should be treated as a single debtor in applying the home country standard, the universalists are on the horns of a dilemma. On the one hand, putting a single court in control of the debtor's worldwide business is the very point of universalism. The basic premise is that reorganization or liquidation of a business requires coordination that only a single court can provide. That suggests that universalism should apply to corporate groups, not corporations, and the search for the "centre of main interests" should be for the center of the group's interests.

Instead, both the EU regulation and the UNCITRAL model law direct that the search be for the home countries of individual corporations, not corporate groups. Thus a British Court held that a

Swedish corporation that owned a subsidiary with an establishment in England did not have an "establishment" in England—its
subsidiary did. [43] A leading commentator states flatly that "international jurisdiction according to the Regulation must exist for
each of the concerned debtors with a separate legal entity."[44] It follows that when the corporations of a group have different home
countries, the bankruptcy of the group's business will be split
among numerous courts.

The problem cannot be solved merely by providing that all
members of the group should file in the home country of the group.
To see why, reconsider my example of the corporate group commonly referred to in the United States as Daimler-Chrysler.[45] The
German parent corporation of that group, Daimler-Benz Corporation, owned subsidiaries that made automobiles in dozens of countries. One of those subsidiaries was Daimler-Chrysler Corporation,
which manufactured automobiles in the United States and in turn
owned sub-subsidiaries that manufactured automobiles in about a
dozen other countries. One of those sub-subsidiaries was Chrysler
De Mexico, S.A., which manufactured automobiles only in Mexico.[46] All of these corporations were members of the same corporate group. If a universalist law required reorganization in the
home country of the group, that probably would mean reorganization in a German court. That in turn would mean the affairs of
Chrysler De Mexico, S.A.—a corporation that did business with
Mexicans in Mexico—would have been adjudicated by a distant
court in a different language. That German court would have
administered German remedies and applied German priorities to
relationships principally among Mexicans. For the German court
to administer Mexican remedies and priorities to the affairs of the
Mexican subsidiary would not be an option. As previously noted,
all commentators agree that the bankruptcy court of one nation
could not competently administer the bankruptcy laws of
another.[47] In this example, the only sensible solution would be to
permit Chrysler De Mexico, S.A., to reorganize in a Mexican court
under Mexican law.

Generalizing on the point, the sensible solution to the corporate group problem is to administer economically integrated group members together in the home country of the integrated group while administering economically independent group members separately in the home countries of the members. But to make the separation, one needs exactly what one cannot have in a world of forum shopping and court competition—unbiased courts that would exercise broad discretion to reject inappropriately filed cases.

As a result of the corporate group problem, the EU regulation began to unravel almost as soon as it went into effect. In May 2000, Daisytek, Inc., a U.S.-based company with about $400 million in assets, filed for bankruptcy reorganization in Dallas, Texas. Later, Daisytek's 14 European subsidiaries filed for bankruptcy administration in England.[48] One of the 14, Daisytek-ISA Limited, was a holding company that owned the other 13. Three of the other 13 were German companies, and one was French. That is, the three German companies operated only in Germany, and the French company operated only in France. The English court—the High Court of Justice in Leeds—nevertheless held that England was the center of main interests for each of the 14 corporations. The court gave as its explanation that various aspects of the businesses of the German and French companies were controlled from England.

German commentators reacted to the English court's decision in Daisytek "with surprise and—to say the least—with anger."[49] In France, the commercial court set up a challenge to English jurisdiction by authorizing a competing main proceeding for the French subsidiary. A French appellate court reversed the commercial court's ruling, correctly saying that it violated the EU regulation.[50] The regulation requires that when an EU member state opens a main proceeding—here the proceeding in England—the courts of other countries must recognize it.[51] The decision of the court that initially gets the case is final.[52]

Notice that if creditors of the German and French subsidiaries of Daisytek had filed against those subsidiaries in Germany and France before Daisytek filed their cases in England, the German and French courts could have determined their countries to be the home countries. The English court would have been bound by those findings. In the context of international court competition, the effect of the EU regulation is the opposite of its intent. The effect is to give the case to the country that grabs first.

The ruling in Daisytek was not an isolated instance. An English commentator described how an English court took jurisdiction over the case of Enron's Spanish subsidiary.

> Enron Directo was a Spanish company with Spanish operations and Spanish employees, and most of its day-to-day operations were performed in Spain. However, some of its strategic decisions were taken in London at Enron's European headquarters and certain board meetings were held in London. Accordingly, the argument was that the debtor's head office functions were in London. At the unopposed hearing, the UK court accepted that as being the test for [centre of main interests] and opened UK administration proceedings.[53]

In another case, an Italian court ruled that Italy was the center of main interests of a Dutch subsidiary of an Italian firm, Cirio Del Monte. The objective was apparently to protect the Dutch subsidiary against a Dutch creditor in circumstances where a Dutch court would not have done so.[54] In the Parmalat bankruptcy, an Italian court is battling with an Irish court over the bankruptcy of Eurofoods, the Irish subsidiary of Parmalat. Because the two courts have entered conflicting orders, the Irish Supreme Court has passed the case along to the European Court of Justice in Luxembourg.

The competition for cases generated by Europe's attempt at universalism makes the Luxembourg court's task a virtually impossible one. If that court rules—as it probably must—that the decision of the first court to hear the case is binding on later courts, it will be a green light for court competition. As one commentator summed up the European experience with universalism:

> We are now nearly 18 months into the Regulation and decisions have been made which were not contemplated on 31 May 2002. The long arm of the Regulation has reached further than was

anticipated. There can be no doubt that, as far as the Member states are concerned, they have handed control over the affairs of companies with their registered office in their jurisdiction to whichever Member State the proceedings are opened in.[55]

The problems of the rest of the world under the UNCITRAL model law will be worse. Both the EU regulation and the UNCITRAL model law adopt the universalist "centre of main interests" test. But the European Union has a viable government structure that can order and coordinate a retreat from its universalist regulation. The rest of the world does not.

It is worth noting that the corporate group problem is easily solved in a cooperative territorial system. A cooperative territorial system is one in which each country's courts administer the assets located in the country and authorize a representative to cooperate with representatives appointed in foreign proceedings.[56] In a cooperative territorial system, once cases were filed and representatives appointed in each of the countries involved, the representatives could meet to determine whether cooperation could increase the total recovery of the group. In most cases, the answer would be no, because the group was compartmentalized by country prior to bankruptcy. If the answer were yes, the negotiators should be able to reach agreement for the simple reason that they could share the increase in recovery among them. The circumstances of KPNQwest illustrate how cooperative territoriality would work.

The KPNQwest group owned cables in Europe and across the Atlantic Ocean, the main ones being in the form of rings. For example, one ring ran through Germany, France, Belgium and The Netherlands, connecting major cities in these countries. However, the part of the ring that was situated in Germany was owned by a German subsidiary, the part of the ring situated in France by a French subsidiary, and so forth. When the Dutch parent company, KPNQwest N.V., went into bankruptcy many of the subsidiaries had to enter insolvency proceedings as well. Interestingly, the KPNQwest N.V. bankruptcy was one of the first to fall under the scope of the Regulation since it was adjudicated on 31 May 2002, the date on which the Regulation entered into force. However, the trustees of the Dutch bankruptcy did not hold any powers with respect to bankrupt subsidiaries in other member states, and it proved to be very difficult to coordinate the sale of the rings. As it turned out, the KPNQwest group disintegrated and it is likely that the proceeds of the sale of the assets were much lower than they would have been if the enterprise had been sold as a whole.[57]

Universalism failed KPNQwest. In a cooperative territoriality regime, insolvency proceedings would have been initiated and a representative appointed in each of the involved countries. Those representatives would have had the power—subject to whatever creditor and court approvals were required under the laws of each country—to join in a common sale effort. Each would realize that he or she faced a choice: join in the common sale effort within the time constraints of the market and share in the proceeds of the common sale or conduct a separate sale of the assets located in the country. Each representative would be free to take the course it believed would produce the greatest distribution for those claiming in the country's insolvency case. By contrast, in a universalist system, creditors must concern themselves not only with the desirability of the common sale but also with which court will conduct it. It might be in a group of creditors' interests to oppose an advantageous sale by the court of a country that would accord the particular group of creditors a low priority. In a cooperative territorial regime, venue would never be an issue. Venue with respect to any particular asset would be in the courts of the country that had power over the asset by sovereignty.

Changing Home Countries

The indeterminacy of the home country standard and the intractability of the corporate group problem are alone enough to doom universalism. But universalism has a much bigger problem with which to grapple. However universalists define a multinational's home country, the multinational can change it.

To illustrate how easily multinationals can change their locations, Fruit of the Loom—which filed for bankruptcy in 1999—had most of its operations in the United States as late as 1995. That year it closed six U.S. plants and laid off more than 3,000 workers.[58] The company moved that production to its own plants in the Carribean and Central America.[59] Then, shortly before filing bankruptcy, Fruit of the Loom incorporated a new holding company in the Cayman Islands and transferred the stock of itself and its foreign subsidiaries to that holding company.[60] These changes converted Fruit of the Loom from a clearly American company to a truly multinational one.

Singer, N.V., a firm that began as the U.S. manufacturer of the Singer sewing machine in 1851 and quickly became a U.S.-based multinational, provides another example. When Hong Kong–based Akai bought Singer in 1989, the new owner changed Singer's place of incorporation to the Netherlands Antilles and its headquarters to Hong Kong. By the time Singer filed for bankruptcy in 1999, three-quarters of its employees were in Asia, Europe, Africa, or the Middle East. By whatever standard one applied, Singer was no longer an American firm.

Singer wanted, however, to reorganize in the United States. Shortly before filing in the New York bankruptcy court, Singer hired a CEO in New York and declared New York its headquarters. But even after the New York court assumed jurisdiction over Singer's worldwide operations, Singer remained concerned whether the courts of other nations would recognize the U.S. proceeding and enforce the plan against "numerous international creditors who might assert that they were not subject to U.S. jurisdiction."[61] The problem was that Singer's parent company, Singer, N.V., was still a Netherlands Antilles company.

To solve the problem, Singer's advisers came up with this strategy.

Singer filed a motion seeking authority to create a new wholly-owned U.S. subsidiary of Singer NV, Singer USA LLC (Singer USA). After Singer USA was formed, the proposal was to transfer all of Singer NV's assets (Singer NV's equity interests in its subsidiaries) to Singer USA and to cause Singer USA to guarantee all of Singer NV's liabilities. Thereafter, Singer NV's sole asset would consist of its equity interest in Singer USA, resulting in a simplified corporate structure as follows:

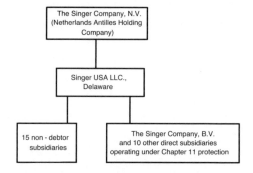

The next step would be for Singer USA to file its own chapter 11 petition, thus bringing Singer USA within the protection of the U.S. bankruptcy court. The final step was to propose a chapter 11 plan of reorganization for Singer USA that eliminated Singer NV's equity interest and issued 100% of the new equity in Singer USA to Singer USA's creditors, i.e., the holders of the obligations of Singer NV that Singer USA had guaranteed.[62]

Stripped of the legalisms, Singer's strategy was to replace the Netherlands Antilles corporation with a newly minted U.S. one and bankrupt the new corporation immediately. The New York bankruptcy court confirmed Singer's plan, and it appears that no one challenged it elsewhere.

Like an immigrant applying for U.S. citizenship, Singer became an American company. Singer's purpose was to file bankruptcy in the United States. Under both the EU regulation and the model law, changing home countries in anticipation of bankruptcy is fair game. The court determines the home country of a multinational company based on the company's characteristics at the time of bankruptcy.[63] Neither law contains any provision prohibiting changes in those characteristics on the eve of bankruptcy or authorizing the court to ignore such changes. Some commentators take the position that the court should "ignore the steps taken purely to avoid the appropriate jurisdiction."[64] But so subjective a limit would play into the hands of competing judges, who could determine the subjective issue of intent in their own personal interests.

Numerous examples in this book have already shown the ease with which multinational companies can change their places of incorporation and the locations of their headquarters. The locations of assets and operations are more difficult to change. But even the multinational's center of assets and operations can be changed—without moving any assets or operations.

Corporate groups can accomplish that through acquisitions and divestitures. For example, a firm with principal assets in England that wished to reorganize in the United States could arrange for its acquisition by a previously unrelated firm already headed for U.S. bankruptcy. In most cases, the English firm would be insolvent and its stock would have only a nominal value, making the "acquisition" mostly a paper transaction. Alternatively, a U.S. parent that would be pulled into the English bankruptcy by its larger English subsidiary could spin off the subsidiary by distributing its stock to the parent's stockholders. If the English subsidiary were insolvent, the transaction would have no economic substance; the stock would be canceled in the bankruptcy case anyway. But distributing that worthless stock before bankruptcy would split the group, leaving the parent with a clear entitlement to file in the United States.

Groups could change their centers by strategically dissolving subsidiaries. For example, the center of Chrysler De Mexico's main interests would be in Mexico. But if that corporation were dissolved before bankruptcy, Chrysler De Mexico's assets would be owned by the much larger, U.S.-based Daimler Chrysler. Despite Daimler Chrysler's acquisition of the Mexican assets, the bulk of Daimler Chrysler's assets and operations would still be in the United States. If Daimler Chrysler then filed bankruptcy in the United States the assets formerly owned by Chrysler De Mexico would be administered in that bankruptcy—in the United States, according to U.S. law.

The case of Derby Cycle Corporation, first discussed in chapter 6, provides an example of how a firm can forum shop by changing the location of the bulk of its assets. Derby Cycle was the manufacturer of Raleigh and Diamondback bikes. At the time its managers arrived at the offices of the firm's U.S. bankruptcy lawyers,

Derby was operated from England, and the group's principal assets were in the Netherlands.[65] The lawyers conceived an integrated plan by which Derby first sold the Netherlands assets for about $120 million and distributed the proceeds to creditors. The managers then put the U.S.-incorporated parent company—whose remaining assets were concentrated in the United States—into bankruptcy in Delaware.[66] The managers availed themselves of Delaware's lax sale procedures to sell the remainder of the company to themselves for $40 million—leaving more than $100 million in debt unpaid.[67] By selling the Netherlands assets first, Derby made itself an American company.

In attempting to deal with the corporate group problem, the ALI principles recommend that the courts immediately begin allowing subsidiaries from anywhere in the world "to file for insolvency in the parent's home country, even if they would not ordinarily be allowed to do so, so they can be reorganized on a group basis."[68] The principles leave no doubt that they intend the court to apply the law of its own country to the reorganization or liquidation of those subsidiaries.

If the courts take this principle seriously, it will open the floodgates to international forum shopping. Parent corporations are often "holding companies" that have no assets other than the stock of their subsidiaries. No matter what attributes determine the center of a holding company's main interests, the holding company can easily change them. Hiring a single employee, for example, fixes the location of the holding company's workforce. Moving the corporate records to the Bahamas and placing them under the control of that single employee there makes the Bahamas the holding company's principal place of business. Under the ALI principles, such a simple ruse would entitle the entire group to file in the Bahamas.

Global and Out of Control?

In combination, the inherent ambiguity of the "centre of its main interests" test, the uncertainty over whether the relevant unit is the corporation or the group, and the ability of both corporations and corporate groups to quickly and easily relocate make forum shopping easy in a universalist system. Because the chosen court can apply its own law to people and events throughout the world and its decisions will be entitled to worldwide recognition, the benefits international shoppers can gain will far exceed the benefits that drive rampant shopping in the United States. The universalist meltdown has already begun in the European Union.

Provided one's own money is not at stake and one is not put off by the corruption of the world's bankruptcy judges, the dynamic of adjustment will be interesting to observe. In the initial stage, participants in the system—governments, courts, professionals, executives, creditors, and other stakeholders—will develop strategies for seeking individual advantage. Debtors will forum shop, creditors will seek to ally with them, and courts will compete for cases. Countries will change their laws to advantage their courts in the competition. Eventually, the minus-sum nature of the game will become apparent, and there will be calls for reform.

Theorists will then repeat the debates that are now occurring with respect to forum shopping and court competition in the United States. Three resolutions seem possible. First, the system may backtrack by adopting an international bankruptcy convention grounded in cooperative territoriality. That seems unlikely. For that to occur, a lot of important people would have to confess error and recommend reversal of a course they themselves set.

Second, the universalists may seize on the chaos they themselves caused as an excuse for forcing the countries of the world to "harmonize" their laws. *Harmonization* is a euphemism for forcing commercially less important countries to adopt the remedies and priorities of the commercially more important countries. (Some Machiavellians may have endorsed universalism in the first place hoping it would lead to this forced harmonization.) That harmonization would be painful for people in countries that would be forced to change the basic rules of their economic cultures—for example, elevating secured banks to priority over employees. Such harmonization would greatly reduce the incentives for forum shopping. But it would hardly eliminate the international competition for cases. Harmonization has already taken place among the states of the United States, but domestic forum shopping and court competition still flourish here.

Third, the advocates of court competition may prevail, leaving multinational companies free to chose the courts in which they will reorganize or liquidate and the law that will govern the rights of their creditors and other stakeholders. As a condition of lending, large creditors and stakeholders will demand a say in their borrowers' choices of bankruptcy courts. Responding to market forces, the competing countries and their courts will adopt rules and practices that heap advantages on the case placers. The losers will be the corporate outsiders who have no means of controlling their debtor's choice of courts: tort victims, employees, suppliers, customers, other stakeholders with small interests, and—as with every strategy game—the less sophisticated players.

9

Ideology

Competition between different parts of government is a good
thing, because it helps keep government under scrutiny.

—Bankruptcy lawyer Stephen H. Case,
commenting on the bankruptcy court competition (2004)

Maybe our national faith in free markets is so strong that
people just don't want to talk about a case in
which markets went spectacularly bad.

—Paul Krugman, referring to the California energy crisis (2002)

In recent decades, Americans have become strong believers in
markets. Professor Lynn Stout recently wrote:

> [E]fficient markets theory had, by the 1970s, captured the imagi-
> nation of a generation of economists and finance theorists. . . .
> Soon after, it captured the imaginations of legal scholars and
> lawmakers as well. By the mid-1980s, "market efficiency" had
> become a mantra not only of finance economists, but also of
> securities scholars, regulators and even judges and practicing
> lawyers.[1]

In part, this came about as a result of the intrinsic appeal of economic thinking. To some degree, it results from a heavier emphasis
on economics in high school, college, and professional school education. Corporate leaders have fueled the fire by spending their
own and their corporations' money to persuade the public of the
main message of classical economics—free markets from regulation and they automatically will serve the public interest. For
example, in just over two decades, the Olin Foundation spent $50

234234 *Courting Failure*

million to $60 million promoting classical economics in a dozen or
so elite law schools.

This newfound confidence in markets strongly colored reaction
to the bankruptcy court competition. Over the past four years, I
have described the competition to literally hundreds of judges,
lawyers, professors, and journalists. Those who have come to the
competition's defense—like Steve Case in the quote at the beginning of this chapter—have done so almost exclusively in economic
terms.

The defenders regard the accumulation of cases in Delaware and
New York and the national changes in court practices discussed in
this book as the products of free market competition. The competition, as they see it, is a market for judges, analogous to the markets for the services of other professionals such as lawyers or
investment bankers. The best lawyers, they say, are the lawyers
who attract the most sophisticated clients. The Delaware and New
York bankruptcy judges attract the most sophisticated bankrupts,
and so it follows that they must be the best judges.

For such defenders of competition, the high failure rates in
Delaware and New York are no more than an interesting anomaly.
The defenders offer a variety of possible explanations, but all have
one thing in common: they begin with the assumption that the
Delaware and New York courts are efficient. You can't argue with
the market.

The Corporate Charter Competition

Attitudes toward the bankruptcy court competition were shaped in
large part by already existing attitudes toward an earlier and in
some ways analogous competition—the corporate charter competition. The early stages of the charter competition were described in
the prologue. They hardly suggest economic efficiency. The governments that won—New Jersey and then Delaware—did so by
selling the right to do things in other states that violated the laws
and policies of those other states. Muckraking journalist Lincoln
Steffens, Supreme Court Justice Louis Brandeis,[2] and President

Woodrow Wilson were three of the competition's staunchest opponents. New Jersey voters were so shamed by New Jersey's role in the competition that the state voluntarily withdrew from the competition while it was in the lead.

In response to New Jersey, the federal government passed its own antitrust and fair trade laws.[3] That eliminated the specific strategies by which New Jersey had won. No state could ever use them again. The federal government did not, however, take any action to prevent the charter competition from continuing with respect to other, subtler issues.

In 1913, Delaware picked up the lead that New Jersey had dropped. For two reasons, that lead never changed hands again. The first is that once Delaware was solidly in front, network effects kicked in. Lawyers who represented large public companies made the effort and investment necessary to learn Delaware corporate law and procedures. As problems arose under Delaware law, those problems were resolved by Delaware courts. A large body of precedent developed providing answers to questions that could not be answered under the laws of other states. Delaware corporate law became a staple of study in the elite law schools that churned out Wall Street lawyers. Law firms, document retrieval companies, and other companies providing services related to incorporation set up shop in Delaware. The Delaware court system grew.

These network effects did not result from any virtue unique to Delaware. Had some other state taken a substantial lead in the competition, these things would have happened in that state. But once these things happened in Delaware, they provided Delaware with a decisive advantage in the competition. For another state to best Delaware in the competition, that state not only had to have corporate law more attractive than Delaware's law, but that law had to be so much more attractive that it compensated for the loss of the network effects.

By about 1920, offering so attractive a law had become impossible. No state could best Delaware by dropping public protections from the state's corporation law because Delaware's corporation law no longer contained public protections. Nor was it likely that any state could best Delaware by offering managers and shareholders freedom they didn't already have. Delaware corporate law, like the corporate law of most other states, imposed virtually no restrictions on corporations. The relationship between managers and shareholders could be whatever the corporation specified in its charter request. Even if some other state had matched Delaware law on every issue and came up with an innovation sufficient to outweigh the network benefits of Delaware, that other state would not have won the competition. Delaware would simply have copied the innovation and offered it in addition to the network effects.

To avoid losing even more incorporations to Delaware, the other states copied the management-friendly provisions of Delaware law. All 50 states ended up with pretty much the same corporation law. Realizing they would not get the benefit of any innovations they might make, the other states didn't try to innovate. Since New Jersey abandoned the competition a century ago, the only state to make more than a halfhearted attempt to compete with Delaware was Nevada. Nevada didn't try to innovate; it simply adopted Delaware corporate law wholesale—including all of its case precedent—and tried to attract incorporations by charging lower fees. Nevada's success was modest.

Thus, the corporate laws of the states were not forged in a century-long contest to produce the best. They were written by James B. Dill and put in place almost a century ago. As two prominent academics recently put it: "[T]he very notion that states compete for incorporations is a myth. Other than Delaware, no state is engaged in significant efforts to attract incorporations of public companies."[4]

The Corporate Charter Debate

The fact that no real competition was going on did not deter the academics from debating the competition's economic efficiency. In 1974, the *Yale Law Journal* published an article by Professor William L. Cary. In it, Cary argued that the corporate charter competition had been a "race for the bottom"[5] in which the states had competed to make laws allowing corporate managers to take advantage of shareholders.

Cary's reliance on the exploitation of shareholders—rather than on the exploitation of the public that actually drove the early competition—provided the perfect foil for competition advocates arguing economic efficiency. In 1977, Professor Ralph Winter responded that the race had not been to the bottom but to the top.[6] Winter argued that the kind of exploitation Cary charged was theoretically impossible. Shareholders could easily discover a corporation's state of incorporation before investing. If the managers of Delaware corporations had been exploiting the shareholders of Delaware corporations, those shareholders would have known about it in advance and adjusted accordingly the amounts they were willing to pay for their shares.

Winter's reasoning was hardly flawless. It assumed that shareholders were perfectly informed and didn't make mistakes. Recognize the obvious falsity of those assumptions and it becomes clear that managers can profit from the exploitation of shareholders when the managers give more attention to the manager-shareholder relationship than the shareholders do. If the profits managers could extract from shareholders before shareholders reacted were large enough, those profits alone might explain the attraction of Delaware.

How large those profits are depends on how long wrong ideas can survive in the marketplace. Suppose, for example, that financial analysts reach the erroneous conclusion that shareholders don't really need or benefit from laws protecting them from managers. They further erroneously conclude that effective provisions for shareholder voting—which Delaware does not have—are unnecessary because managers know they must remain loyal to shareholders to maintain their own personal value in the marketplace. Thus, shareholders don't need an expensive process for electing managers. Nor, the financial analysts wrongly conclude, do shareholders benefit from the right to sue managers because managers don't act against the interests of shareholders with sufficient frequency to warrant the expense of the many bogus lawsuits individual shareholders will bring if corporate law allows them. Suppose further that, based on these beliefs, the financial analysts conclude that, because Delaware law makes elections impossible for insurgents to win and bans shareholders from suing managers, Delaware law is more efficient. The financial analysts recommend investment in Delaware corporations.

On the analysts' recommendations, investors would be willing to pay more for Delaware corporations until someone discovered the error. Who would discover it and how? No investor or analyst would have a sufficiently wide view to be able to weigh the advantages of corporate democracy or shareholder litigation against their costs.

The kinds of empirical studies of Delaware incorporation conducted to date would not discover such an error. Those studies all have assumed that the market values stocks correctly. That is, the beliefs of market participants, as reflected in stock prices, are an accurate measure of economic performance.

The studies essentially are of two kinds. The first, known as "event studies," determined whether the stock price of corporations went up or down in reaction to the corporations' announcements that they were changing their places of incorporation to Delaware.[7] The event studies did not measure the companies' performances. (Everyone seems to acknowledge that firms incorporated in Delaware do not perform better than firms incorporated elsewhere.)[8] Instead, the researchers used stock price as a surrogate for performance. In so doing, they implicitly assumed that the market knew the true value of Delaware incorporation. If stock traders erroneously believed companies incorporated in Delaware would perform better, an event study would confirm that erroneous belief.

The other kind of study—which employs a concept known as "Tobin's Q"—examines how much corporate shares trade for in relation to the book value behind them. This kind of study also equates the value of a company to the amount people are willing to pay for its stock and thus implicitly assumes that markets don't make mistakes about value.[9]

Good economists recognize that markets do make mistakes and that those mistakes can be huge. The stock market is generally lauded as the most efficient of markets and therefore as the market least prone to such errors. But few leading economists today would claim that markets accurately value stocks. As Professor Lynn Stout notes:

> The seeds of doubt were first sown widely on October 19, 1987, when the Dow Jones Index of industrial stocks mysteriously lost twenty three percent of its value in a single trading session. More recently we have seen the appearance and subsequent bursting of a remarkable price bubble in technology stocks that rivals the famous Dutch Tulip Bulb Craze of 1637. To some extent, the entire stock market seemed to have been caught in the turbulence: in the Spring of 2000, the Standard & Poors 500 Index of 500 leading companies topped 1,500. By October 2002, the S&P Index was hovering near 775, a nearly fifty percent decline in value.[10]

Stout's point was that the market's evaluation of the entire stock of U.S. corporations had changed by 23 percent in one instance and 48 percent in another, with no apparent intervening reason. The market may have been right in its evaluation before the change or right in its evaluation afterward, but it couldn't have been right both times.

Leave the realm of stock markets and the record of market competition is considerably worse. Consider, for example, the deregulation of the wholesale market for electrical power that led to the California energy crisis or the deregulation of savings and loan associations that led to the savings and loan scandal of the 1980s.

Even if the empirical studies had shown a clear market preference for companies incorporated in Delaware—which the studies did not[11]—that preference would have remained suspect. Markets are great at reflecting the beliefs of market participants but not very good at assessing complex systems like the corporation laws of a state.

The increasing number of academics, policymakers, judges, lawyers, students, and others who came to believe in market efficiency since the 1970s did not view the evidence so critically. Yale law professor Roberta Romano declared the charter competition to have been "the genius of American corporate law,"[12] and the new believers in economic efficiency overwhelmingly endorsed that view. In a growing segment of American leadership, the idea that the charter competition had been a "race to the top" became the conventional wisdom. That segment proposed to conduct similar races to determine the best legal regimes for international security regulation,[13] environmental regulation,[14] antitrust regulation,[15] computer information transactions regulation,[16] commercial dispute resolution,[17] and other regulatory problems.

The Bankruptcy Court Competition Debate

The bankruptcy court competition that erupted in the 1990s bore a striking resemblance to the corporate charter competition. Most obviously, Delaware was the leader in both. Both competitions involved large public companies choosing legal regimes that would then judge the companies' conduct. In both competitions, managers or their representatives effectively made the companies' choices.

Even some of the dynamics of the competition were similar. New Jersey launched its charter competition effort with a crude appeal to corporate interests, the public be damned. In the Continental Airlines case, Delaware launched its bankruptcy competitive effort with a crude appeal to corporate interests, creditors be damned. Both strategies succeeded in initially distinguishing the strategist from the pack and propelling it to the lead in its respective competition. Neither initial strategy remained viable for long. A fierce political backlash forced New Jersey to abandon its initial pro-corporate strategy. Delaware began moderating its pro-debtor strategy almost as soon as it obtained a pro-debtor reputation. As the competitions progressed, the legal differences between Delaware and its rivals shrank to the almost imperceptible, but the network effects enabled Delaware not only to hang on but to prosper.

When Delaware emerged as the leader in the bankruptcy court

competition, bankruptcy academics were quick to make the analogy to the charter competition.[18] But despite overall similarities, the two competitions were different in one crucial respect.

In the competition for corporate charters, states sought to appeal to corporations relatively early in their life cycles. At those stages, the managers who chose the state of incorporation had substantial reason to concern themselves with the interests and preferences of shareholders. If the business being incorporated was a new start-up, the shareholders might not yet have invested. If the shareholders did not like the state of incorporation selected, they might not invest at all. If the business was already incorporated in another state and the managers wished to change the state of incorporation to Delaware, the existing corporate charter probably required an affirmative vote of the shareholders to go forward.[19] Shareholders would be inclined to vote in accord with the managers' recommendations, but even that might change if the chosen state's laws obviously favored managers over shareholders. Thus managers have substantial reason to consider the interests of shareholders in selecting a state of incorporation.

In the bankruptcy competition, the courts seek to appeal to corporations that are insolvent and considering reorganization or liquidation. The managements of most of these companies have no reason to concern themselves with the interests or preferences of shareholders in selecting a court. The shares are underwater in most cases, and the court will cancel the shares as part of the bankruptcy case. Until that occurs, the chosen court will protect the managers from shareholder efforts to meet and vote the managers out of office.

Nor would the managers have much reason to concern themselves with the interests or preferences of creditors. Creditors don't elect managers and thus can't oust managers. Creditors have legal remedies against their debtors, but most of those remedies are suspended during bankruptcy. If the company reorganizes, creditors are likely to be the shareholders of the emerging company. In that capacity they might later be able to punish managers for the managers' choice of a bankruptcy court. Most managers facing bankruptcy, however, are more concerned with the short run. They seek a court that will not investigate them too carefully, will pay them bonuses, and will allow them to negotiate a graceful exit—or a court that will let them sell the company to someone who will employ the managers afterward.

Some creditors do have the power to participate in the corporation's venue decision. A majority of large public companies need additional financing during the bankruptcy case. That money comes from debtor-in-possession (DIP) lenders (who might or might not already be creditors of the debtor) or suppliers. To attract cases, a bankruptcy court has to protect those new lenders along with the managers and professionals. But the court does not have to protect ordinary creditors along with them. Even if the ordinary creditors vote against the company's reorganization plan, the court can impose it on them through cramdown.

Theoretically, one could still argue that prepetition creditors have considerable power, even on the eve of bankruptcy, and that one way or another, they could use that power to prevent their debtors from selecting courts inimical to their interests. If so, the prepetition creditors might be able to veto bankruptcy courts that pandered to managers just as Professor Ralph Winter asserted that shareholders were able to veto incorporation states that pandered to managers. I waited to see if any of the bankruptcy academics would make that argument in Delaware's defense.

Professors Rasmussen and Thomas made a very limited version of that argument, applicable only to prepacks.

> We claim that prepackaged bankruptcies do, in fact, promote efficiency. . . . Managers are unlikely to file prepackaged bankruptcies in Delaware in an attempt to enrich themselves at the expense of creditors. A majority of creditors must consent for a prepackaged bankruptcy to succeed. Creditors, as a group, are unlikely to agree to being shortchanged.[20]

But they remained "agnostic" with respect to the large majority of cases, which are not prepackaged.[21] "In the situation of a prepackaged bankruptcy," Rasmussen and Thomas explained, "[the managers] have to get the creditors to agree with them. This is not the case in the traditional Chapter 11 bankruptcy."[22]

Professor Marcus Cole wrongfully attributed to me the view that the creditors were the ones pushing for Delaware venue.[23] He then proceeded, on the basis of interviews with 50 bankruptcy lawyers, to refute it. (He excepted secured creditors from his conclusion.)[24] Thus Cole was acknowledging that unsecured creditors had no effective control over their debtors' choices of bankruptcy courts.

Professor David Skeel's concession was most directly to the point: "When a troubled firm files for bankruptcy in Delaware, on the other hand—and, as a Delaware enthusiast, I say this at the risk of making an admission against interest—the firm's managers (and their lawyers) may simply be looking out for their own interests."[25] Nobody was even claiming that court competition took the interests of ordinary creditors into account.

If court competition did not take the interests of creditors and other corporate constituencies into account, there was no longer any reason to believe that the courts were engaged in a race to the top. The courts' incentives were to serve managers and those managers' lawyers and contract allies. When any of those interests come into conflict with the interests of prepetition unsecured creditors, employees, taxing authorities, regulatory authorities, pensioners, and other corporate constituencies, competition forces the courts to squeeze the latter groups. The bankruptcy court competition is not a market but a market failure.

But Won't the Market Recover?

Some market advocates believe markets will recover from any obstacles placed in their way. If creditors are ignored in the choice of bankruptcy venue and exploited in the aftermath, creditors won't just stand for the loss. They will react. That reaction might come in the form of higher interest rates on unsecured lending or loan contracts that control any later choice of a bankruptcy venue.

Such adjustments are certainly possible. But they will be a long time coming. Even when they arrive, they will be incomplete. Before the adjusting can begin, creditors must realize that some part of the loss they are suffering results from the pro-case-placer biases of the leading bankruptcy courts. Few have that realization today. However the creditors choose to react, they will encounter resistance and delay. For example, if wizened lenders were to raise interest rates for potential bankrupts, they would initially lose business to other credit extenders who had not yet realized the increased risk associated with court competition. Eventually, the market enthusiasts tell us, those others would be bankrupted by their lack of foresight. But by then, the foresighted creditors may be bankrupted as well. And while these adjustments are occurring, the conditions they address may be changing as well. Market equilibrium is a moving target. Before the market can arrive at its destination, the reason for going there may disappear.

Effective markets—from the New York Stock Exchange to eBay—seldom arise spontaneously. People invent effective markets and impose rules on participants to give those markets structure. When the rules and structure are inadequate, clever participants devise strategies for taking advantage of other participants, and the market stumbles. Effective markets require constant tending—regulation—both to define the rules for interaction and to assure that the markets serve the interests of society as a whole. Courts are regulators. Their job is to enforce the rules by which markets operate. By putting the bankruptcy courts in competition for the business of large public companies, the bankruptcy venue rule makers accidently turned the referees into players.

10

Conclusions

In a multi-judge district, it's imperative the integrity of the
blind allocation system is maintained. [Delaware
assignment practices] are absolutely appalling to me.

—Florida bankruptcy judge Alexander Paskay (1997)

[The rules of venue should not] be changed on the ground
that it is somehow "fairer" to stake millions of jobs and
billions of dollars on the luck of the draw in filing a case . . . .
Bankruptcy is not a crap game.

—Delaware Bar Association Report (1996)

As of this writing, the bankruptcy court competition continues
to hang in the balance. The cases filed in 2003 and early 2004 were
distributed about one-quarter in Delaware, about one-quarter in
New York, and about half through the rest of the country. After its
big year in 2002, Chicago sank back into obscurity. Houston, with
two filings in 2003, was the only court other than Delaware and
New York to get more than one that year.

Congress will decide what happens next. As of this writing, legislation that would increase the number of Delaware bankruptcy
judges from two to six still teeters on the brink of enactment.
Enactment would create the huge infrastructure in Delaware necessary to make that state the permanent bankruptcy capital of the
United States.

The Delaware court's wait for its new judges has been uncomfortable. Delaware's claim to four additional judges retains validity
only as long as Delaware's caseload justifies them. In other words,
Delaware's two-judge court must continue to do the work of six

judges until Congress gets around to voting on the bill. So far, Delaware's two judges have accomplished that by working herculean hours and receiving assistance from other judges inside and outside Delaware. It is a delicate balancing act, and it is unclear how long the two judges can keep it up. They have already scaled back their effort by surrendering some of their smaller megacases to other districts.

The wait should be over soon. Despite huge increases in the total numbers of bankruptcy filings, Congress has not increased the total number of bankruptcy judges nationwide since 1992. The pressure for more judges nationally has been building, and it seems inevitable that a bill authorizing additional judges will pass in 2005, if not earlier. Unless Congress singles out Delaware in an effort to end the bankruptcy court competition, Congress will authorize Delaware's new bankruptcy judges along with the rest. With those judges, the Delaware bankruptcy court will have the capacity to process two to three times the number of cases it does today.

Two scenarios then seem plausible. In the first, Delaware's market share again climbs to near 90 percent. This time it remains there. In three or four years, the shift becomes irreversible. The skills and experience necessary to process big bankruptcy cases have grown in Delaware and disappeared from the rest of the United States. Many of the top professionals working in the bankruptcy field have moved to Delaware. Others have been replaced by ambitious young bankruptcy professionals already in Delaware. The bankruptcy courtroom construction begun in Delaware in 2003 has been completed and yet more courtroom construction begun. The bankruptcy court competition ends with Delaware's victory—just as the corporate charter competition did around 1920.

In the second plausible scenario, the New York bankruptcy court fights back. The New York court's location in lower Manhattan—convenient to the world's leading bankruptcy professionals and numerous corporate headquarters—provides a powerful advantage. Few leading bankruptcy professionals would prefer to live and work in Delaware, and so they make an effort to keep as many cases as possible in New York. (Living in New York while doing the cases in Delaware is a possibility, but contrary to the glib assertions sometimes made, it takes substantially longer for a New York professional to travel to Penn Station, take the Metroliner 125 miles to Delaware, and then walk eight blocks to the Wilmington courthouse than it does to travel to the New York court in lower Manhattan.)[1]

Despite the New York professionals' work site preference, the New York court would not win the competition. The New York professionals would keep the Delaware court alive as a check on the New York court. With the two courts in competition, the case placers could play them off against one another to increase the cases placers' power over both. In this scenario, the New York professionals would reward the New York court for "good" behavior by doling out cases to the court in much the same way that a biologist doles out kernels of corn when training a chicken to do a pirouette. Eventually, both courts might be dancing to the case placers' tune—pretty much without regard to bankruptcy law.

Will Delaware's New Judges Be with the Program?

In both of the preceding scenarios, I made the assumption that the new judges appointed to the Delaware bankruptcy court will compete on Delaware's behalf as competently and enthusiastically as those already sitting. The Delaware bankruptcy court is, however, a federal court. The United States Court of Appeals for the Third Circuit chooses the Delaware bankruptcy court's judges. The Third Circuit includes not only Delaware but also New Jersey, Pennsylvania, and the Virgin Islands. The Third Circuit judges have life tenure and thus have little reason to promote Delaware's effort to dominate big-case bankruptcy reorganization. Given the prominence of the Delaware bankruptcy court, the Third Circuit will have highly qualified applicants from which to select the Delaware court's judges. What is to prevent the Third Circuit from reasserting federal control over the Delaware bankruptcy court by selecting bankruptcy judges of high quality and integrity who are from outside Delaware and have no precommitment to Delaware's competitive effort?

I expect the Third Circuit to appoint such judges. But I don't think the effect will be a return of the Delaware court to federal control. After their appointment, the new judges will take up residence in Wilmington, become part of the Wilmington social and business community, and work at the downtown Wilmington courthouse. The court will assign large public company bankruptcies to the new judges; that is pretty much the only kind of work the court has. The new judges will then have to decide whether to join in Delaware's plot to become the bankruptcy capital of the world or to exert their independence as have the judges in Boston and some other places.

Joining in the competition is the only plausible choice. First, tremendous political and social pressure will be applied to compel the appointees to do so. As a Delaware corporate lawyer put it: "If these bankruptcy judges wanted to buck the system, they would find life in Delaware very unpleasant and lonely. It's just not reasonable to expect them to act differently than all of the other lawyers and judges here."[2] Second, the new judges will quickly realize that the quality of their jobs depends on Delaware's continuing competitive success. If the new judges don't do what is necessary to attract new cases, the cases may not come. If that happened, the new judges would not lose their jobs. The legislation guarantees them employment for 14-year terms.[3] But how Delaware fares in the competition will determine what those judges would do during those 14 years.

If Delaware succeeds, the new judges will be members of the most prestigious bankruptcy court in the world. They will rule over the multibillion-dollar reorganizations of companies whose names are household words. The new judges' exploits will be discussed in newspapers, in magazines, and on television. The new judges will determine the fees of the great New York law firms and investment banks, which will make them and their families members of the East Coast business and social establishment.

If Delaware fails in the competition, the initial effect will be that the new judges will have nothing to do. Eventually, the officials with the power to do so will begin temporarily reassigning them to other courts—perhaps to the courts that replaced Delaware as the winners of the competition. To their new courts, they will be as they were to the Delaware court: toxic judges and social outcasts. The judges who drove the cases out of Delaware. As visiting judges, they will get the least desirable case assignments in their new districts. They will serve out their terms as itinerants and probably will not be reappointed for the simple reason that they will not be needed.

In other words, the new judges' interests will be aligned with the interests of Delaware. For that reason, I am confident they would see Delaware's side of matters and join in Delaware's competitive effort.

The Future of Bankruptcy Court Competition

The initial round of court competition is only now coming to a close. In that round, the courts focused principally on procedural matters such as establishing omnibus hearings, assuring quick action on first-day motions, and paying professionals monthly. The courts interested in competing have already made these changes. The case placers no longer shop for these practices; they can find them in almost any big city court. Courts interested in improving their market shares now must offer something more.

The most attractive procedural change an ambitious court could offer would be to abandon the random draw as the primary method of assigning big reorganization cases to judges. The random draw is a powerful tradition in state and federal courts. It guards against corruption by making it impossible for case placers to choose particular judges. The random draw also promotes harmony among the judges of a panel by protecting each against discrimination in case assignments.

To the case placers, however, the random draw is anathema. The case placers want predictability. That is, they want to know what the judge will do with their case before they irrevocably surrender it by filing. The best way to know what the judge will do is to know who the judge will be. Recall from chapter 3 that when the Delaware bankruptcy court went from one judge to two, it began telling debtors which judge they would get before the debtors filed. Under a random draw, one toxic judge on a panel of five or ten is usually enough to drive cases away.

No law requires the bankruptcy courts to assign cases by random draw. The chief judge of a panel can assign them in whatever manner the judge chooses. Competitive pressures have already begun to erode the practice of random assignment. Both the Houston and Chicago bankruptcy courts have established separate draws for "complex cases." Judges of those two courts are excluded from the complex case draws only if they so request. In Houston, one has. But if the court competition continues, it is only a matter of time before courts seize the competitive advantage that would come from involuntarily eliminating their least attractive judges from the draws. When that occurs, it will signal that the bankruptcy court competition has entered its final, desperate stages. Not only will the case placers be in a position to play off courts against other courts, they will be in a position to play off judges of a court against other judges of the same court.

If Congress allows the bankruptcy court competition to continue, the substantive changes already visible in the competing courts' practices will accelerate. To the extent that the courts have placed any limits on incumbent managers' pay, authority, or job security, the courts will remove them. The same will be true of limits on pay, conflict-of-interest restrictions, or liability releases of bankruptcy lawyers and investment bankers. The courts will facilitate sales of companies that enable managers and their new investors to make a quick profit by externalizing costs to employees, the Pension Benefit Guarantee Corporation, local governments, and customers who already own the firms' products. The bankruptcy courts will actively seek new ways in which they can protect the case placers from investigations by criminal prosecutors, the Securities and Exchange Commission, other regulatory agencies, class action lawyers, and anyone else who threatens them.

The appeals courts will try to control the competing bankruptcy courts but will have limited success. Appeals courts decide only the few narrow issues of law presented to them. Because the bankruptcy courts deal in the rehabilitation of fragile businesses, time is often of the essence. Appeals become moot long before they can be heard. Moreover, the structure of the legal system assumes independent lower courts, unconstrained by competition and therefore free to follow the appellate courts' lead in good faith. The structure is designed to herd cattle, not cats. Bankruptcy courts that seek ways around the restrictions placed on them by appellate courts will find them.

The competitive pressures from U.S. bankruptcy court competition will not be confined to the United States. In the hopes of stemming their outflows of cases, other countries are already changing their bankruptcy laws to more closely resemble those of the United States. Consistent with the thesis I have presented in this book, a main emphasis of those efforts has been to increase the power of debtors' managers and professionals.

The existence of the international competition will impede political efforts to curb the domestic competition. Competition advocates argue that Delaware and New York courts must be allowed free rein in order to compete internationally. Attempts to restrict those courts, competition advocates will correctly note, will risk driving multinational bankruptcies to other countries, with attendant loss of jobs, industry, and tax base in the United States.

Recommendations for Change

A well-structured competition can do wonders, pushing people and institutions to higher levels of performance. Because it is poorly structured, the current bankruptcy court competition has had principally the opposite effect. In the bankruptcy court competition, the contest is not to do the best job of reorganizing the companies, to maximize economic benefit, or even to maximize economic benefit to the parties to the case. The contest is to maximize benefits to the case placers.

Two basic approaches exist for dealing with this structural problem. One is to restructure the competition through the adoption of rules that permit additional parties to participate in court selection. Courts would then have incentives to serve a wider constituency. The nature of that restructuring is, however, difficult to imagine. Debtors are often in urgent need of relief when they file bankruptcy cases. One cannot simply suspend the reorganization process for the week or two necessary to permit broad participation in court selection.

The more practical approach would be to limit the case placers' choice of courts. If the case placers had little choice in courts, the courts would have little incentive to compete for cases. The competition would die out.

Congress could limit the case placers' choice in either of two ways. First, Congress could adopt venue rules similar to those proposed by the National Bankruptcy Review Commission in 1997. The new rules should delete the debtor's place of incorporation from the list of proper venues and provide for the mandatory transfer of misfiled cases to the proper venue. With few exceptions, Delaware would no longer be a proper venue.

These new rules should also eliminate the venue hook—the ability of a parent company to file in the court where the bankruptcy of a subsidiary is pending. Members of a corporate group should be allowed to reorganize together only at the location of the parent company or the group.

These changes would effectively require a company to file its bankruptcy at the location of the company's headquarters or principal assets. Companies with headquarters and principal assets in different districts would still be able to choose between the two districts. Companies would also remain free to move their headquarters or principal assets to the district in which they chose to file. That means some shopping could continue, enabling companies to escape particularly bad courts. But such shoppers would not exist in sufficient numbers to corrupt courts that hoped to attract them.

One problem with requiring companies to file in their local bankruptcy courts is that few of those local courts would have much expertise in the reorganization of large public companies. To put the same point another way, the big-case expertise of the American bankruptcy courts would be spread among so many judges that few or none could develop substantial expertise.

As an alternative to the rules just discussed, Congress might establish specialized bankruptcy courts at three or four locations in the United States to handle only the largest cases. Each of the specialized courts would serve a specified territory. Companies over a specified size would all file their bankruptcy cases with a single judge. Working from information required to be filed with the petition, that judge would assign each case to the most appropriate of the four courts based on geographical considerations. The assignment would be made on the same day the company filed the case.

One might be tempted to urge such concentrations of expertise—or even the continuation of the current bankruptcy court competition—as an advantage for the United States in competing with foreign courts for multinational reorganization cases. But for the United States to participate in and encourage international bankruptcy competition would be unwise. Such a competition would be less likely to pass control of international bankruptcy to the United States than to pass it to the multinational companies and their case placers.

The potential for economic harm would be tremendous. In a system that permitted international competition for bankruptcy cases, the stakes for creditors and shareholders would be much greater than in domestic competition. The competitors—some of whom would be traditional havens—would be bolder than any state of the United States could be. Countries might compete for cases by offering financially embarrassed multinationals an entirely secret reorganization process. (Insuring, among other things, that no book like this one could ever be written again.) Most important, if the international competition went awry, no world government exists to correct it.

Current U.S. law requires the U.S. bankruptcy courts to administer assets located in the United States. The U.S. courts can surrender control of U.S. assets to foreign courts to assure an economical and expeditious administration—but only if the particular foreign proceeding is likely to produce results substantially in accord with U.S. law.[4] That standard requires that the U.S. bankruptcy courts evaluate requests for recognition or cooperation on a case-by-case basis. The standard is a sound one.

The broad commitment to automatic recognition of foreign proceedings sought by the universalists would lead to rampant international forum shopping, court competition, and perhaps economic chaos. Efforts toward international cooperation in the bankruptcy field should focus on cooperation in specific cases and the harmonization of laws and procedures among countries and should avoid broad, anticipatory grants of recognition to whatever decisions foreign courts might hand down. Universalist impulses should be reined in until the countries of the world have similar bankruptcy laws.

The Case against Court Competition

Bankruptcy insiders who know the full extent of the case against the bankruptcy court competition will probably breathe a sigh of relief when they read this book and realize the limited extent to which I was able to penetrate their world. Many of the facts crucial to the case against competition are protected by the lawyers' professional obligation to hold the secrets of their clients in confidence. One New York lawyer I interviewed told me essentially that. After providing me with some interesting leads for discovering facts he knew but could not tell me, he said: "I should be writing this book." Then quickly he added: "But of course, I could never do that."

From what I was able to discover, the case is essentially this. In 1974 and 1975 the Bankruptcy Rules Committee adopted venue rules that gave big bankrupt companies a wide choice of courts. In so doing, the committee inadvertently triggered the court competition. Forum shopping was a modest 20 percent to 40 percent during the first 15 years after the rules were adopted. Had we known what to look for in the statistics of that era, we could have seen what was coming. Bankruptcy Judge Burton R. Lifland was the principal destination for forum shopping. An eye-popping 57 percent of the companies he reorganized refiled.

The sleepy, one-judge Delaware court that had attracted not a single big case in the decade of the 1980s entered the competition in 1990. It did so by ripping the Continental Airlines case out of the jaws of the Houston bankruptcy court and flaying Continental's secured creditors and lessors. Impressed with what they saw, the case placers brought the Delaware court more. By the end of 1996, the Delaware court had 87 percent of the big-case bankruptcy market nationwide. The results of Delaware's reorganizations were disastrous. Depending on how one measured, the Delaware-reorganized companies were two to ten times as likely to fail as companies reorganized in other courts (i.e., courts other than Delaware and New York). The apparent causes of the high failure rates were the very same reasons the case placers chose Delaware: speed of the proceedings and the judges' willingness to approve whatever the debtor and its allies proposed.

Delaware's success sucked the most lucrative part of the bankruptcy business out of the rest of the country. Bankruptcy lawyers in other cities pressured their courts to do whatever was necessary to keep the cases at home. Many of the courts responded by copying the practices that had produced the Delaware disaster, thus producing mini-disasters of their own. The bankruptcy courts were in full-blown competition. If the case placers didn't see it on display, they could probably get it by asking for it.

Courts authorized larger fees for bankruptcy professionals and relaxed their conflict-of-interest standards. Instead of squeezing failed executives out, the courts allowed more of them to stay and even approved multimillion-dollar bonuses to "retain" them. Instead of reorganizing companies—which required full disclosure to creditors—managers took to selling their companies to investors who would hire the managers to continue running them and give the managers as much as 5 to 10 percent of the equity. The courts approved the deals even when the prices offered were apparently inadequate and only a single bidder showed up for the auction.

The bankruptcy court competition contributed to the corporate scandals of 2001 and 2002. When Houston-based Enron filed its bankruptcy in New York, the New York court retained the case over the objection of some of Enron's major creditors. The court allowed Kenneth Lay, the apparent perpetrator of one of the biggest frauds in history, to remain as CEO long enough to choose a successor who flatly refused to take action against him. Ignoring a motion for appointment of a trustee filed by major creditors, the New York court left unindicted members of Enron's corrupt management in control through the crucial stages of the case. Apparently pleased with what they saw, the fraudulent managements of three other big companies, Global Crossing, Adelphia, and Worldcom, filed those companies' cases in New York. The four cases together pushed New York past Delaware to become the nation's leading bankruptcy court The court rewarded the Enron professionals with more than a billion dollars in fees, probably five times the amount authorized in any prior bankruptcy case.

Even with the facts in front of them, many leading judges, lawyers, academics, and journalists could not grasp what was happening. They saw the court competition as a market for judicial services in which the customers were some of the most financially sophisticated firms and investment banks in the nation. That this competitive market was racing to the bottom rather than the top seemed to them unimaginable. They could not explain the data, but they were sure that somehow there must be an explanation consistent with their preconceptions. They applauded the competition and declared it a race to the top. Told that markets don't fail massively—something virtually no economist believes today—the experts could not see the massive market failure in front of them.

The Human Costs of the Bankruptcy Court Competition

This book tells the story of a competition gone bad. In it, I have written about the bankruptcy system; the strategies by which lawyers, judges, and others have sought to manipulate it; and the financial consequences. One thing missing is the stories of the millions of people whose lives have been adversely affected by the course of these reorganizations. In part, those stories are missing because of the vantage point from which I observe the competition. As an empirical researcher, I examine accounting and statistical data drawn from Securities and Exchange Commission filings and bankruptcy court files—records in which those stories seldom appear.

In part those stories are missing because they are not the kinds of stories that play most easily on human emotions—the dramatic and sudden destruction of lives and dreams by a single, easily identifiable cause. Such destructions did occur as a result of the bankruptcy court competition. Some retired Enron employees lost their entire pensions. Polaroid canceled the heath care coverage of its disabled employees. The owner of Riscomp lost his business because United Airlines breached its promise to put him on the critical vendor list. And many of the older employees who lost their jobs in filings and refilings will not be hired by someone else, even if the economy does produce more jobs elsewhere.

The vast majority of the victims of court competition, however, did not lose their entire lives and dreams. They lost only time, money, and a little bit of their faith in the future. They, like everyone else, had personal tragedies. The bungled bankruptcies of these companies contributed to them, but so did lots of other things, from the war in Iraq to the cancellation of their favorite TV shows. I made a judgment that such death from a thousand blows— including a hit from bankruptcy court corruption—was not a story that would break my readers' hearts. (It didn't make the newspapers either.)

The bankruptcy judges are more visible yet perhaps less sympathetic victims of the competition. Over the past 15 years, hundreds of them have had to decide whether to compete for the big cases. As I believe the Chicago bankruptcy judges learned the hard way, the competition is not for the squeamish. The case placers want good judges, but they want more than that. Like most litigants, they want to win without regard to whether they are right.

Bankruptcy judges are generally good people of high integrity.

Probably few enter the competition with the idea that they will trade their integrity for cases. More likely, they believe that they can find solutions sufficiently clever to serve justice and the market simultaneously. (The problem will not even exist for those who start from the belief that justice and the market are the same thing.) As the demands of justice and the market diverge, the judges at first seek to straddle them. But if they stick to their strategy long enough, they eventually succumb to corruption.

Refusing to participate in the competition is no solution. Judges who refuse to compete offend their local communities and bring their own competence into question. Many end up isolated, irrelevant, and toxic. At least two judges have lost their jobs for refusing to meet the demands of the competition. For the judges, the bankruptcy court competition is a no-win situation.

On Market Solutions

The bankruptcy court competition is slowly but surely transferring power over the bankruptcy courts from elected officials to case placers. This ongoing transfer is interfering with two crucial bankruptcy functions: restructuring debt and saving companies. Thirty-day prepacks and critical vendor orders have distorted the debt restructuring process. The retention and enrichment of failed executives, together with the courts' abdication of their responsibility for the feasibility of plans, have destroyed companies that could otherwise have been saved. As long as the competition continues unregulated, these effects are only likely to get worse.

The lesson is that markets do not automatically serve the public interest. Markets are structured by law, culture, and technology. The particular structure chosen can cause markets to serve the public interest, private interests in conflict with the public interest, or no one's interests at all. As a result, the social use of markets requires thoughtful design and continuous evaluation. This is particularly true of complex markets such as the market for bankruptcy courts. In the final analysis, some social problems are simply not amenable to market solutions.

Recognition of the limitations of markets is especially important at this point in history because the national faith in markets has never been stronger. Market advocates are proposing market solutions to every kind of problem from the selection of legal regimes to the protection of the environment and the distribution of medical services. Yet the limitations of markets are real. Our choice is to seek them out and acknowledge them or to stumble over those limitations in the darkness.

Notes

Prologue

1. Lincoln Steffens, *New Jersey: A Traitor State, Part II,* 25 McClure's Magazine, May 1905, at 43.

2. *Id.* at 41–47.

3. *See, e.g.,* Santa Clara County v. Southern Pacific R.R. Co., 118 U.S. 394, 394 (1886) ("The court does not wish to hear argument on the question whether the provision in the Fourteenth Amendment to the Constitution, which forbids a State to deny to any person within its jurisdiction the equal protection of the laws, applies to these Corporations. We are all of the opinion it does.").

4. Steffens, *supra* note 1, at 42.

5. *Id.* at 44–45.

6. William E. Kirk III, *A Case Study in Legislative Opportunism: How Delaware Used the Federal-State System to Attain Corporate Pre-Eminence,* 10 Journal of Corporation Law 233, 240 (1984) (explaining how the ability to purchase other corporations undermined the antitrust protections of the time).

7. Edward Q. Keasbey, *New Jersey and the Great Corporations,* 13 Harvard Law Review 198, 207 (1899).

8. Kirk, *supra* note 6, at 247 (Republican governor); Joel Seligman, *A Brief History of Delaware's General Corporation Law of 1899,* 1 Delaware Journal of Corporate Law 249 (1976) ("reform" governor); Harold W. Stoke, *Economic Influences upon the Corporation Laws of New Jersey,* 38 Journal of Political Economy 551, 572 (1930).

9. Seligman, *supra* note 8, at 265–66 (describing the provisions of the law).

10. Santa Clara County v. Southern Pac. R.R., *supra* note 3.

11. Lincoln Steffens, Autobiography of Lincoln Steffens 195 (1931).

12. Seligman, *supra* note 8, at 267.

13. *Id.* at 268.

14. Steffens, *supra* note 1.

15. Seligman, *supra* note 8, at 268.

16. *Id.* at 268.

17. Note, 33 AMERICAN LAW REVIEW 418–19 (1899).

18. *Id.* at 419.

19. *Id.*

20. Kirk, *supra* note 6, at 254.

21. Steffens, *supra* note 1.

22. Stoke, *supra* note 8, at 577.

23. *Id.*

24. Kirk, *supra* note 6, at 256.

25. Seligman, *supra* note 8, at 270.

26. Feb. 17, 1913, at 7.

27. *Id.*

28. *Broad Street Gossip,* WALL STREET JOURNAL, Mar. 18, 1913, at 4.

29. *New Jersey's Loss, New York's Gain,* NEW YORK TIMES, Jan. 17, 1915, at C2 ("For the first time in the history of New Jersey there was in 1914 a reduction in the number of corporations assessed for taxation.").

30. Seligman, *supra* note 8, at 270.

31. James F. Dorrance, *The Lawyer Who Earned Title of Being Father of the Trusts,* WALL STREET JOURNAL, Dec. 28, 1907, at 6.

32. James B. Dill, *National Incorporation Laws for Trusts,* 11 YALE LAW JOURNAL 273, 279 (1902) (emphasis in original).

33. Dorrance, *supra* note 31.

34. *Ex-Judge J. B. Dill Dies in Jersey Home,* NEW YORK TIMES, Dec. 3, 1910, at 11.

35. DEFAC Worksheet, May-04 DEFAC Meeting, at 1, *available at* http://www.state.de.us/finance/publications/DEFAC.shtml (total of Franchise Tax Less Refunds, Corporate Fees, Limited Partnerships and LLCs, and Uniform Commercial Code is 26.8 percent of Net Receipts).

Introduction

1. Court-approved professional fees in the Enron bankruptcy are expected to exceed $1 billion, substantially more than those in Worldcom and any other case. *Enron Fees to Exceed $1 Billion,* UNITED PRESS INTERNATIONAL, November 14, 2003.

2. For explanations of "large" and "public" see A Note on the Statistics in This Book, *supra.*

3. Final Report of Neal Batson, Court-Appointed Examiner, Appendix D, filed Nov. 24, 2003, Docket No. 14455, at 51–52, In Re Enron Corp., Case No. 01-16034, in the United States Bankruptcy Court for the Southern District of New York [hereafter "Final Report of Neal Batson, Appendix D"] ("The Board heard a presentation about the Rhythms transaction, and approved necessary components relating to the use of Enron stock, on June 28, 1999 at a specially called meeting. The board also ratified a determination by Enron's Office of the Chairman (meaning Lay and Skilling) under the company's Code

of Ethics that Fastow's role as general partner of LJM1 would 'not adversely affect the interests of the company'"); *id.* at 68–69 ("The Finance Committee and the full Board reviewed and approved the formation of Raptor I in May 2000. The Executive Committee approved the formation of Raptor II in June 2000, and the Finance Committee and the full Board approved the formation of Raptor IV in August 2000. . . . Lay and Skilling were present at each meeting and participated in explaining the transactions and they voted in favor of the transactions").

4. Final Report of Neal Batson, Appendix D, *supra* note 3, at 28 ("During the four year period 1998 through 2001, Lay had gross proceeds of over $209 million from Enron stock sales.").

5. Final Report of Neal Batson, Court-Appointed Examiner, Annex 1 to Appendix D, filed Nov. 24, 2003, Docket No. 14455, at 13, In re Enron Corp., Case No. 01-16034, in the United States Bankruptcy Court for the Southern District of New York [hereafter "Final Report of Neal Batson, Annex 1 to Appendix D"] ("Oregon law was clear at the time of these transactions: committees of the Board were not permitted to approve repurchases of company stock without specific authority from the Board. In this instance, that authority was apparently never granted to the Compensation Committee [that approved the repurchases].").

6. PETER C. FUSARO & ROSS M. MILLER, WHAT WENT WRONG AT ENRON 201 (2002) (reproducing memo in full).

7. Theo Francis & Ellen Schultz, *Enron Faces Suits by 401(k) Plan Participants,* WALL STREET JOURNAL, Nov. 23, 2001 ("Amid growing disclosures of financial problems in recent weeks, the company 'locked down' the retirement plan from October 17 to Nov. 19 . . . which prevented employees from selling Enron shares as the share price collapsed.").

8. *Id.*

9. New York Stock Exchange Composite Transactions, WALL STREET JOURNAL, Oct. 18, 2001 (Enron Corp. [ENE] Closing Price of $32.20 for October 17, 2001); New York Stock Exchange Composite Transactions, WALL STREET JOURNAL, Nov. 20, 2001 (Enron Corp. [ENE] Closing Price of $9.06 for November 19, 2001).

10. Final Report of Neal Batson, Annex 1 to Appendix D, *supra* note 5, at 7.

11. Complaint to Avoid Certain Pre-Petition Loan and Annuity Transactions as Fraudulent Transfers, Docket No. 1, dated Jan. 31, 2003, In re Enron Corp. (The Official Committee of Unsecured Creditors of Enron Corp. v. Kenneth L. Lay and Linda P. Lay), Case No. 01-16034, Adversary No. 03-02075, at 15, in the United States Bankruptcy Court for the Southern District of New York.

12. Indictment, filed Mar. 7, 2002, Docket No. 1 at para. 13, United States v. Arthur Andersen, Case No. 02-121, in the United States District Court for the Southern District of Texas.

13. Final Report of Neal Batson, Appendix D, *supra* note 38, at 3–4.

14. Order Pursuant to 11 U.S.C. §§ 1104(c) and 1106(b) Directing Appoint-

ment of Enron Corp. Examiner, dated April 8, 2002, Docket No. 2838, In re Enron Corp., Case No. 01-16034, in the United States Bankruptcy Court for the Southern District of New York (reflecting compromise that gave examiner some information privileges but left examiner an outsider in other respects).

15. Commodities Futures Trading Commission v. Weintraub, 471 U.S. 343 (1985) (holding trustee in bankruptcy to be the owner of the debtor's attorney-client privilege).

16. 11 U.S.C. § 1104(a)(1).

17. In re Bibo, Inc., 76 F.3d 256 (9th Cir. 1996) ("The statute plainly gives the bankruptcy judge authority to appoint a trustee in Chapter 11 proceedings [when no party has made a request].").

18. *Houston, We Know We Have a Problem (But We're Working on It!)*, BANKRUPTCY COURT DECISIONS NEWS AND COMMENT, Feb. 8, 2000.

19. In re Enron Corp., 274 B.R. 327, 337 (Bankr. S.D.N.Y. 2002).

20. *See also* In re Marvel Entertainment Group, Inc., 140 F.3d 463, 469 (3rd Cir. 1998) ("The district court appointed Gibbons as trustee on December 22, 1997 . . . ."); Transcript of Omnibus Hearing Before Honorable Mary F. Walrath United States Bankruptcy Judge, dated Feb. 12, 2002, Docket No. 1457, at 41, In re Coram Healthcare, Case No. 00-3299, in the United States Bankruptcy Court for the District of Delaware (later case in which a Delaware bankruptcy judge appointed a trustee pursuant to the *Marvel* standard).

21. In re Enron Corp., *supra* note 19.

22. *E.g.*, Motion of Absolute Recovery Hedge Fund LP and Regents of the University of California for Order (i) Directing the Appointment of a Chapter 11 Trustee, (ii) Pending the Appointment of a Permanent Chapter 11 Trustee, Directing the Appointment of an Emergency "Gap" Trustee, and (iii) Directing the Debtors to Cooperate with the Trustee, dated Jan. 25, 2002, Docket No. 1125, In re Enron Corporation, Case No. 01-16034, in the United States Bankruptcy Court for the Southern District of New York; Motion of the Florida State Board of Administration for Order Appointing a Chapter 11 Trustee Pursuant to Section 1104 of the Bankruptcy Code, dated Feb. 14, 2002, Docket No. 1472, In re Enron Corp., Case No. 01-16034, in the United States Bankruptcy Court for the Southern District of New York.

23. Memorandum from Entwistle & Cappucci LLP, to Our Institutional Clients 2 (April 10, 2002), *available at* http://www.entwistle-law.com/news/institutional/enron/enron9.htm, (last visited August 8, 2004) ("After the FSBA filed its Trustee Motion, presiding Judge Arthur J. Gonzalez convened a conference call to facilitate discussions between the [parties]. At Judge Gonzalez' request, we pursued a course of negotiations with the Debtors' counsel to resolve the trustee issue.").

24. *See* chapter 6.

25. *See, e.g.*, Regulations of the Judicial Conference of the United States for the Selection, Appointment, and Reappointment of United States Bankruptcy Judges, Sec. 5.02, March 1997, *available at* http://www.ncbj.org/faq1bktcylaw/bankrupt.htm (providing for public notice and the solicitation of comments on an application for reappointment).

26. Stan Bernstein, The Reappointment of Bankruptcy Judges: A Preliminary Analysis of the Present Process (Oct. 15, 2001) (unpublished manuscript, on file with the author).

27. *Id.* at 2 ("[Q]uite a significant number of applicants for reappointment were put through the wringer.").

28. In re Lauriat's Inc., 219 B.R. 648 (Bankr. D. Mass. 1998).

29. *See, e.g.*, 1 ALMANAC OF THE FEDERAL JUDICIARY 38–41 (2003) (lawyers' comments on the Boston bankruptcy judges).

30. The rates for each of these cities are significantly different from those for all other cities at the .05 level. For each city, the odds of so great a difference from the norm occurring by chance are less than one in 20.

Chapter 1

The case under consideration in the quotation at the beginning of the chapter was S.L. Industries, Inc. v. NLRB, 673 F.2d 1, 7 (1st Cir. 1982).

1. H.R. No. 95-595 (1st Session 1977), at 233.

2. Paul Elias & Rinat Fried, *Some Judges Are Slower than Others,* CAL LAW NEWS ALERT, Dec. 15, 1999.

3. Jean Braucher, *Lawyers and Consumer Bankruptcy: One Code, Many Cultures,* 67 AMERICAN BANKRUPTCY LAW JOURNAL 501, 532 (1993).

4. *No Judge Shopping Allowed,* NATIONAL LAW JOURNAL, May 5, 1997.

5. Randall Samborn, *Chicago Judge Sanctions Firm,* NATIONAL LAW JOURNAL, April 18, 1994.

6. Note, *Forum Shopping Reconsidered,* 103 HARVARD LAW REVIEW 1677, 1688 (1990).

7. Lynn M. LoPucki & William C. Whitford, *Venue Choice and Forum Shopping in the Bankruptcy Reorganization of Large, Publicly Held Companies,* 1991 WISCONSIN LAW REVIEW 11, 33.

8. *Id.* at 28 n.60.

9. *Id.* at 50 n.135, 61.

10. United States v. Bestfoods, 524 U.S. 51, 69 (1998) ("[D]irectors and officers holding positions with a parent and its subsidiary can and do 'change hats' to represent the two corporations separately, despite their common ownership.").

11. Voluntary Petition for Relief Under Chapter 11, Title 11, United States Code, filed Mar. 9, 1989, Docket No. 1, In re Ionosphere Clubs, Inc., Case No. 89-10448, in the United States Bankruptcy Court for the Southern District of New York (indicating "Total assets $1,933,643.00").

12. NATIONAL BANKRUPTCY REVIEW COMMISSION, BANKRUPTCY: THE NEXT TWENTY YEARS 775 (1997) ("At the time of LTV's filing, there was no indication that Chateaugay Corporation was in need of bankruptcy protection.").

13. In re Enron Corp., 274 B.R. 327, 338 (Bankr. S.D.N.Y. 2002).

14. 28 U.S.C. § 1412.

15. Claudia MacLachlan, *Anger Rises over Bankruptcy Fees,* NATIONAL LAW JOURNAL, Mar. 9, 1992, at 1 (reporting the discovery of a lawyer who billed 27 hours in a single day in the Carter Hawley Hale bankruptcy case);

Doug Bailey, *FDIC Challenges Lawyer Fees in Bank of N.E. Bankruptcy Case,* BOSTON GLOBE, Nov. 20, 1991, at 45 (reporting lawyers billing for more than 24 hours in a single day in the Bank of New England bankruptcy case).

16. David A. Scholl v. United States, 54 Federal Claims 640, 641 (2002) ("By a memorandum dated March 1, 2000, Chief Judge Becker informed all active Third Circuit judges that the Court had initially approved Judge Scholl's application and would go forward with the required 'public comment' period concerning his reappointment."); *id.* at 642 ("[After the public comment period] Chief Judge Becker informed Judge Scholl . . . that the Third Circuit has refused to reappoint him. . . . The Chief Judge offered no formal or even informal explanation for the Court's adverse decision.").

17. In re Evans Products, 69 Bankr. 68, 69 (Bankr. S.D. Fla. 1986).

18. In re Wilson Foods Corp., 36 Bankr. 317, 321 (Bankr. W.D. Okla. 1984).

19. In re Frontier Airlines, 74 Bankr. 973, 976 (Bankr. D. Colo. 1987).

20. In re Washington Manufacturing, 101 Bankr. 944, 952 (Bankr. M.D. Tenn. 1989).

21. Seth Lubove, *A Bankrupt's Best Friend,* FORBES, Apr. 1, 1991, at 99 ("Lifland's pro-debtor reputation is so widespread that companies which want to stiff their creditors are known to 'forum shop' to get their cases before him.").

22. Amy Dockser, *The Eastern Bankruptcy Filing: Chief Judge, Veteran of Big Cases, Gets Airline's Chapter 11 Petition,* WALL STREET JOURNAL, Mar. 10, 1989.

23. *Morris and Judge Balick Respond to Professors' Forum Shopping Study,* BANKRUPTCY COURT DECISIONS NEWS AND COMMENT, May 12, 1998.

24. *Professor LoPucki Responds to Clerk of Court Cecelia Morris and Judge Balick,* BANKRUPTCY COURT DECISIONS NEWS AND COMMENT, Nov. 17, 1998.

Chapter 2

The quotation at the beginning of the chapter is from Robert K. Rasmussen & Randall S. Thomas, *Whither the Race? A Comment on the Effects of the Delawarization of Corporate Reorganizations,* 54 VANDERBILT LAW REVIEW 283, 283 (2001).

1. U.S. CONST. art. IV, § 1.

2. DEFAC Worksheet, May-04 DEFAC Meeting, at 1, *available at* http://www.state.de.us/finance/publications/DEFAC.shtml (total of Franchise Tax Less Refunds, Corporate Fees, Limited Partnerships and LLCs, and Uniform Commercial Code is 26.8 percent of Net Receipts).

3. Marquette National Bank of Minneapolis v. First of Omaha Service Corp., 439 U.S. 299 (1978).

4. Depository Institutions Deregulation and Monetary Control Act of 1980, Pub. L. 96-221.

5. Matt Swalley, *A Bite out of the Big Apple: Citicorp in South Dakota,* UNITED PRESS INTERNATIONAL, Sept. 5, 1982 ("Citibank had 300 employees [in South Dakota] at the beginning of 1981 and now employs 725.").

6. James L. Rowe, Jr., *Citicorp Moving Its Credit Unit: New York Bank*

to Move Credit-Card Unit to S.D., WASHINGTON POST, Mar. 27, 1980, at B1 ("South Dakota now has a usury ceiling of 24 percent but after May 1 will impose no ceilings on bank charges.").

7. Jeff Gerth, *New York Banks Urged Delaware to Lure Bankers*, NEW YORK TIMES, Mar. 17, 1981.

8. *E.g.*, John F. Berry, *Delaware Wears New Business Heart on Its Sleve; Delaware: Its Love Affair With Business*, WASHINGTON POST, Mar. 9, 1981, at 1. ("To qualify [under the FCDA] a bank must be newly chartered in Delaware with a single office that won't attract customers from the general public—a provision that protects the home banks."); David B. Swayze & David B. Ripsom, *The Delaware Banking Revolution: Are Expanded Powers Next?* 13 DELAWARE JOURNAL OF CORPORATE LAW 27, 43 (1988) ("In the FCDA, Delaware opened the . . . window wide enough to permit an out-of-state holding company to establish a single office bank subsidiary empowered to accept deposits and offer both consumer and commercial credit throughout the United States (*excepting the solicitation of such business in Delaware*) without any usury ceiling.") (emphasis added).

9. Swayze & Ripsom, *supra* note 8, at 44.

10. Jonathan D. Epstein, *State Still Top Employer, but MBNA Is New No. 2*, NEWS JOURNAL (Wilmington, DE), Mar. 17, 2002, at 11J.

11. DEFAC Worksheet, *supra* note 2, at 1 (showing $141.5 million in Bank Franchise Tax revenues, which is 5.8 percent of Delaware's net receipts of $2,436.4 million).

12. *E.g.*, Lawrence v. Goldberg, 279 F.3d 1294 (11th Cir. 2002) (upholding contempt order against debtor who did not comply with court order to turn over assets held in an offshore asset protection trust).

13. Barry S. Engel, *Does Asset Protection Planning Really "Work"?* JOURNAL OF ASSET PROTECTION, Sept./Oct. 1998, at 18.

14. Alaska Trust Act, 1997 Alaska Sess. Laws A.L.S. ch. 6, § 7 (codified at Alaska Stat. § 34.40.110) (Michie Supp. 1997).

15. Qualified Dispositions in Trust Act, 71 De. Laws A.L.S. ch. 159 (1997) (codified at Del. Code Ann. Tit. 12 §§ 3570–3576).

16. Christine Dugas, *Asset Protection Not Automatic*, USA TODAY, Mar. 1, 2002 (quoting an officer of Wilmington Trust).

17. A copy of the brochure is on file with the author.

18. Lynn M. LoPucki, Bankruptcy Research Database, *available at* http://lopucki.law.ucla.edu (search for "DE" as incorporation state).

19. 28 U.S.C. § 1408(1).

20. *Compare* David A. Skeel, Jr., *Bankruptcy Judges and Bankruptcy Venue: Some Thoughts on Delaware*, 1 DELAWARE LAW REVIEW 1, 15 (1998) (arguing that the bankruptcy venue statute allows filing at the place of incorporation) *with* Kristin Kendra Going, Fixing the Bankruptcy Venue Problem: The Solution Has Been There All Along (unpublished manuscript) (arguing that the bankruptcy venue statute does not allow filing at the place of incorporation) and James F. Queenan, *Rethinking the Legality of Delaware Venue*, 22 Bankr. Ct. Dec. 3 (2001) (same). *E.g.*, In re EDP Medical Computer Sys-

tems, Inc., 178 B.R. 57, 62 (M.D. Pa. 1995) (citing conflicting cases on the point).

21. *E.g.,* In re EDP Medical Computer Systems, Inc., 178 B.R. 57, 62 (M.D. Pa. 1995) (raising but not deciding the issue).

22. In re Ocean Properties of Delaware, Inc., 95 B.R. 304 (Bankr. Del. 1988).

23. In re Delaware & H.R. Co., 96 B.R. 467 (Bankr. Del. 1988).

24. *E.g.,* Sidney Rutberg, *The Man Who's Judging Macy's: Chief Bankruptcy Judge Burton R. Lifland,* WOMEN'S WEAR DAILY, Feb. 9, 1994, at 4 ("He also had Eastern Airlines, which turned out to be a disaster. . . . Critics say Lifland allowed the losses to mount at Eastern before eventually closing down the business.").

25. Kenneth Jennings, *Eastern's Final Days,* TRANSPORTATION JOURNAL, Mar. 22, 1992, at 27.

26. In re Amdura Corporation, 121 B.R. 862 (Bankr. D. Colo. 1990) (withdrawing appointment of Winston & Strawn as counsel for the debtors because the debtors had conflicts of interest among themselves).

27. *Adversary Watch,* BCD NEWS AND COMMENT, Aug. 1, 1995, *available at* LEXIS, Library News, File Allnws ("The examiner, David Shapiro, concluded that there were between $200 million and $400 million worth of intercompany transactions for which there was insufficient consideration paid by Continental to Eastern Airlines. The examiner's list included acquisition of [System One Direct Access] and Eastern Airlines Automated Services Inc.].").

28. Bankruptcy Rule 1014(b).

29. Temporary Restraining Order to Show Cause, filed Dec. 19, 1990, at 2, In re Continental Airlines, Case No. 90-932 (Continental Airlines, Inc. v. American General Corporation), Adversary No. 90-119, in the United States Bankruptcy Court for the District of Delaware.

30. Joint Stipulation of Debtors and American General for Relief from the Automatic Stay, dated Jan. 8, 1991, In re Continental Airlines, Case No. 90-932 (American General Corporation v. Continental Airlines, Civil Action 90-755), in the United States District Court for the District of Delaware.

31. Letter from Honorable R. F. Wheless, Jr., United States Bankruptcy Judge for the Southern District of Texas, to Honorable Helen S. Balick, United States Bankruptcy Judge for the District of Delaware (Jan. 9, 1991) (on file with the author).

32. A portion of the O'Neill Group story is recounted in Frank R. Kennedy & Gerald K. Smith, *Postconfirmation Issues: The Effects of Confirmation and Postconfirmation Proceedings,* 44 SOUTH CAROLINA LAW REVIEW 621, 736–37 n.421 (1993).

33. Telephone interview with Marty Harper, partner in Shugahart Thomson & Kilroy P.C., Phoenix, Arizona, May 24, 2004 (reporting that the O'Neill Group pilots got lifetime passes, equity in Continental worth $20 million to $25 million, and payment of their attorneys' fees over a period of six months).

34. In re Mahurkar Double Lumen Hemodialysis, 140 B.R. 969 (N.D. Ill. 1992).

35. *Id.*

36. 11 U.S.C. § 1110(a).

37. 11 U.S.C. § 1110(a)(1).

38. In re Braniff, Inc., 110 B.R. 980 (Bankr. M.D. Fla. 1990).

39. In re Pan Am Corp., 929 F.2d 109 (2nd Cir. 1991), affirming 125 B.R. 372 (S.D.N.Y. 1991) (which in turn affirmed the bankruptcy court).

40. In re Continental Airlines, 932 F.2d 282 (3rd Cir. 1991) [hereafter "Continental I"] (affirming the district court that had reversed the bankruptcy court).

41. *Id.*

42. *Id.* at 284 n.1 ("Subsequent to the district court's ruling, Continental reached agreements covering 57 of these aircraft, under which Continental will defer rental payments until September, 1991.").

43. United Savings Ass'n of Texas v. Timbers of Inwood Forest Assocs., 484 U.S. 365, 370 (1988).

44. In re Continental Airlines, 91 F.3d 553, 562 (3rd Cir. 1996) [hereafter "Continental IV"] ("The condition the Trustees sought in lieu of a stay was the establishment of a segregated account for $117 million, the full amount of their adequate protection claim, or alternatively at least $22 million, which they claim was the admitted decline in the value of the collateral.").

45. In re Continental Airlines, Inc., 154 B.R. 176, 178 (Bankr. D. Del. 1993) [hereafter "Continental III"].

46. *Id.* at 176.

47. In re Continental Airlines, 146 B.R. 536, 542 (Bankr. D. Del. 1992) [hereafter "Continental II"]. ("Finally, the court does not agree that adequate protection may only be sought in conjunction with a lift stay motion. . . . [T]he existence of section 363(e) would imply that adequate protection may be sought independently") (at 540).

48. Continental IV, *supra* note 44, at 557.

49. *Adversary Watch, supra* note 27.

50. Shanon D. Murray, *Patton Pending,* DAILY DEAL, Aug. 9, 2001, *available at* LEXIS, Library News, File Allnws.

51. In re Chateaugay Corp., 109 B.R. 51 (Bankr. S.D.N.Y. 1990).

52. Sherry R. Sontag, *It's Harder to Trade in Old Debts,* NATIONAL LAW JOURNAL, June 11, 1990, at 3.

53. In re Chateaugay Corp., 961 F.2d 378 (2nd Cir. 1992).

54. Order Extending the Exclusive Periods, entered Nov. 16, 1994, Docket No. 2799, In re Columbia Gas System, Inc., Case No. 91-803, In the United States Bankruptcy Court for the District of Delaware; *Bankruptcy Court Again Extends Exclusivity Periods for Columbia Gas Companies to File Reorganization Plans,* FOSTER NATURAL GAS REPORT, Nov. 17, 1994, at 14, *available at* LEXIS, Library News, File Allnws ("This is the ninth such extension.").

55. Section 363 sales are discussed in chapter 6.

56. 11 U.S.C. § 1126(b).

57. 11 U.S.C. § 1102.

58. 11 U.S.C. § 1103(a)

59. 11 U.S.C. § 1129(a)(11).

60. Hilary Rosenberg, The Vulture Investors 260 (2000 ed.).

61. *Id.* at 259–63.

62. 28 U.S.C. § 154.

Chapter 3

The quotation at the beginning of the chapter is from *What Delaware's Withdrawal of the Reference Means,* Consumer Bankruptcy News, Feb. 27, 1997, *available at* LEXIS, Library News, File Allnws.

1. National Bankruptcy Review Commission, Minutes of Meeting Held Friday, February 23, 1996, Washington D.C., and Saturday, February 24, 1996, Washington D.C.

2. National Bankruptcy Review Commission, Bankruptcy: The Next Twenty Years 35 (1997) (Recommendation 3.1.5).

3. Understanding the Federal Courts: Judicial Councils and Conferences, http://www.uscourts.gov/understanding_courts/89914.htm.

4. Gordon Bermant et al., Federal Judicial Center, Chapter 11 Venue Choice by Large Public Companies: Report to the Committee on the Administration of the Bankruptcy System 1 (1997).

5. *Id.* at 62.

6. *Id.* at 37.

7. *Id.* at 61.

8. *Id.* at 40–41.

9. In re USG Corporation, 368 F.3d. 289, 309 (4th Cir. 2004).

10. Code of Conduct for United States Judges, Introduction, 28 U.S.C.A. Appendix ("This Code applies to . . . Bankruptcy Judges . . . .").

11. *Id.* at Canon 3.A.(4).

12. *See generally* In re Kensington International Ltd., 368 F.3d. 289 (4th Cir. 2002) ("We have previously described ex parte communications as 'anathema in our system of justice.' One leading reason is that ex parte meetings are often, as they were here, unrecorded. Consequently, there is no official record of what was said during those meetings.").

13. Vern Countryman, *Scrambling to Define Bankruptcy Jurisdiction: The Chief Justice, the Judicial Conference, and the Legislative Process,* 22 Harvard Journal on Legislation 1, 2 (1985).

14. Northern Pipeline Constr. Co. v. Marathon Pipe Line Co., 458 U.S. 50, 87 (1982).

15. Countryman, *supra* note 13, at 29–42.

16. 28 U.S.C. § 1334(a) and (b) (giving the district courts jurisdiction over bankruptcy cases).

17. 28 U.S.C. § 157(a) and (b)(1) (authorizing the district courts to refer bankruptcy cases to the bankruptcy courts).

18. *E.g.,* Allen R. Kamp, *Court Structure Under the Bankruptcy Code,* 90 Commercial Law Journal, 203, 208 (May 1985) ("To my knowledge, all districts have promulgated a general order referring all bankruptcy cases to the bankruptcy judges.").

19. Order Regarding Referral of Title 11 Proceedings to the United States Bankruptcy Judges for This District (Jan. 23, 1997, *reprinted in* BANKRUPTCY COURT DECISIONS NEWS AND COMMENT, Feb. 4, 1997), at A1, A8.

20. *See* William B. Sullivan, *Shaking the Jurisdictional System: Will Revocation of Automatic Reference Become the Norm?* BANKRUPTCY STRATEGIST, Mar. 1997, at 1 (describing possible rationales for Judge Farnan's order).

21. *See* A Note on the Statistics in This Book, *supra* (defining "big" as exceeding $220 million in assets and thus eligible for inclusion in the Bankruptcy Research Database [BRD]).

22. ADMINISTRATIVE OFFICE OF THE U.S. COURTS, FEDERAL JUDICIAL WORKLOAD STATISTICS, Table F-2 (December 31, 1995, and December 31, 1996).

23. *Delaware District Court Reinstates Chapter 11 Reference,* BCD NEWS AND COMMENT, Jan. 10, 2001.

24. Claudia MacLachlan, *Ex Parte Contacts Behind Del. Bankruptcy Shakeup?* NATIONAL LAW JOURNAL, Feb. 10, 1997, at A10.

25. Sullivan, *supra* note 20, at 1.

26. *Id.; What Delaware's Withdrawal of the Reference Means,* CONSUMER BANKRUPTCY NEWS, Feb. 27, 1997.

27. Sullivan, *supra* note 20.

28. *Id.* (quoting District Court Clerk Peter T. Dalleo).

29. *E.g.,* Robert J. Feinstein, *The New Delaware,* DAILY DEAL, Aug. 16, 2001 ("[T]he federal district judges in the state turned out to be reliable, available and devoted to understanding the complexity of [bankruptcy] megacases.").

30. In cases confirmed from 1997 to 2000, four of 13 debtors whose plans were confirmed by district judges (31 percent) refiled within five years. For the two bankruptcy judges, the corresponding figures were eight of 23 (35 percent).

31. *Why Forum Shopping Shifted from New York to Delaware: The Impact of Delaware's Chief District Judge Withdrawing the Reference,* BANKRUPTCY COURT DECISIONS NEWS AND COMMENT, Apr. 21, 1998 (stating that "[t]he bankruptcy judges had not asked for any assistance and Chief Bankruptcy Judge Balick resigned shortly after Judge Farnan's order."). *See also* Jeff Feeley, *Key Bankruptcy Post to Be Filled,* NATIONAL LAW JOURNAL, May 18, 1998 (stating that Judge Balick "stepped down in January in part because she lost her power to assign cases last year").

32. *Morris and Judge Balick Respond to Professors' Forum Shopping Study,* BANKRUPTCY COURT DECISIONS NEWS AND COMMENT, May 12, 1998, at A3.

33. Marcus Cole, *"Delaware Is Not a State": Are We Witnessing Jurisdictional Competition in Bankruptcy?* 55 VANDERBILT LAW REVIEW 1845, 1892 (2002) (referring to Judge Walrath as "purportedly appointed to buck [the Delaware] culture"); Feeley, *supra* note 31, at B5 (quoting an unnamed lawyer as saying "Ms. Walrath's status as an outsider in Wilmington's legal circles may have helped her get the job. It's seen as being a little too incestuous down here").

34. Cole, *supra* note 33, at 1859 ("Most lawyers [interviewed] also sug-

gested that if they had to file a petition tomorrow, they would be satisfied with either Judge Walsh or Judge Walrath . . . .").

35. Shanon D. Murray, *About-Face on Judges,* NATIONAL LAW JOURNAL, Oct. 8, 2001, at A17 ("Since 1997, the district judges were allowed to preside over bankruptcy cases in an arrangement unique to Delaware. Robinson ended that practice in February.").

36. *Delaware: Reference Revoked after Visiting Judge Questions Venue,* BANKRUPTCY COURT DECISIONS NEWS AND COMMENT, Apr. 25, 2001.

37. *Delaware District Court Reinstates Chapter 11 Reference,* BANKRUPTCY COURT DECISIONS NEWS AND COMMENT, Jan. 10, 2001.

38. Report of the Proceedings of the Judicial Conference of the United States, Mar. 11, 1997 (recommending additional judgeships for districts other than Delaware).

39. U.S. House of Representatives Committee on the Judiciary Subcommittee on Commercial and Administrative Law and U.S. Senate Committee on the Judiciary Subcommittee on Administrative Oversight and the Courts Joint Oversight Hearing on "Bankruptcy Judgeship Needs," 106th Congress (Nov. 2, 1999) (testimony of Michael N. Castle, congressman), *available at* http://www.house.gov/judiciary/cast1102.htm.

40. Theodore Eisenberg & Lynn M. LoPucki, *Shopping for Judges: An Empirical Analysis of Venue Choice in Large Chapter 11 Reorganizations,* 84 CORNELL LAW REVIEW 967, 997–99 (1999).

41. *Id.* at 1003.

42. Report of the Proceedings of the Judicial Conference of the United States, Sept. 15, 1998.

43. Report of the Proceedings of the Judicial Conference of the United States, Mar. 16, 1999.

44. 28 U.S.C. § 1412 (2004); In re A & D Care, Inc., 86 B.R. 43 (Bankr. M.D. Pa. 1988) (bankruptcy court can transfer case under 28 U.S.C. § 1412).

45. REPORT OF THE DELAWARE STATE BAR ASSOCIATION TO THE NATIONAL BANKRUPTCY REVIEW COMMISSION IN SUPPORT OF MAINTAINING EXISTING VENUE CHOICES 17, n.38, Oct. 3, 1996.

46. Murray, *supra* note 35, at A17 (noting a "rumor that Delaware judges lately have been sending out 'vibes' . . . that the bankruptcy court is only interested in handling the mega-Chapter 11 cases of $1 billion or more and that smaller cases should go elsewhere").

47. Shanon D. Murray, *Visiting Judge Rankles Bankruptcy Court,* DEAL, Apr. 11, 2001; *Delaware: Reference Revoked after Visiting Judge Questions Venue,* BANKRUPTCY COURT DECISIONS NEWS AND COMMENT, Apr. 25, 2001.

48. *Reaction to Delaware District Court's Actions,* BANKRUPTCY COURT DECISIONS NEWS AND COMMENT, May 16, 2001.

49. *Id.*

50. Case No. 02-12218-JCA.

Chapter 4
The quotation at the beginning of the chapter is from Maureen Milford, *Study Attacks Delaware Bankruptcy Court,* NATIONAL LAW JOURNAL, March 25,

2002, at B1 (reporting on the release of the LoPucki-Doherty follow-up study on refilings by companies reorganized in the Delaware and New York bankruptcy courts).

1. Lynn M. LoPucki & William C. Whitford, *Patterns in the Bankruptcy Reorganization of Large, Publicly Held Companies,* 78 CORNELL LAW REVIEW 597, 608 (1993).

2. 11 U.S.C. § 1129(a)(11).

3. Edith Schwalb Hotchkiss, *The Post Bankruptcy Performance and Management Turnover,* 50 JOURNAL OF FINANCE 3 (1995).

4. Robert K. Rasmussen & Randall S. Thomas, *Timing Matters: Promoting Forum Shopping by Insolvent Corporations,* 94 NORTHWESTERN UNIVERSITY LAW REVIEW 1357, 1386–91 (2000) (arguing that Delaware gets the most prepackaged bankruptcies because it is faster and has other unspecified advantages over other courts); David A. Skeel, Jr., *Bankruptcy Judges and Bankruptcy Venue: Some Thoughts on Delaware,* 1 DELAWARE LAW REVIEW 1, 28 (1998) (arguing that Delaware venue should be maintained because the Delaware bankruptcy court "has successfully addressed the single biggest problem with Chapter 11 in recent years—the inordinate time and expense of the reorganization process").

5. Lynn M. LoPucki & Sara D. Kalin, *The Failure of Public Company Bankruptcies in Delaware and New York: Empirical Evidence of a "Race to the Bottom,"* 54 VANDERBILT LAW REVIEW 231, 270 (2001).

6. *Id.* at 267.

7. John F. Manser, *First State Practitioners Criticize Study That Claims Companies Reorganized Here Often Slide Back,* DELAWARE LAW WEEKLY, August 22, 2000.

8. Peter Aronson, *Study Faults Delaware Court,* NATIONAL LAW JOURNAL, Sept. 18, 2000, at B4.

9. Harvey R. Miller, *Chapter 11 Reorganization Cases and the Delaware Myth,* 55 VANDERBILT LAW REVIEW 1987, 2004 (2002).

10. Marcus Bernard Butler III, Valuation Conflicts in Corporate Bankruptcy (2002) (unpublished Ph.D. dissertation, University of Chicago) (finding that "primary sample firms not filing in Delaware refiled at roughly half the rate of Delaware firms (28% vs. 58%)").

11. Miller, *supra* note 9, at 2016 ("[D]istress debt traders may sacrifice the long-term viability of a debtor for the ability to realize substantial and quick returns on their investments.").

12. Janet Kidd Stewart, *Competing Players Pursue Myriad Goals,* CHICAGO TRIBUNE, Dec. 16, 2001, at C1 (quoting Klee that "There's a euphoria when a company comes out that the problems are solved and the bondholders can flip the debt and get out").

13. David Marcus, *Wilmington Whitewash?* CORPORATE CONTROL ALERT, May 2001, at 10 (quoting Trost that "When [distress debt traders] get in, they need something to happen fast. . . . so sometimes cases are resolved too quickly").

14. *Chapter 22: Who's to Blame?* BANKRUPTCY COURT DECISIONS NEWS AND COMMENT, July 5, 2001 [hereafter *Chapter 22 Blame*].

15. Manser, *supra* note 7.

16. *Id.*

17. Marcus, *supra* note 13, at 10.

18. *Id.*

19. *Evaluating Plan Feasibility: Whose Responsibility Is It?* BANKRUPTCY COURT DECISIONS NEWS AND COMMENT, Aug. 8, 2001 [hereafter *Evaluating Plan Feasibility*].

20. *Id.*

21. *Id.*

22. *Chapter 22 Blame, supra* note 14.

23. *Evaluating Plan Feasibility, supra* note 19.

24. *Id.*

25. 11 U.S.C. § 1129(a)(11) (provision known as the "feasibility requirement").

26. Miller, *supra* note 9, at 2000.

27. *What Other Legal Scholars Think of the LoPucki/Kalin Study,* BANKRUPTCY COURT DECISIONS NEWS AND COMMENT, Aug. 10, 2000.

28. *E.g.*, Marcus, *supra* note 13, at 11 ("Finally, there's the possibility that LoPucki's figures reflect Balick's pro-debtor orientation rather than that of the Delaware court . . . .").

29. E-mail from Jesse M. Fried, Professor of Law, University of California at Berkeley to Lynn M. LoPucki, Sept. 19, 2000.

30. Robert K. Rasmussen & Randall S. Thomas, *Whither the Race? A Comment on the Effects of the Delawarization of Corporate Reorganizations,* 54 VANDERBILT LAW REVIEW 283, 336 (2001).

31. *Chapter 22 Blame, supra* note 14.

32. *Chapter 22: Does It Matter?* BANKRUPTCY COURT DECISIONS NEWS AND COMMENT, Aug. 1, 2001.

33. Lynn M. LoPucki, *Can the Market Evaluate Legal Regimes?* 54 VANDERBILT LAW REVIEW 331, 336–38 (2001).

34. Lynn M. LoPucki & Joseph W. Doherty, *Why Are Delaware and New York Bankruptcy Reorganizations Failing?* 55 VANDERBILT LAW REVIEW 1933, 1939 (2002).

35. *Id.* at 1939–42.

36. *Id.* at 1944–45.

37. *Id.* at 1942–44.

38. Miller, *supra* note 9, at 2004; David A. Skeel, Jr., *What's So Bad About Delaware?* 54 VANDERBILT LAW REVIEW 309, 319 (2001) ("[T]he firms that file for bankruptcy in Delaware may have more complicated capital structures.").

39. *E.g.*, THEODORE EISENBERG, BUSINESS INSOLVENCY LAW: CREATING AN EFFECTIVE SWEDISH RECONSTRUCTION LAW (Stockholm: Studieförbundet Näringsliv och Samhälle, Center for Business Policy Studies, Occasional Paper No. 75, 1995) (reporting that U.S. Chapter 11 confirmation rates decrease monotonically with firm size: the rate is 96 percent for firms with assets greater than $100 million, 36 percent for firms with assets between $1 million and $100 million, and 20 percent for firms with less than $1 million).

40. LoPucki & Doherty, *supra* note 34, at 1951–52.

41. Skeel, *supra* note 38, at 319.

42. LoPucki & Doherty, *supra* note 34, at 1977 (statistically significant at the .008 level).

43. Barry E. Adler & Henry N. Butler, *On the Delawarization of Bankruptcy Debate,* 52 EMORY LAW JOURNAL 1309, 1317 (2003) ("Perhaps the explanation is simply that reorganization plans for which proximity to the bankruptcy court matters are the more complicated cases.").

44. LoPucki & Doherty, *supra* note 34, at 1953.

45. Lynn M. LoPucki & Joseph W. Doherty, *The Determinants of Professional Fees in Large Bankruptcy Reorganization Cases,* 1 JOURNAL OF EMPIRICAL LEGAL STUDIES 111, 131 (2004) (stating that the difference was not statistically significant).

46. LoPucki & Doherty, *supra* note 34, at 1976–77.

Chapter 5

The first quotation at the beginning of the chapter is from Robert A. Mark, Chief's Corner: *What Would Della Wear?* BANKRUPTCY BAR ASSOCIATION, SOUTHERN DISTRICT OF FLORIDA, NEWS AND VIEWS, Nov./Dec. 2000, at 6.

The second quotation at the beginning of the chapter is from *Keep Megacases in Your District with Case Management Procedures,* BANKRUPTCY COURT DECISIONS NEWS AND COMMENT, Nov. 4, 2003, at A5 [hereafter *Keep Megacases*] (quoting statement made by Judge Fitzgerald on a panel at the National Conference of Bankruptcy Judges Annual Meeting).

1. *Houston, We Know We Have a Problem (But We're Working on It!),* BANKRUPTCY COURT DECISIONS NEWS AND COMMENT, Feb. 10, 2000.

2. *Id.*

3. *Id.*

4. Amy Merrick, *Chicago Court Adeptly Attracts Chapter 11 Cases,* WALL STREET JOURNAL, Dec. 10, 2002, at B1 (reporting that Judge Sonderby commissioned the focus group). The quoted language is from the title of the report.

5. Procedural Guidelines for Prepackaged Chapter 11 Cases in the United States Bankruptcy Court for the Southern District of New York, VIII. B. and XI; United States Bankruptcy Court for the Central District of California, General Order 02-01(h).

6. *Keep Mega-cases, supra* unnumbered note, at 1.

7. Kristi O'Brien, *Northern District of Illinois Is Rich in Major Bankruptcy Cases,* CHICAGO LAWYER, Feb. 2003, at 8 (quoting Chicago bankruptcy judge Eugene Wedoff).

8. This estimate is based on the size and expected duration of the actual cases filed. I compiled it using a computer program Joseph Doherty and I developed, based on a study of professional fees and expenses in 48 recent cases. The simple, easy-to-use program is posted at http://lopucki.law .ucla.edu/feecalculator.asp.

9. Nathan Koppel, *Local Counsel Rule Keeps Delaware in the Dough,* DELAWARE LAW WEEKLY, May 7, 2003, at D4.

10. Report of the Proceedings of the Judicial Conference of the United States, March 16, 1999.

11. Judicial Conference Committee on the Administration of the Bankruptcy System and the Federal Judicial Center, Conference on Large Chapter 11 Cases (2004), at 1, *available at* http://www.fjc.gov/newweb/jnetweb.nsf/pages/582) (the "recommendation would have prohibited corporate debtors from filing for bankruptcy in a district based solely on the debtor's state of incorporation or based solely on an earlier filing by a subsidiary in the district").

12. Administrative Office of the U.S. Courts, Need for Additional Bankruptcy Judges at a Critical Level, May 22, 2003 (recommending four additional bankruptcy judgeships for Delaware), *available at* http://www.uscourts.gov/Press_Releases/Index.html (last visited Oct. 15, 2004).

13. *Supra* note 11, at 41.

14. Report of the Proceedings of the Judicial Conference of the United States, September 24, 2002, at 39.

15. *E.g.,* Order Transferring Chapter 11 Proceedings, dated June 20, 2003, Docket No. 14, In re Touch America Holdings, Inc., Case No. 03-11915, in the United States Bankruptcy Court for the District of Delaware ("transferring" case to Philadelphia bankruptcy judge Kevin J. Carey without transferring the case to the Eastern District of Pennsylvania).

16. Merrick, *supra* note 4 (quoting Judge Sonderby).

17. *Talent, Efficiency and Common Sense Draw Mega-cases to Chicago,* BANKRUPTCY COURT DECISIONS NEWS AND COMMENT, January 28, 2003.

18. Spiegel's and National Equipment.

19. Bill W. Hornaday, *Lesser Debtholders Challenge Conseco; TOPRs Class Claims Company Has Manipulated Valuation,* INDIANAPOLIS STAR, May 19, 2003 (noting that the TOPRs class was objecting to the managers' releases).

20. *Financial Services Brief: Conseco Inc.,* WALL STREET JOURNAL, Aug. 1, 2003 (noting Conseco's settlement with the trust preferred securities [TOPRs]).

21. Bill W. Hornaday, *Legal Releases Threaten Conseco Plans,* INDIANAPOLIS STAR, July 11, 2003 ("A federal judge put Conseco on notice Thursday that unless it makes a better case why its third amended bankruptcy plan calls for legal releases even broader than those in an earlier plan, it may be rejected altogether."); *Judge Gives Parties More Time by Deferring Ruling on Plan,* WALL STREET JOURNAL, Aug. 4, 2003 ("Judge Carol A. Doyle . . . said she had objections to wording in the plan that would have creditors release these executives from liability. . . .").

22. Jonathan Berke, *Conseco Pairs Bankruptcy with Deal,* DAILY DEAL, Dec. 19, 2002 ("Sprayregen expects Conseco to exit bankruptcy by the end of the second quarter of 2003.").

23. Capital Factors, Inc. v. Kmart Corporation, 291 B.R. 818 (N.D. Ill. 2003); *affirmed* In re Kmart Corporation, 359 F.3d 866 (7th Cir. 2004) [hereafter "Kmart District Court Opinion"].

24. In re Kmart Corporation, 359 F.3d 866 (7th Cir. 2004) (describing the order as "open-ended permission to pay any debt to any vendor [Kmart] deemed 'critical' in the exercise of unilateral discretion"); *id.* at 868 (Kmart used its authority to pay in full the prepetition debts to 2,330 suppliers, which collectively received about $300 million).

25. *See* Kmart District Court Opinion, *supra* note 23 ("[I]t is clear that however useful and practical these payments may appear to bankruptcy courts, they simply are not authorized by the Bankruptcy Code. Congress has not elected to codify the doctrine of necessity or otherwise permit pre-plan payment of prepetition unsecured claims.").

26. In re Kmart Corporation, 359 F.3d 866 (7th Cir. 2004).

Chapter 6

The case under consideration in the quotation at the beginning of the chapter is In re TW, Inc., Case No. 03-10785, hearing of Aug. 25, 2002, in the United States Bankruptcy Court for the District of Delaware (not transcribed).

1. Lynn M. LoPucki & Joseph W. Doherty, *The Determinants of Professional Fees in Large Bankruptcy Reorganization Cases,* 1 JOURNAL OF EMPIRICAL LEGAL STUDIES 111 (2004) (study of 48 cases showing fees averaging between 1 and 2 percent of assets).

2. Lynn M. LoPucki, *Can the Market Evaluate Legal Regimes?* 54 VANDERBILT LAW REVIEW 331, 336–38 (2001) (showing that firms refiling bankruptcy lost an average of 18 percent of assets merely in operating losses between the two bankruptcies).

3. Gary Young, *U.S. Bankruptcy System Blasted,* NATIONAL LAW JOURNAL, July 26, 2004, at 7 (quoting Case).

4. Lynn M. LoPucki & William C. Whitford, *Venue Choice and Forum Shopping in the Bankruptcy Reorganization of Large, Publicly Held Companies,* 1991 WISCONSIN LAW REVIEW 11, 32–33.

5. Marcus Cole, *"Delaware Is Not a State": Are We Witnessing Jurisdictional Competition in Bankruptcy?* 55 VANDERBILT LAW REVIEW 1845, 1866 ("A slight majority of attorneys thought that fees played some role . . . .").

6. Judicial Conference Committee on the Administration of the Bankruptcy System and the Federal Judicial Center, Conference on Large Chapter 11 Cases (2004), at 5, *available at* http://www.fjc.gov/newweb/jnetweb.nsf/pages/582); *id.* at 27–33 (discussing the bankruptcy courts' fee policies as a venue driver).

7. *Houston, We Know We Have a Problem (But We're Working on It!),* BANKRUPTCY COURT DECISIONS NEWS AND COMMENT, Feb. 10, 2000.

8. Amy Merrick, *Chicago Court Adeptly Attracts Chapter 11 Cases,* WALL STREET JOURNAL, Dec. 10, 2002, at B1.

9. Robert A. Mark, Chief's Corner: *What Would Della Wear?* BANKRUPTCY BAR ASSOCIATION, SOUTHERN DISTRICT OF FLORIDA, NEWS AND VIEWS, Nov./Dec. 2000, at 5.

10. Administrative Order M-219, United States Bankruptcy Court for the Southern District of New York.

11. General Order 02-02(f), United States Bankruptcy Court for the Central District of California.

12. Local Rule 7016-1, United States Bankruptcy Court for the Northern District of Illinois.

13. General Order 00-7, at 3, United States Bankruptcy Court for the Northern District of Texas.

14. Administrative Order No. 02-03 (2002), United States Bankruptcy Court for the District of Maryland.

15. E-mail from Judge Randall J. Newsome, Bankruptcy Judge, N.D. Cal., to Lynn M. LoPucki (Oct. 10, 2003) (on file with the author).

16. Lynn M. LoPucki & Joseph W. Doherty, *The Determinants of Professional Fees in Large Bankruptcy Reorganization Cases*, 1 JOURNAL OF EMPIRICAL LEGAL STUDIES 111, 136 (2004).

17. A list of such cases appears *infra* note 25.

18. Lynn M. LoPucki & William C. Whitford, *Corporate Governance in the Bankruptcy Reorganization of Large, Publicly Held Companies*, 141 UNIVERSITY OF PENNSYLVANIA LAW REVIEW 669, 723–37 (1993).

19. Stuart C. Gilson, *Management Turnover and Financial Distress*, 25 JOURNAL OF FINANCIAL ECONOMICS 241 (1989); Edith Shwalb Hotchkiss, *Postbankruptcy Performance and Management Turnover*, 50 JOURNAL OF FINANCE 3 (1995).

20. Lynn M. LoPucki & Joseph W. Doherty, CEO Turnover in Large Bankruptcy Cases (2004) (unpublished manuscript, on file with the author) [hereafter "CEO Turnover"].

21. *See, e.g.,* Joann S. Lublin, Management: *White Knights Asked to Save Companies Find Boards Are Getting Harder to Please,* WALL STREET JOURNAL, Apr. 27, 1994 (reporting an increase in first-year CEO firings by troubled companies from 11 percent to 21 percent from 1988 to 1993); Drake Beam Morin, CEO Turnover and Job Security 9 (2000) *available at* http://dbmext.dbm.com/portal/public/dbmnav.nsf (search for "CEO Turnover" then select "File Attachment Library: CEO") (reporting a trend toward shorter CEO tenure in the United States and the world from the 1980s to the 1990s).

22. Gilson, *supra* note 19.

23. Ethan S. Bernstein, All's Fair in Love, War & Bankruptcy? Corporate Governance Implications of CEO Turnover in Financial Distress (2003) (unpublished manuscript, on file with the author).

24. LoPucki & Doherty, *supra* note 20.

25. Associated Press, *U.S. Court Takes Control of Eastern from Lorenzo*, NEW YORK TIMES, Apr. 19, 1990, at 1 ("A Federal bankruptcy judge appointed a special trustee yesterday to take over Eastern Airlines, removing control of the carrier from Frank Lorenzo, chairman of Eastern's parent, the Texas Air Corporation."); *Bonneville Pacific Accused of Sham Transactions; Trustee Appointed,* INDEPENDENT POWER REPORT, June 19, 1992, at 1, *available at*

LEXIS, Library News, File Allnws ("The U.S. Bankruptcy Court in Salt Lake City has appointed a trustee to take over day-to-day operations of Bonneville Pacific Corp. . . ."); *Court-Appointed Trustee to Oversee Reorganization of Colorado-Ute*, ELECTRIC UTILITY WEEK, Aug. 13, 1990, at 3, *available at* LEXIS, Library News, File Allnws ("Reorganization of debt-ridden Colorado-Ute Electric Assn. will go forward under a trustee to be appointed by the U.S. Bankruptcy Court at Denver. . . ."); Debtor's Amended Disclosure Statement, dated Mar. 5, 1985, at 41, In re Pizza Time Theatre, Inc., Case No. 584-00941, in the United States Bankruptcy Court for the Northern District of California, San Jose Division ("During the week of the scheduled hearing on the Trustee Motion, the Creditors' Committee proposed that John B. R. Leisner be appointed as the President and Chief Executive Officer of Pizza Time, with very broad powers and not subject to the control of Pizza Time's Board of Directors. [The court approved that arrangement.]).

26. Tom Hamburger et al., *Staff Saw Document Shredding at Enron,* WALL STREET JOURNAL, Jan. 22, 2002.

27. Sue Herrera, *Stephen Cooper's Ability to Turn Enron Around Is Questioned,* CNBC NEWS TRANSCRIPTS, Jan. 30, 2002 ("By hiring Cooper, Enron's board of directors and largest creditors are hoping to squelch an effort to persuade U.S. Bankruptcy Court Judge Arthur Gonzalez to appoint a trustee to run the company"); Jonathan Berke, *Enron Names CEO, Chief Restructurer,* DAILY DEAL, Jan. 29, 2002 (referring to the hiring of Cooper as a "last ditch effort" to avoid the appointment of a trustee).

28. Rebecca Smith & Joann S. Lublin, *Accounting for Enron: Enron's Top Choice for Acting CEO Is Stephen Cooper,* WALL STREET JOURNAL, Jan. 25, 2002, at A4 ("Mr. Cooper . . . is set to fly to Houston from New York today.").

29. Lisa Sanders, *Enron's Acting Chief Says Turnaround Is Achievable,* CBS.MARKETWATCH, Jan. 30, 2002.

30. Permanent Subcommittee on Investigations of the Committee on Governmental Affairs United States Senate, Role of the Board of Directors in Enron's Collapse, July 8, 2002, 107th Cong., 2nd Sess., at 3.

31. *E.g.,* Mary Fagan, *Enron Rescue Strategy Disclosed,* SUNDAY TELE-GRAPH (LONDON) May 5, 2002, at 2.

32. Debtors' Disclosure Statement for Amended Joint Plan of Affiliated Debtors Pursuant to Chapter 11 of the United States Bankruptcy Code, dated Sept. 18, 2003, Docket No. 12823, at 215–16, In re Enron Corp., Case No. 01-16034, in the United States Bankruptcy Court for the Southern District of New York (discussing reconstitution of the board of directors of Enron Corporation).

33. Marc L. Steinberg, *Curtailing Investor Protection Under the Securities Laws: Good for the Economy?* 55 SOUTHERN METHODIST UNIVERSITY LAW REVIEW 347, 350–51 (2002) (describing actions taken by Congress, the courts, and the SEC during the 1990s to make class action securities litigation more difficult for plaintiffs to bring and win); Lynn A. Stout, *The Investor*

Confidence Game, 68 BROOKLYN LAW REVIEW 407, 433 (2002) (referring to the Private Securities Litigation Reform Act of 1995 as "explicitly designed to make it more difficult for plaintiffs to bring securities fraud class actions in federal courts").

34. Mary Flood, *The Fall of Enron / Lawyers Ask for Efficiency to Save Cash,* HOUSTON CHRONICLE, Dec. 12, 2003 (reporting on negotiations intended to prevent duplicative discovery).

35. *Id.* (reporting that the examiner had requested that the bankruptcy court permit him to "shred the documents he has collected to prepare his report").

36. Newby v. Enron Corp., et al., Civil Action No. H-01-3624, in the United States District Court for the Southern District of Texas, Houston Division, Order of Consolidation entered Dec. 12, 2001, at 17 (noting that some of the consolidated cases were "actions filed derivatively on behalf of Enron against its present or former directors").

37. FRANKLIN A. GEVURTZ, CORPORATION LAW 387 (2000) (explaining derivative suits by saying: "If the courts were to leave exclusive control over corporation litigation in the hands of the board, then enforcement of the directors' duty to the corporation would be confined to those relatively rare cases in which the corporation goes broke and a bankruptcy trustee asserts the claim, or else there is a change in management and the new directors decide the corporation should act").

38. Final Report of Neal Batson, Court-Appointed Examiner, Appendix D, filed Nov. 24, 2003, Docket No. 14455, at 8, In re Enron Corp., Case No. 01-16034, in the United States Bankruptcy Court for the Southern District of New York [hereafter "Final Report of Neal Batson, Appendix D"].

39. Complaint to Avoid Certain Pre-Petition Loan and Annuity Transactions as Fraudulent Transfers, dated Jan. 31, 2003, Docket No. 1, In re Enron Corp. (Official Committee of Unsecured Creditors of Enron Corp v. Kenneth Lay), Case No. 01-16034, Adversary Proceeding No. 03-02075, in the United States Bankruptcy Court for the Southern District of New York (presenting fraudulent transfer claims but no claim that Enron had voided the sales).

40. Final Report of Neal Batson, Appendix D, *supra* note 38, at 178–79.

41. Final Report of Neal Batson, Appendix D, *supra* note 38, at 117–20 (arguing that Enron's board might have dealt more effectively with the problems if Lay and Skilling had not misled them with respect to the special purpose entity transactions).

42. Jennifer Frey & Hannah Rosin, *Enron's Green Acres,* WASHINGTON POST, Feb. 25, 2002, at C1.

43. *See, e.g.,* In re Coates, 242 B.R. 901 (Bankr. N.D. Tex. 2000) (holding debtor entitled to exempt a homestead after paying the mortgage against it by means of transfers intended to defraud creditors); In re Reed, 12 B.R. 41 (Bankr. N.D. Tex. 1981) (same).

44. Havoco of America v. Hill, 790 So.2d 1018 (Fla. 2001) (holding that a homestead acquired by a debtor with the specific intent to hinder, delay, or

defraud creditors is not excepted from homestead protection under the Florida Constitution).

45. Nancy Rivera Brooks, *Enron Execs Were Paid to Remain,* LOS ANGELES TIMES, Dec. 7, 2001, at C3; Mitchell Pacelle, *Despite Lawsuits, Enron Bonuses Haven't Been Returned,* WALL STREET JOURNAL, Nov. 3, 2003, at C1.

46. Second Interim Report of Neal Batson, Court-Appointed Examiner, Annex 2 to Appendix P, filed Mar. 5, 2003, Docket No. 9551, at 8, In re Enron Corp., in the United States Bankruptcy Court for the Southern District of New York.

47. Pacelle, *supra* note 45.

48. Francoise C. Arsenault, *Enron Executives Sued for $21 Million,* TURNAROUNDS AND WORKOUTS, Dec. 15, 2003, at 2 ("Everyone in Group 1 [current employees] has now settled.").

49. *Id.* at 1 ("To date, over $7 million has been brought into the estate as a result of the negotiations and settlements."); Pacelle, *supra* note 45, at C1 ("Most bonus recipients haven't surrendered any of their pay-outs, which totaled roughly $73 million.").

50. Pacelle, *supra* note 45 (noting that Jeffrey McMahon "was awarded a $1.5 million bonus, in exchange for a commitment to remain at the company for 90 days").

51. Third Interim Report of Neal Batson, Court-Appointed Examiner, dated June 30, 2003, Docket No. 11960, at 54, 63, In re Enron Corp., Case No. 01-16034, in the United States Bankruptcy Court for the Southern District of New York.

52. 11 U.S.C. § 546(a).

53. Order Approving the Appointment of Neal Batson as the Examiner for Enron Corp., dated May 24, 2002, Docket No. 4003, In re Enron Corp., Case No. 01-16034, in the United States Bankruptcy Court for the Southern District of New York.

54. John Emshwiller & Mitchell Pacelle, *In His Own Defense: Was Enron Inquiry Worth $90 Million?* WALL STREET JOURNAL, Mar. 18, 2004, at C1, C5 ("Mr. Batson was appointed about six months after Enron's bankruptcy-court filing. He says this delay added time pressure—and required throwing more attorneys into the fray—because under federal statutes certain claims to recover money have to be made within two years of the bankruptcy filing.").

55. *See, e.g.,* Order Authorizing the Filing of an Amended Complaint Under Seal for a Limited Period, dated Nov. 26, 2003, Docket No. 6, In re Enron Corp. (Enron Corp. v. Citigroup, Inc.), Case No. 01-16034, Adversary Proceeding No. 03-09266, in the United States Bankruptcy Court for the Southern District of New York (allowing Enron's lawsuit against Citigroup to be filed secretly until the examiner's report on which it was based could be filed).

56. Stuart C. Gilson, *Management Turnover and Financial Distress,* 25 JOURNAL OF FINANCIAL ECONOMICS 241, 254–55 (1989).

57. *Id.* at 255.

58. Kmart Corporation, Form DEF 14A, filed as of Apr. 4, 2001, at 11–17, *available at* http://www.sec.gov/edgar/searchedgar/companysearch.html (last visited June 20, 2004) (describing Conaway's compensation).

59. Pacelle, *supra* note 45 ("Kmart Corp. . . . is attempting to claw back some $30 million of 'retention loans' paid to executives prior to its Chapter 11 filing.").

60. Amy Merrick, *Chicago Court Adeptly Attracts Chapter 11 Cases,* WALL STREET JOURNAL, Dec. 10, 2002, at B1.

61. Joel J. Smith, *Ex-CEO Conaway May Get $9 Million,* DETROIT NEWS, May 16, 2002 ("But the bankruptcy judge called the matter routine business that shouldn't take up the time of the court and told Kmart management it had the authority to pay the settlement."); Brent Snavely, *Kmart Execs Cash in While Business Falters,* CRAIN'S DETROIT BUSINESS, May 27, 2002 ("Conaway already has received a $4 million severance payment. Kmart has also agreed to forgive the remaining balance of a $5 million loan granted to him when he was hired.").

62. Karen Dybis, *Ex-Kmart Exec Must Give up Data,* DETROIT NEWS, May 13, 2003 ("Kmart has since terminated employee contracts with all of these [25] executives and asked them to return the money. Only three have complied."); Kathleen Kerwin, *Creditors Take on Kmart's "Frat Boys,"* BUSINESS WEEK ONLINE, Nov. 21, 2003 (noting that Kmart creditors' trust sued six of the 25 executives and that "at least three other former managers . . . have returned their loans").

63. William J. Rochelle III, FULBRIGHT & JAWORSKI L.L.P. DAILY BANKRUPTCY NEWS, Apr. 23, 2004 ("Restaurant operator Denny's Corp. says it is talking with the holders of its $592 million in 11.25% senior notes of '08 about a debt for equity swap.").

64. Kmart Corporation, Form 10-K for the year ended Jan. 30, 2002, at 63 (reporting services agreement providing for $1 million annual fee).

65. *E.g.,* Joann S. Lublin, *Multiple Seats of Power,* WALL STREET JOURNAL, Jan. 23, 2001, at B1 ("Outside board members of the 200 biggest industrial and service concerns commanded an average of $137,410 in cash and equity awards per directorship last year . . . according to a proxy analysis by New York pay consultants Pearl Meyer & Partners.").

66. Kmart Corporation, Form 10-K for the year ended Jan. 30, 2002, at 63–64.

67. *Id.* at 67.

68. *Id.* at 68 ("a cash lump sum equal to the sum of 300% of Mr. Adamson's base salary and 100% of his target bonus . . . minus the amount of the entire inducement payment").

69. Nelson D. Schwartz, *Greed-mart, Attention, Kmart Investors. The Company May Be Bankrupt, but Its Top Brass Have Been Raking It In,* FORTUNE MAGAZINE, Oct. 14, 2002, at 139.

70. Kmart Corporation, Form 10-K afor the year ended Jan. 30, 2002, at 64 ("The employment agreement was subject to Court approval, which was received on April 23, 2002. . . .").

71. Lorene Yue, *Kmart Execs to Get Millions in Pay Under Bankruptcy,*

CHICAGO TRIBUNE, Apr. 24, 2002 ("Instead, Judge Susan Pierson Sonderby said the contract needed approval only from the company's board of directors.").

72. Kmart Corporation, Form 10-K for the year ended Jan. 29, 2003, at 78 (reporting $3.6 million settlement).

73. Ann Davis, *Want Some Extra Cash? File for Chapter 11*, WALL STREET JOURNAL, Oct. 31, 2001 (quoting a restructuring and executive pay expert saying that the "wide use of pay-to-stay bonuses is a shift from the last economic slowdown in the early 1990s").

74. In re Geneva Steel Co., 236 B.R. 770 (Bankr. D. Utah 1999) (refusing to approve a retention program on ground that it was not an exercise of sound business judgment because the debtor did not have the approval of a union equally critical to successful reorganization); Order Granting Debtor's Motion to Approve Amended Key Employee Retention Program, dated Sept. 16, 1999, Docket No. 416, In re Geneva Steel, Case No. 99C-21130, in the United States Bankruptcy Court for the District of Utah.

75. Bankruptcy Rule 2004 (providing for the examination of "any entity" with respect to "the operation of any business and the desirability of its continuance, the source of any money or property acquired or to be acquired by the debtor for the purposes of consummating a plan . . . and any other matter relevant to the case or to the formulation of a plan").

76. 7 COLLIER ON BANKRUPTCY § 1103.05[1] (15th ed. 2003) ("[T]he members of a committee have a fiduciary duty to their constituents . . . ."). *Id.* at § 1103.05[2] ("A member of a committee owes a fiduciary duty to the class the committee represents.").

77. HILARY ROSENBERG, THE VULTURE INVESTORS 260 (2002 ed.).

78. *Id.*, at 261–62.

79. General Order 02-02, Chapter 11 Procedures, United States Bankruptcy Court, Central District of California, Apr. 17, 2002.

80. Lynn M. LoPucki & Joseph W. Doherty, *Why Are Delaware and New York Bankruptcy Reorganizations Failing?* 55 VANDERBILT LAW REVIEW 1933, 1973 (2002) (finding that prepackaged bankruptcies were significantly more likely to fail than nonprepackaged bankruptcies).

81. Lynn M. LoPucki, *Can the Market Evaluate Legal Regimes? A Response to Professors Rasmussen, Thomas, and Skeel,* 54 VANDERBILT LAW REVIEW 331, 336–38 (2001) (showing that operating losses between bankruptcies average 23 percent for prepackaged bankruptcies leading to refiling but only 11 percent for nonprepackaged bankruptcies leading to refiling).

82. Thomas J. Salerno, *The Mouse That Roared Or, Hell Hath No Fury Like a Critical Vendor Scorned,* 2003 ABI JOURNAL, LEXIS 114 ("The concept of 'critical vendors' has gone from an extraordinary remedy to something that is simply done as a matter of course in almost all cases."); Charles Jordan Tabb, *Emergency Preferential Orders in Bankruptcy Reorganizations,* 65 AMERICAN BANKRUPTCY LAW JOURNAL 75, 92–93, 98–99 (citing cases); In re Kmart Corporation, 359 F.3d 866,871 (7th Cir. 2004) ("Every circuit that has considered the question has held that this statute does not allow a bankruptcy

judge to authorize full payment of any unsecured debt, unless all unsecured creditors in the class are paid in full."); In re Ionosphere Clubs, Inc., 98 B.R. 174, 176 (Bankr. S.D.N.Y. 1989) (referring to the "'necessity of payment' doctrine").

83. *E.g.,* Blackwelder Furniture Company case 7 B.R. 328 (Bankr. W.D.N.C.1980) (ordering the supplier to sell to the reorganizing debtor for cash on ordinary business terms).

84. Salerno, *supra* note 82.

85. In re Kmart Corporation, 359 F.3d 866, 869 (7th Cir. 2004) ("They and 43,000 additional unsecured creditors eventually received about 10¢ on the dollar, mostly in stock of the reorganized Kmart.").

86. *Id.,* at 871.

87. Memorandum Order, dated July 16, 2003, Docket No. 32, at 2, In re Mirant Corp., Case No. 03-46590, United States Bankruptcy Court for the Northern District of Texas, Fort Worth Division.

88. In re Lionel Corporation, 722 F.2d 1063, 1071 (2nd Cir. 1983) (requiring a "good business reason" to grant such an application); In re White Motor Credit Corporation, 14 B.R. 584 (Bankr. N.D. Ohio 1981) (requiring an "emergency").

89. *E.g.,* H.R. Rep. No. 95-595, 95th Cong., 1st Sess. (1977), at 181–84 (legislative history of § 363 focused on the protection of secured creditors' interests in collateral and not mentioning the sale of an entire business).

90. First Amended Disclosure Statement Accompanying First Amended Chapter 11 Plan of the Derby Cycle Corporation, dated Dec. 17, 2001, Docket No. 174, at 16, In re The Derby Cycle Corporation, Case No. 01-10200, in the United States Bankruptcy Court for the District of Delaware [hereafter "Derby Cycle Disclosure Statement"] ("[T]he debtor retained Alan J. Finden-Crofts (who was the Debtor's chief executive officer until January 1, 1999) as its chief executive officer . . . .").

91. Mark Patterson, *Buyout Aims to Revive Raleigh,* NOTTINGHAM EVENING POST, June 5, 2001, at 1 ("The chief executive of Raleigh's debt-ridden American owners has offered to lead a management buyout . . . .").

92. Motion for Orders Under 11 U.S.C. §§ 105, 363, 365, and 1146(c), dated Aug. 21, 2001, Docket No. 14, In re The Derby Cycle Corporation, Case No. 01-10200, in the United States Bankruptcy Court for the District of Delaware [hereafter "Derby Sale Motion"], at 6–7.

93. Derby Cycle Disclosure Statement, *supra* note 90, at 17 (stating price and describing the application of proceeds).

94. Derby Sale Motion, *supra* note 92, at 7.

95. *Id.,* at 8.

96. *Id.*

97. The Derby Cycle Corporation, Form 8-K, Oct. 26 [sic], 2001, at 1.

98. Objection of the United States Trustee to Motion for Orders, dated Aug. 31, 2001, Docket No. 47, at paragraph 13, In re The Derby Cycle Corporation, Case No. 01-10200, in the United States Bankruptcy Court for the District of Delaware [hereafter "U.S. Trustee Objection to Sale"].

99. Jonathan Berke, *Judge OKs Derby Cycle's Liquidation Plan,* DAILY DEAL, Feb. 1, 2002 ("The assets had been shopped by both Lazard for the debtor and Jefferies & Co. on behalf of the creditors committee, but Cycle Bid was the only buyer that came forth.").

100. Application for Final Approval and Allowance of Compensation and Reimbursement of Expenses of Jefferies & Company, Inc., dated Mar. 11, 2002, Docket No. 248, In re The Derby Cycle Corporation, Case No. 01-10200, in the United States Bankruptcy Court for the District of Delaware (listing and describing eight categories of services rendered).

101. U.S. Trustee Objection to Sale, *supra* note 98, at paragraph 9 ("The bidding procedures for which the Debtor seeks approval contain a 'no-shop' provision which requires that the debtor not solicit any initial inquiry or the making of any initial proposal that constitutes or may reasonably be expected to lead to a bid for the purchased property. . . .").

102. Jeffrey Krasner, *Insiders Landed out of Running at Polaroid,* BOSTON GLOBE, Dec. 9, 2001, at E1.

103. Jeff Krasner, *Suitors Say Polaroid Unit Sale Rules Unfair; Management Bid Favored, They Say,* BOSTON GLOBE, Nov. 2, 2001, at E3.

104. Krasner, *supra* note 102.

105. *Id.*

106. Deposition of William L Flaherty, July 1, 2003, at 162, Exhibit 107 to the Examiner's Report, Docket No. 2954, In re Polaroid Corporation, Case No. 01-10864, in the United States Bankruptcy Court for the District of Delaware ("Generally, if the new equity owners of the company wish to retain management, it's customary for management to receive some equity participation in the company."); Deposition of David Neal Goldman, June 24, 2003, at 108–10, Exhibit 109 to the Examiner's Report, Docket No. 2956, In re Polaroid Corporation, Case No. 01-10864, in the United States Bankruptcy Court for the District of Delaware (discussing exhibit showing OEP's intention prior to purchase of Polaroid to give management 10 percent of the company's equity); Transcript of Confirmation Hearing Before Honorable Kevin J. Carey, United States Bankruptcy Judge, dated Oct. 21, 2003, Docket No. 3148, at 74, In re Exide Technologies, Case No. 02-11125, in the United States Bankruptcy Court for the District of Delaware ("You'll hear a lot from the Debtors about how it's typical in a bankruptcy case for five to ten percent of the equity of a reorganized company to go to management . . . ."); *id.* at 78 (showing equity of this company committed to management valued at $1.5 billion).

107. Transcript of Sale Hearing Before Honorable Peter J. Walsh, United States Chief Bankruptcy Judge, June 28, 2002, Docket No. 1255, at 39, In re Polaroid Corporation, Case No. 01-10864, in the United States Bankruptcy Court for the District of Delaware [hereafter "Polaroid Sale Hearing Transcript"] (80 prior to the stalking horse bid and another 90 afterward).

108. *Id.* at 42 (40–44 prior to the stalking horse bid and 19 afterward).

109. *Id.*, at 173.

110. *Id.*, at 73–74.

111. *Id.,* at 177.

112. Tom Becker & Lingling Wei, *Questions Mount in Chapter 11 Case of Former Polaroid,* WALL STREET JOURNAL ONLINE, Jan. 28, 2003 (stating Flaherty testified in June 2002 that he expected sales to decrease by 25 percent to 30 percent each year through 2004).

113. Jeffrey Krasner, *Once-Ailing Polaroid Pays off for New Owners,* BOSTON GLOBE, Sept. 18, 2003.

114. Disclosure Statement with Respect to Third Amended Joint Plan of Reorganization of Primary PDC, Inc. (f/k/a Polaroid Corporation) and Its Debtor Subsidiaries and the Official Committee of Unsecured Creditors, Appendix D, Entered Sept. 11, 2003, Docket No. 3024, at 32, In re Polaroid Corporation, Case No. 01-10864, in the United States Bankruptcy Court for the District of Delaware (hereafter "Appendix D").

115. Deposition of Neal David Goldman at 86 (he discussed employment with OEP "between the auction and the closing of the transaction"). The deposition transcript is Exhibit 109 to the Report of Perry M. Mandarino, CPA, Examiner, dated Aug. 22, 2003, Docket No. 2934, In re Polaroid Corporation, Case No. 01-10864, in the United States Bankruptcy Court for the District of Delaware [hereafter "Deposition of David Neal Goldman"].

116. *Id.* at 84–85.

117. Appendix D, *supra* note 114, at 28.

118. *Id.* at 162–66; Deposition of Neal David Goldman, *supra* note 115, at 110.

119. Appendix D, *supra* note 114, at 28.

120. Order Under 11 U.S.C. §§ 105 and 363 and Federal Rules of Bankruptcy Procedure 6004(I) Approving Bidding Procedures, Termination Payment, and Expense Reimbursement, dated May 10, 2002, Docket No. 982, at 8, In re Polaroid Corporation et al., Case No. 01-10864, in the United States Bankruptcy Court for the District of Delaware ("The provisions of Section 9.02 of the Purchase Agreement relating to the Termination Payment in the amount of $5,000,000 are hereby approved . . . .").

121. Tom Becker & Lingling Wei, *Questions Mount in Chapter 11 of Former Polaroid,* WALL STREET JOURNAL ONLINE, Jan. 28, 2003.

122. Krasner, *supra* note 113.

123. Kris Frieswick, *What's Wrong with This Picture?* CFO MAGAZINE, Jan. 2003, at 41.

124. Krasner, *supra* note 113. (quoting Delahunt as saying that the latest disclosures showed the new company "was built from assets diverted from its employees, retirees, shareholders, and creditors").

Chapter 7

The first quotation at the beginning of the chapter is from Reuters, *Foreign Firms Seek Chapter 11 in U.S.; Emphasis Here on Reorganization Is a Strong Lure,* CHICAGO TRIBUNE, Apr. 21, 2003, at 6, *available at* LEXIS, Library News, File Allnws.

The second quotation at the beginning of the chapter is from Freshfields Bruckhaus Deringer, *Cenargo: The End of the Saga,* RESTRUCTURING AND

INSOLVENCY BULLETIN, Autumn 2003, at 1, *available at* LEXIS, Library News, File Allnws, and at http://www.freshfields.com/publications/en.asp (search for "Cenargo") (last visited June 20, 2004).

1. Jay Lawrence Westbrook, *Theory and Pragmatism in Global Insolvencies: Choice of Law and Choice of Forum,* 65 AMERICAN BANKRUPTCY LAW JOURNAL 457, 484 (1991) ("Disagreements about the proper choice-of-country rule proved fatal to the U.S.-Canadian efforts at a bankruptcy treaty.").

2. Scandanavian Convention, 155 League of Nations Treaty Series 115, 133 (1935); Bustamante Code (Julio Romanach, Jr., ed., Lawrence Publishing Co. 1996).

3. Council Regulation (EC) No. 1346/2000, European Union Regulation on Insolvency Proceedings, 2000 O.J. (L. 160).

4. *E.g.,* DAVID A. SKEEL, JR., DEBT'S DOMINION: A HISTORY OF BANKRUPTCY LAW IN AMERICA 241 (2001) (predicting that other countries will adopt reorganization frameworks like Chapter 11); *id.* at 243 ("All around the world, other nations are beginning to adopt some of the features of U.S. bankruptcy law.").

5. *E.g.,* In re Spanish Cay Co., Ltd., 161 B.R. 715, 721 (Bankr. S.D. Fla. 1993); In re McTague, 198 B.R. 428, 429 (Bankr. W.D.N.Y. 1996).

6. In re Cenargo International, PLC, 294 B.R. 571, 576–77 (Bankr. S.D.N.Y. 2003) ("Some [international shipping companies], including Global Ocean Carriers, Limited, Gold Ocean Group Ltd., and Amer Reefer, had successfully restructured their balance sheets in Chapter 11 cases, notwithstanding that they, like Cenargo, did not have substantial assets or conduct business in the United States.").

7. In re Petroleum Geo-Services ASA, Case No. 03-14786, in the United States Bankruptcy Court for the Southern District of New York, Manhattan Division.

8. In re Aerovias Nacionales de Colombia S.A. Avianca, Case No. 03-11678, in the United States Bankruptcy Court for the Southern District of New York, Manhattan Division.

9. In re TV Filme, Inc., Case No. 00-00342 (PJW), in the United States Bankruptcy Court for the District of Delaware.

10. In re Seven Seas Petroleum Inc., Case No. 02-45206-H2-11, in the United States Bankruptcy Court for the Southern District of Texas, Houston Division.

11. In re Tamarijn Hotel Corporation, N.V., Case No. 91-13587, in the United States Bankruptcy Court for the Southern District of Florida.

12. In re Cenargo International, PLC, 294 B.R. 571 (Bankr. S.D.N.Y. 2003).

13. In re Global Ocean Carriers Limited, 251 B.R. 31 (Bankr. D. Del. 2000).

14. *Id.*

15. *Id.* at 38–39.

16. *See, e.g.,* Third Amended Disclosure Statement for Second Plan of Reorganization of Global Ocean Carriers Limited, et al., Dated Nov. 3, 2000, Under Chapter 11 of the Bankruptcy Code, Docket No. 416, and Order Confirming Third Amended Plan of Reorganization of Global Carriers Limited, et al., dated Dec. 15, 2000, Docket No. 463, In re Global Ocean Carriers Limited, et al., Case No. 00-956, in the United States Bankruptcy Court for the District of Delaware.

17. EEOC v. Arabian American Oil Co., 499 U.S. 244, 248 (1990) ("It is a longstanding principle of American law that legislation of Congress, unless a contrary intent appears, is meant to apply only within the territorial jurisdiction of the United States.").

18. 11 U.S.C. § 541(a).

19. *E.g.,* In re Nakash, 190 B.R. 763 (Bankr. S.D.N.Y.).

20. In re Filipek, 35 B.R. 339 (Bankr. D. Haw. 1983) (citing to the legislative history).

21. In re McLean Indus., 68 B.R. 690 (Bank. S.D.N.Y. 1986).

22. In re Nakash, 190 B.R. 763 (Bankr. S.D.N.Y. 1996).

23. *Id.* at 766 ("an Israeli banking institution").

24. *Id.*

25. *Id.* at 771 ("[T]his court finds the Receiver in violation of the automatic stay.").

26. In re Cenargo International, PLC, 294 B.R. 571 (Bankr. S.D.N.Y. 2003).

27. *Id.* at 589 ("I accordingly entered an order to show cause . . . on whether an order should not be entered enforcing the automatic stay and assessing damages against Lombard . . . .").

28. Shinichiro Abe, *Recent Developments of Insolvency Laws and Cross-Border Practices in the United States and Japan,* 10 AMERICAN BANKRUPTCY INSTITUTE LAW REVIEW 47, 75–76 (2002).

29. Arnold M. Quittner, *Cross-Border Insolvencies—Ancillary and Full Cases: The Concurrent Japanese and United States Cases of Maruko Inc.,* 4 INTERNATIONAL INSOLVENCY REVIEW 171, 179 (1995) ("[T]he provisions of the Japanese reorganization law are deemed not to extend beyond Japan.").

30. In re McLean Indus., *supra* note 21, at 700 ("We further find that a contempt citation should issue . . .").

31. Mark Magnier, *Firm Told to Release USL Ships: $5,000-a-Day Fine Levied Until Liens Lifted from Two Vessels,* JOURNAL OF COMMERCE, January 2, 1987, *available at* LEXIS, Library News, File Allnws.

32. In re McLean Indus., *supra* note 21, at 693.

33. Quittner, *supra* note 29, at 182–83 ("[N]one of the Maruko properties in Australia or Canada were threatened with any action by the Japanese banks once the United States Chapter 11 was initiated.").

34. Jacob S. Ziegel, *Canada's Phased-In Bankruptcy Law Reform,* 70 AMERICAN BANKRUPTCY LAW JOURNAL 383, 391 (1996) ("There is no automatic stay of proceedings by creditors even after reorganization proceedings have been initiated; both the availability of a stay and its terms are subject to the court's discretion.").

35. In re Cenargo International, PLC, 294 B.R. 571, 577–78 (Bankr. S.D.N.Y. 2003) ("Cenargo and CWT believed that [Lombard] had sufficient assets or conducted sufficient business in the United States to be bound, in practical terms, by the automatic stay . . . .").

36. *Id.* at 578 ("Lombard submitted an affidavit in the Stay Litigation asserting that it does not have any assets or business in the U.S.").

37. *Id.* at 584 ("Lombard's application to the English Court acknowledged that Lombard was violating the automatic stay . . . .").

38. *Id.* at 586 ("Lombard's stated concern about drawn out jurisdictional litigation in the U.S. ignored, moreover, well-developed law in this Circuit according comity to the interests of foreign creditors in Lombard's position . . . .").

39. *Id.* at 606 ("[T]here are no material assets of the Cenargo debtors remaining in the United States or under the Court's practical control; thus [the professionals who represented Cenargo in the New York court] cannot be assured that they will receive the fees and expenses herein allowed.").

40. *Id.* at 589 ("I accordingly entered an order . . . in the interim, enjoining Lombard and the [joint provisional liquidators] from acting in furtherance of the provisional liquidations.").

41. *Id.* at 590 ("Lombard agreed to a standstill for as long as the administrators reasonably believed there was a reasonable prospect of a timely restructuring that left Lombard's rights unimpaired.").

42. Tony Gray, *High Court Go-Ahead for Cenargo,* Lloyd's List, Dec. 19, 2003, at 2.

43. Stacy Notaras, *Cenargo's Cross-Border Conundrum,* Turnarounds and Workouts, Feb. 15, 2004, at 1, 2 ("The lesson to be learned for U.S. bankruptcy advisers is to think very carefully about using Chapter 11 proceedings for a non-American company with no substantive connection to the U.S.").

44. *Why the Big Restructurings Are Going to Delaware,* Global Turnaround, April 2000, at 6.

45. David Cay Johnston, *U.S. Corporations Are Using Bermuda to Slash Tax Bills,* New York Times, Feb. 18, 2002.

46. *E.g., Elaine Walker Discusses Some of the Companies That Have Relocated to Bermuda to Save Money on Taxes, All Things Considered,* National Public Radio, Aug. 2, 2002, transcript *available at* LEXIS, Library News, File Allnws.

47. *Id.*

48. Felixstowe Dock & Railway Co. v. United States Lines Inc., [1989] Queen's Bench 360, 374 (citing Dicey & Morris, Conflict of Law 741 [10th ed. 1980]). The same rule appears in the most recent edition. 2 Dicey & Morris on the Conflict of Laws 1141 (Lawrence Collins ed., 13th ed. 2002).

49. In re National Warranty Insurance Risk Retention Group, 42 Bankruptcy Court Decisions 179 (2004).

50. Donna Harris, *Dealerships: Warranty Accounts Drained; More Fallout from National Warranty Failure,* Automotive News, Mar. 1, 2001 (reporting funds backing "Smart Choice" service contracts missing); *Central Texas Digest,* Austin American Statesman, Jan. 16, 2004, at D2 (reporting the surrender of Warranty Gold's license to do business in Texas after the filing of its bankruptcy case).

51. Mark Kawar & Steve Jordon, *Low Carb Chain,* Omaha World Herald, Feb. 21, 2004, at 1d.

52. In re National Warranty Insurance Risk Retention Group, 42 BANK-RUPTCY COURT DECISIONS 179 (2004).

53. *Id.*

54. *Id.*

55. National Warranty Insurance Risk Retention Group v. Bullmore, _ F.3d _ (8th Cir. 2004).

56. *E.g.,* Cayman Islands Legal Practitioners Law § 12(2) (2002 Revision) (requiring Caymani status or residence in the Cayman Islands during the period of practice).

57. The Cayman Islands, The Companies Law § 86 (2001 Second Revision).

58. *ICO Appoints Chief Commercial Officer to Lead Company to Full Global Mobile Services Launch in 2000,* M2 PRESSWIRE, Sept.18, 1997, *available at* LEXIS, Library News, File Allnws.

59. Debtors' Amended Disclosure Statement Pursuant to 11 U.S.C. § 1125, dated Mar. 22, 2000, Docket No. 621, at 40, In re ICO Global Communications Services Inc., Case No. 99-2933, in the United States Bankruptcy Court for the District of Delaware [hereafter "ICO Disclosure Statement"].

60. *Id.* at 41. *Chapter 11 Meets Liquidation in the Middle of the Atlantic,* GLOBAL TURNAROUND, Feb. 2000, at 4 (stating that the ICO "business is run out of Hammersmith, England") [hereafter *Chapter 11 Meets Liquidation*].

61. ICO Disclosure Statement, *supra* note 59, at 41.

62. *Id.,* at 41.

63. *Id.* at 1.

64. *Id.* at 38–39. The Disclosure Statement does not nullify the possibility of employees other than the 240 listed as working in England and the United States, but the ICO group had only 260 employees a year before bankruptcy. Gautam Naik & Quentin Hardy, *ICO Global Communications to Award $130 Million Pact to Computer Sciences,* WALL STREET JOURNAL, June 26, 1998 ("[ICO] currently has 260 employees . . . .").

65. ICO Disclosure Statement, *supra* note 59, at 1.

66. *Id.*

67. United States Bankruptcy Court for the District of Delaware, cases numbered 99-02933 (lead) to 99-02936.

68. *Chapter 11 Meets Liquidation, supra* note 60, at 4.

69. Harris Collingwood (ed.), *Did Commodore Run Away from Home?* BUSINESS WEEK, Jan. 16, 1989.

70. Commodore International Limited Form 20-F for the year ended June 30, 1993, at 4–5.

71. Paul B. Carroll, *Commodore Faces IRS Tax Claim of $74.1 Million,* WALL STREET JOURNAL, Jan. 4, 1989.

72. Disclosure Statement by the Official Committee of Unsecured Creditors with Respect to Its Chapter 11 Plan of Liquidation of Commodore Business Machines, Inc., dated Feb. 10, 2004, Docket No. 407, at 11, In re Commodore Business Machines, Inc., Case No. 94-42187, in the United States Bankruptcy Court for the Southern District of New York [hereafter "Com-

modore Business Machines Disclosure Statement"] ("Many of the Commodore subsidiaries were, thereafter, either forced into involuntary liquidation proceedings or voluntarily filed proceedings in their countries of residence.").

73. In re Commodore Business Machines, 246 BR. 476, 478 (S.D.N.Y. 2000) (describing a protocol "which purported to set forth the conduct of the liquidation proceedings in the Bahamas and the United States").

74. Commodore Business Machines Disclosure Statement, *supra* note 71, at 18 ("[T]he parties achieved a settlement which . . . provide[s] for an immediate distribution to [Commodore Business Machines] Creditors . . . .").

75. For an overview, see LYNN M. LOPUCKI & ELIZABETH WARREN, SECURED CREDIT: A SYSTEMS APPROACH 609–47 (4th ed. 2003).

76. 11 U.S.C. § 507(a)(1).

77. 11 U.S.C. § 507(a)(4).

78. 11 U.S.C. § 507(a)(8).

79. AMERICAN LAW INSTITUTE, INTERNATIONAL STATEMENT OF MEXICAN BANKRUPTCY LAW 98 (2003) ("The first and foremost priority is that of employee claims for unpaid salaries and indemnifications."); *id.* at 101–02 (describing implementation of employees' priority over secured creditors).

80. *Id.* at 98–99 (describing the tax priority as "de facto").

81. *Id.* at 99–100 (describing priority of various expenses of administration over secured creditors).

82. In re Treco, 239 B.R. 36, 39 (S.D.N.Y. 1999). (In particular, BNY asserted that, under Bahamian law as opposed to U.S. law, BNY's interest will be subordinated to (i) the administrative costs of the liquidation, (ii) taxes, (iii) prepetition wages, and (iv) personal injuries to workmen.)

83. Jay Lawrence Westbrook, *Multinational Enterprises in General Default: Chapter 15, The ALI Principles, and the EU Insolvency Regulation,* 76 AMERICAN BANKRUPTCY LAW JOURNAL 1, 9 (2002).

84. Lernout & Hauspie Speech Products, N.V., Form 10-K for the year ended Dec. 31, 1999, at 2.

85. *Lernout & Hauspie Completes Acquisition of Dictaphone Corporation,* BUSINESS WIRE, May 8, 2000, *available at* LEXIS, Library News, File Allnws [hereafter *Lernout & Hauspie Completes Acquisition*].

86. Houlihan Lokey Howard & Zulkin, Inc., *Technology Hot Spots,* MERGERSTAT REVIEW, June 2000, *available at* LEXIS, Library News, File Allnws.

87. *Lernout & Hauspie Completes Acquisition, supra* note 85.

88. John Carreyrou & Mark Maremont, *Lernout States It Had "Errors" in Accounting,* WALL STREET JOURNAL, Nov. 10, 2000.

89. Stonington Partners v. Lernout & Hauspie Speech Products, 310 F.3d 118 (3rd Cir. 2002) [hereafter "Stonington Partners"].

90. *Id.* at 123.

91. *Id.* at 122–23 ("[T]he amount of Stonington's claims . . . would, in combination with the other [stock fraud] claims dwarf the unsecured claims if not subordinated.").

92. *Id.* at 122–23.

93. *Id.* at 123 ("In the Belgian court, L&H sought to confirm a reorganization plan that would have subordinated Stonington's claims, but the Belgian court rejected the plan based on principles of Belgian bankruptcy law that required equal treatment, rather than subordination, of such claims."); *id.* at 122 ("Although L&H challenged Stonington's claims in the Belgian proceeding, the Belgian court allowed the claims.").

94. 11 U.S.C. § 510(b).

95. Stonington Partners, *supra* note 89, at 123 ("The bankruptcy court ruled . . . that, should Stonington ever file a proof of claim in these Bankruptcy Cases . . . the claims asserted therein would have the same priority as the common stock of L&H.").

96. *Id.* at 122.

97. *Id.* at 124 ("Stonington is hereby immediately enjoined from further prosecuting the issue of the priority, treatment, and classification of the Dictaphone Merger Claims in Belgium under Belgian law.").

98. *Id.* at 133.

Chapter 8

The quotation at the beginning of the chapter is from *A Question of Firms Quoting Chapter and Verse,* THE TIMES (LONDON), Feb, 20, 2003, at 29.

1. Robert K. Rasmussen, *A New Approach to Transnational Insolvencies,* 19 MICHIGAN JOURNAL OF INTERNATIONAL LAW 1, 33 (1997) ("It is fanciful to expect a court to apply the bankruptcy law of a foreign country with anything approaching an acceptable degree of accuracy."); Jay Lawrence Westbrook, *Theory and Pragmatism in Global Insolvencies: Choice of Law and Choice of Forum,* 65 AMERICAN BANKRUPTCY LAW JOURNAL 457, 481 (1991) ("[T]he difficulty is that a single judge in the midst of litigation is all too likely to err about questions of foreign insolvency law, including reciprocity. The Felixstowe opinion illustrates the difficulty of understanding other insolvency regimes, even those from relatively similar legal systems.").

2. John Lowell, *Conflict of Laws as Applied to Assignments for Creditors,* 1 HARVARD LAW REVIEW 259, 264 (1888).

3. Kurt H. Nadelmann, *Bankruptcy Treaties,* 93 UNIVERSITY OF PENNSYLVANIA LAW REVIEW 58, 61–68 (1948) (cataloging the European treaties).

4. *Id.* at 70–71.

5. *Id.* at 87.

6. Reproduced at 93 UNIVERSITY OF PENNSYLVANIA LAW REVIEW 94 (1948).

7. *Id.* at 94.

8. Nadelmann, *supra* note 3.

9. David Costa Levenson, *Proposal for Reform of Choice of Avoidance Law in the Context of International Bankruptcies from a U.S. Perspective,* 10 AMERICAN BANKRUPTCY INSTITUTE LAW REVIEW 291, 351 (2002) ("Unfortunately, the Act does not specify the choice of principal forum.").

10. Roland Lechner, *Waking from the Jurisdictional Nightmare of Multinational Default: The European Council Regulation on Insolvency Proceed-*

ings, 19 ARIZONA JOURNAL OF INTERNATIONAL AND COMPARATIVE LAW 975, 1006 (". . . MIICA has not been adopted or seriously considered by governments around the world.").

11. Donald T. Trautman et al. *Four Models for International Bankruptcy,* 41 AMERICAN JOURNAL OF COMPARATIVE LAW 573, 578 (1993) ("In 1970 a draft bankruptcy convention was produced . . .").

12. Ian F. Fletcher, CONFLICT OF LAWS AND EUROPEAN COMMUNITY LAW 206 (1982).

13. *E.g.,* Nicola Hobday, *Home Court Advantage,* DAILY DEAL, Apr. 3, 2003 ("The 'center of main interests' is not really a defined term in the regulations, says Sandy Shandro, a partner at Freshfields Bruckhaus Derringer in London. You could have the prospect of a conflict between England and Delaware if both claimed that their proceedings should be the main, or primary, proceeding.").

14. Jay Lawrence Westbrook, *Theory and Pragmatism in Global Insolvencies: Choice of Law and Choice of Forum,* 65 AMERICAN BANKRUPTCY LAW JOURNAL 457, 484 (1991).

15. Jay Lawrence Westbrook, *A Global Solution to Multinational Default,* 98 MICHIGAN LAW REVIEW 2276, 2324–25 (2000) [hereafter Westbrook, *Global Solution*] (requiring only that "the foreign [bankruptcy] law be of the same sort generally as ours").

16. *E.g.,* In re Culmer, 25 B.R. 621 (Bankr. S.D.N.Y. 1982) (ordering surrender of assets to a Bahamian bankruptcy court that would distribute them differently than the United States would have).

17. Jay Lawrence Westbrook, *Fearful Future Far Off,* 33 BANKRUPTCY COURT DECISIONS 5, Mar. 30, 1999 ("The leading case is Judge Lifland's opinion in Culmer . . . which explicitly rejects that the foreign rules have to be the same as ours as a pre-requisite to cooperation and deference.") [hereafter Westbrook, *Fearful Future*]; Westbrook, *Global Solution, supra* note 15, at 2324–25 (2000) (advocating that U.S. courts apply universalist principles today to surrender assets); *id.* at 2324–25 (requiring only that "the foreign [bankruptcy] law be of the same sort generally as ours").

18. In re Treco, 240 F.3d 148 (2nd Cir. 2001).

19. *Id.* at 159.

20. *E.g.,* Jay Lawrence Westbrook, *International Bankruptcy Approaches Chapter 15,* NEW YORK LAW JOURNAL, Aug. 23, 2001, at 1 (asserting that "the most natural and best" reading of Treco "is that a U.S. court will not grant section 304 relief where it finds clear and compelling evidence of maladministration or corruption").

21. UNCITRAL Model Law on Cross Border Insolvency, Article 17, § 1 [hereafter "Model Law"] ("[A] foreign proceeding shall be recognized if . . . [t]he foreign proceeding is a proceeding within the meaning of subparagraph (a) of article 2."); *id.* at Article 17, § 2(a) ([A] foreign proceeding shall be recognized . . . [a]s a foreign main proceeding if it is taking place in the State where the debtor has the centre of its main interests . . . .").

22. Council Regulation (EC) No. 1346/ 2000, European Union Regulation

on Insolvency Proceedings, 2000 O.J. (L. 160) [hereafter "EU Regulation"] Article 3, § 1 ("The courts of the Member State within the territory of which the centre of a debtor's main interests is situated shall have jurisdiction to open insolvency proceedings."); *id.* at Article 16, § 1 ("Any judgment opening insolvency proceedings handed down by a court of a Member State which has jurisdiction pursuant to Article 3 shall be recognised in all the other Member States . . .").

23. Model Law, *supra* note 21, at Article 17(2) ("A foreign proceeding shall be recognized as a foreign main proceeding if it is taking place in the State where the debtor has the centre of its main interests."). EU Regulation, *supra* note 22, at Article 16 ("Any judgment opening insolvency proceedings handed down by a court of a Member State which has jurisdiction pursuant to Article 3 shall be recognised in all the other Member States . . . .").

24. EU Regulation, *supra* note 22, at Article 16, § 1 ("Any judgment opening insolvency proceedings handed down by a court of a Member State which has jurisdiction pursuant to Article 3 shall be recognised in all the other Member States . . . ."); Model Law, *supra* note 21, at Article 21, § 2 ("Upon recognition of a foreign proceeding . . . the court may . . . entrust the distribution of all or part of the debtor's assets located in this State to the foreign representative. . . .").

25. EU Regulation, *supra* note 22, at Article 33(1) (referring to parallel proceedings as "secondary" proceedings and obligating the court in which they are pending to stay them at the request of the liquidator in the main proceedings); proposed § 1528 of the United States Bankruptcy Code (denying extraterritorial effect to parallel proceedings filed in the United States after recognition of a foreign main proceeding).

26. Westbrook, *Fearful Future, supra* note 17.

27. *Id.* ("Therefore, an involuntary proceeding will always be available to give the United States courts reasonable discretion about deferring to a foreign proceeding whenever creditors have a serious concern.").

28. 11 U.S.C. § 303(a) and (b).

29. 11 U.S.C. § 303(i).

30. Jay Lawrence Westbrook, *Multinational Enterprises in General Default: Chapter 15, The ALI Principles, and The EU Insolvency Regulation,* 76 American Bankruptcy Law Journal 1, 35 (2002) [hereafter Westbrook, *Multinational Enterprises*].

31. American Law Institute, Transnational Insolvency: Cooperation Among the NAFTA Countries, Principles of Cooperation Among the NAFTA Countries 8 (2003).

32. *See, e.g.,* Freshfields Bruckhaus Deringer, *Arms of UK Administration Embrace US Companies,* Restructuring and Insolvency Bulletin, May 2003, at 2, *available at* LEXIS, Library News, File Allnws, and at http://www.freshfields.com/publications/en.asp (search for "UK Administration") (last visited Aug. 8, 2004).

33. EU Regulation, *supra* note 22, at Preamble ¶ 22 ("The decision of the first court to open proceedings should be recognised in the other Member

States without those Member States having the power to scrutinise the court's decision."); *e.g.,* Bob Wessels, International Jurisdiction to Open Insolvency Proceedings in Europe, In Particular Against (Groups of) Companies 19 (unpublished manuscript), *available at* http://www.iiiglobal.org/country/ netherlands.html (last visited Aug. 8, 2004) (agreeing with another commentator that this provision of the preamble is law).

34. *See, e.g.,* Nadelmann, *supra* note 3, at 72–73 (noting early bankruptcy treaties that gave venue decision making authority to the court which received the first case or that first declared itself to be a proper venue).

35. Westbrook, *Multinational Enterprises, supra* note 30, at 36 ("The ALI Principles make an approved plan binding to a large extent, although not completely, through two Procedural Principles.").

36. EU Regulation, *supra* note 22, at Article 3(1); Model Law, *supra* note 21, at Article 2(b).

37. In re BRAC Rent-A-Car International Inc., [2003] 1 Weekly Law Reports 1421, [2003], 2 All England Law Reports 201 (Chancery Division).

38. Westbrook, *supra* note 15, at 2316.

39. Jay Lawrence Westbrook, *The Lessons of Maxwell Communication,* 64 FORDHAM LAW REVIEW 2531, 2538 (1996) (asserting that Maxwell's "center of gravity" was in England).

40. Stonington Partners v. Lernout & Hauspie Speech Products, 310 F.3d 118, 122 (3rd Cir. 2002).

41. *Id.* at 133.

42. Exhibit 21, Subsidiaries of the Registrant, General Motors Corp., Form 10-K for the year ended Dec. 31, 2003.

43. *E.g.,* Telia v. Hillcourt, 2002 WestLaw 31523284 (High Court of Justice Chancery Division 2002).

44. Wessels, *supra* note 33, at 18 ("[T]he general rule to open . . . insolvency proceedings against any of the related companies . . . is that international jurisdiction according to the Regulation must exist for each of the concerned debtors with a separate legal entity.").

45. This example is based on the structure as it existed in 1997. Daimler-Benz's new structure has not been fully revealed in its U.S. securities filings.

46. Chrysler Corporation, Form 10-K for the fiscal year ended Dec. 31, 1997.

47. *See* authorities cited *supra* note 1.

48. Wessels, *supra* note 33, at 20.

49. *Id.,* at 22.

50. *Id.,* at 24.

51. EU Regulation, *supra* note 22, at Preamble ¶ 22 (referring to "automatic recognition").

52. EU Regulation, *supra* note 22, at Preamble ¶ 22 ("The decision of the first court to open proceedings should be recognised in the other Member States without those Member States having the power to scrutinise the court's decision.").

53. Freshfields Bruckhaus Deringer, *supra* note 32, at 2. *See also* Wessels, *supra* note 33, at 8 n.35 (referring to an unreported decision in the case of Enron Directo Sociedad Limitada, June 4, 2002).

54. Wessels, *supra* note 33, at n.87 (referring to the Cirio Del Monte [Italy] case along with Enron Directo as one in which "a likewise COMI interpretation was exercised"); *Italian Court Declares Dutch Cirio Del Monte Insolvent*, ANSA ENGLISH CORPORATE SERVICE, Aug. 27, 2003, *available at* LEXIS, Library News, File Allnws ("Cirio Del Monte NV insolvency procedure was started to protect the company from its creditor Dutch bank Rabobank. . . .").

55. Herbert Smith, *The EC Regulation on the Recognition and Enforcement of Insolvency Proceedings—How Elastic Is It? Decisions of the English Courts*, CORPORATE RECOVERY BRIEFING, Nov. 2003, *available at* http://www.herbertsmith.com/publications/list.asp?id=37.

56. Lynn M. LoPucki, *The Case for Cooperative Territoriality in International Bankruptcy*, 98 MICHIGAN LAW REVIEW 2216 (2000); Lynn M. LoPucki, *Cooperation in International Bankruptcy: A Post-Universalist Approach*, 84 CORNELL LAW REVIEW 696 (1999).

57. Robert van Galen, *The European Insolvency Regulation and Groups of Companies* (unpublished manuscript), *available at* http://www.iiiglobal .org/country/european_union.html.

58. Hoover's Company Profiles, Fruit of the Loom (2004), *available at* LEXIS, Library Compny, File Hvrpro ("The company lost nearly $230 million in 1995, partly because of charges incurred from closing six US. Plans and laying off more than 3,000 workers.").

59. *Id.*; Fruit of the Loom, Inc., Form 10-K for the fiscal year ended Dec. 29, 2001, at 9 ("[A]pproximately 13% of all garments sewn for Fruit of the Loom were sewn by contract manufacturers with substantially all of the remaining 87% at facilities owned and operated by affiliated companies.").

60. Fruit of the Loom, Ltd., Form 10-K for the fiscal year ended Jan. 1, 2000, at 1 (describing the reincorporation transaction).

61. Evan D. Flaschen & Leo Plank, *The Foreign Representative: A New Approach to Coordinating the Bankruptcy of a Multinational Enterprise*, 10 AMERICAN BANKRUPTCY INSTITUTE LAW REVIEW 111, 123 (2002).

62. *Id.* at 122–23. Reprinted with permission from the American Bankruptcy Institute (www.abiworld.org).

63. Wessels, *supra* note 33, at 12–13 (taking the position that under the EU Regulation the home country is determined at the moment the court rules on the opening of proceedings and that national laws that would ignore last-minute changes are displaced).

64. Wessels, *supra* note 33, at 12 (agreeing with the statement of Moss).

65. *Boss Shuts Headquarters*, NOTTINGHAM EVENING POST, Jan. 17, 2001, at 20 ("The firm will now be run by Mr. Findon-Crofts, who is based in Guernsey . . . There will be no corporate head office for Derby."), *available at* LEXIS, Library News, File Allnws.

66. Mairin Burns, *Corporate Restructuring Turns TransAtlantic: European Bicycle Maker Derby Cycle Reorganizes Stateside Via Chapter 11*, BANK LOAN REPORT, Nov. 5, 2001, *available at* LEXIS, Library News, File Allnws ("Lawyers at the international firm of Bingham Dana are putting the final

touches on a two-part restructuring, which began with a sale in Europe and shifted to a reorganization under U.S. bankruptcy law, for the UK's Derby Cycle Corp.").

67. Discussed in chapter 6.

68. Westbrook, *supra* note 30, at 38.

Chapter 9

The first quotation at the beginning of the chapter is from Gary Young, *U.S. Bankruptcy System Blasted*, NATIONAL LAW JOURNAL, July 26, 2004, at 7 (quoting Stephen H. Case of New York's Davis Polk & Wardwell).

The second quotation at the beginning of the chapter is from Paul Krugman, *In Broad Daylight*, NEW YORK TIMES, Sept. 27, 2002, at 31A.

1. Lynn A. Stout, *The Mechanisms of Market Inefficiency: An Introduction to the New Finance*, 28 IOWA JOURNAL OF CORPORATE LAW 635, 636 (2003).

2. Liggett Co. v. Lee, 288 U.S. 517, 557 (1933) ("The removal by the leading industrial States of the limitations upon the size and powers of the business corporations appears to have been due, not to their conviction that maintenance of the restrictions was undesirable in itself, but to the conviction that it was futile to insist upon them; because local restriction would be circumvented by foreign incorporation."); *id.* at 567 ("Such is the Frankenstein monster which States have created by their corporation laws.").

3. Mark Roe, *Delaware's Competition*, 117 HARVARD LAW REVIEW 588, 609 (2003) (noting that "[a] year after New Jersey's first liberalization of corporate law for the monopolists, Congress passed the Sherman Act, formally taking away the authority New Jersey had bestowed on its corporations to enter into one type of combination—the interstate corporate merger—if it restrained trade or monopolized a part of American commerce").

4. Marcel Kahan & Ehud Kamar, *The Myth of State Competition in Corporate Law*, 55 STANFORD LAW REVIEW 679, 684 (2002).

5. William L. Cary, *Federalism and Corporate Law: Reflections Upon Delaware*, 83 YALE LAW JOURNAL 663, 705 (1974).

6. Ralph K. Winter, Jr., *State Law, Shareholder Protection, and the Theory of the Corporation*, 6 JOURNAL OF LEGAL STUDIES 251 (1977).

7. Roberta Romano, *Competition for State Corporate Law*, 1 NEW PALGRAVE DICTIONARY OF ECONOMICS AND THE LAW 364, 367 (1998) ("An event study uses standard financial econometrics to investigate the impact of new information on stock prices . . ."); *id.* at 367–68 (discussing event studies of reincorporation to Delaware).

8. *Id.* at 368 ("Because statutory domicile is an endogenous choice of firms, if firms choose their incorporation state to maximize share values . . . we should not expect to find cross-sectional performance differences. And, indeed, none of the studies find differences in performance.").

9. *E.g.*, Robert Daines, *Does Delaware Law Improve Firm Value?* 62 JOURNAL OF FINANCIAL ECONOMICS 525 (2001).

10. Stout, *supra* note 1, at 636.

11. Lucian Bebchuk et al., *Does the Evidence Favor State Competition in Corporate Law?* 90 CALIFORNIA LAW REVIEW 1775, 1820 (2002) (reviewing the empirical studies and concluding that "the evidence does not establish that Delaware incorporation produces an increase in share value").

12. ROBERTA ROMANO, THE GENIUS OF AMERICAN CORPORATE LAW (1993).

13. *E.g.,* Roberta Romano, *Empowering Investors: A Market Approach to Securities Regulation,* 107 YALE LAW JOURNAL 2359 (1998).

14. *E.g.,* Richard L. Revesz, *Rehabilitating Interstate Competition: Rethinking the Race to the Bottom Rationale for Federal Environmental Regulation,* 67 NEW YORK UNIVERSITY LAW REVIEW 1210 (1992).

15. *E.g.,* Frank H. Easterbrook, *Antitrust and the Economics of Federalism,* 26 JOURNAL OF LAW & ECONOMICS 23 (1983).

16. *E.g.,* Brian D. McDonald, *The Uniform Computer Information Transactions Act,* 16 BERKELEY TECHNOLOGY LAW JOURNAL 461, 479 (2001) ("Moreover, despite the fact that this competition among states takes place primarily in the realm of corporate law, this theory can also be applied to other areas of state-led legislative efforts, such as the uniform law process. UCITA is no exception to this rule.")

17. *See, e.g.,* Larry E. Ribstein, *Delaware, Lawyers, and Contractual Choice of Law,* 19 DELAWARE JOURNAL OF CORPORATE LAW 999, 1004 (1994) (discussing a Delaware statute that authorizes contracting parties to specify the application of Delaware law to contracts involving more than $100,000, even if the transaction has no relationship to Delaware).

18. *E.g.,* David A. Skeel, Jr., *Bankruptcy Judges and Bankruptcy Venue: Some Thoughts on Delaware,* 1 DELAWARE LAW REVIEW 1, 21–23 (1998) (drawing the analogy to the corporate charter competition).

19. Lucian Arye Bebchuk, *Federalism and the Corporation: The Desirable Limits on State Competition in Corporate Law,* 105 HARVARD LAW REVIEW 1435, 1458 (1992) ("Reincorporation generally requires a decision by the company's board and approval by the company's shareholders.").

20. Robert K. Rasmussen & Randall S. Thomas, *Timing Matters: Promoting Forum Shopping by Insolvent Corporations,* 94 NORTHWESTERN UNIVERSITY LAW REVIEW 1357, 1387, 1390 (2000).

21. Robert K. Rasmussen & Randall S. Thomas, *Whither the Race? A Comment on the Effects of the Delawarization of Corporate Reorganizations,* 54 VANDERBILT LAW REVIEW 283, 289 (2001).

22. *Id.* at 290.

23. Marcus Cole, *"Delaware Is Not a State": Are We Witnessing Jurisdictional Competition in Bankruptcy?* 55 VANDERBILT LAW REVIEW 1845, 1868 ("Creditor pressure, one of the factors the Delaware Skeptics believe is driving the convoy to Delaware, received a mixed reception from both debtors' and creditors' counsel.").

24. *Id.* at 1869 ("Secured creditors . . . can influence many of the debtor's key decisions, including venue selection.").

25. David A. Skeel, Jr., *What's So Bad About Delaware,* 54 VANDERBILT LAW REVIEW 309, 315 (2001).

Chapter 10

The first quotation at the beginning of the chapter is from *Delaware's Withdrawal of the Reference: What It Means,* BANKRUPTCY COURT DECISIONS NEWS AND COMMENT, Feb. 11, 1997, available at LEXIS, Library News, File Allnws.

The second quotation at the beginning of the chapter is from Delaware Bar Association Report to the National Bankruptcy Review Commission 35 (1996).

1. Marcus Cole, *"Delaware Is Not a State": Are We Witnessing Jurisdictional Competition in Bankruptcy?* 55 VANDERBILT LAW REVIEW 1845, 1867 (2002) ("One lawyer quipped that the bankruptcy court in Wilmington is 'just a two-hour train ride from most company headquarters in New York; then again, the same is true for the bankruptcy court in Manhattan.'").

2. Cole, *supra* note 1, at 1891 (quoting an anonymous interviewee).

3. *Compare* 28 U.S.C. § 152 (2004) (providing that "[e]ach bankruptcy judge shall be appointed for a term of fourteen years" and may be removed only for cause) *with* H.R. 975, 108th Cong. (2003) § 1223 (providing that the first four vacancies "resulting from the death, retirement, resignation, or removal of a [Delaware] bankruptcy judge shall not be filled").

4. 11 U.S.C. § 304(c)(4).

Glossary

10-K   The annual report each public company files with the Securities and Exchange Commission

30-day prepack   A prepackaged bankruptcy case in which the court confirms a plan in about 30 days. See *prepackaged bankruptcy.*

§ 363 sale   Debtor's sale of its business during bankruptcy without the proposal or confirmation of a reorganization plan

adequate protection   Payments or contract rights awarded to protect a secured creditor against loss or decline in the value of collateral during a bankruptcy case

administrators   In foreign bankruptcy systems, persons appointed by the court to administer the debtor's business during bankruptcy

affiliate   A corporation that is a member of a corporate group. See *corporate group.*

ALI principles   Principles of Cooperation in Transnational Insolvency Cases among the Members of the North American Free Trade Association, adopted by the American Law Institute in 2002

ancillary proceeding   In international bankruptcy, a bankruptcy case that is subordinate to a main proceeding filed in another country involving the same debtor. See *main proceeding.*

automatic reference   An order of a U.S. district court that transfers all bankruptcy cases filed with the district court to the bankruptcy court of the same district

automatic stay   An injunction against any attempt to collect a debt owing from the bankrupt. The stay comes into existence automatically upon the filing of every bankruptcy case.

bankruptcy bill   See *omnibus bankruptcy bill.*

bankruptcy case   A case pending in a bankruptcy court

Bankruptcy Code   Title 11 of the United States Code, which contains most of the laws governing bankruptcy

bankruptcy professionals The lawyers, investment bankers, accountants, turnaround managers, financial advisers, and other professionals who work in large public company bankruptcy cases

bankruptcy reorganization A debt restructuring that takes place in connection with a bankruptcy case

Bankruptcy Research Database (BRD) A database maintained by the author that contains information on all large public company bankruptcy cases filed in the United States from October 1, 1979, to the present; *available at* http://lopucki.law.ucla.edu

big bankruptcy The bankruptcy case of a debtor that reported assets in excess of $220 million (in current dollars) before filing

BRD See *Bankruptcy Research Database.*

case placers The individuals who jointly or individually choose the court in which a bankruptcy case is filed. They are usually the company's top executives, board members, and bankruptcy lawyers but may also include investment bankers, debtor-in-possession lenders, or the creditors' committee in a prepackaged case.

caseload The workload of a court

center of its main interests A test commonly used in international bankruptcy to determine the debtor's home country. See *home country.*

Chapter 7 Provisions of current U.S. bankruptcy law under which any person or company can file for liquidation

Chapter 11 Provisions of current U.S. bankruptcy law under which any person or company can file for reorganization or liquidation

Chapter 11 trustee Individual appointed by the United States Trustee to administer a bankrupt company

Chapter X Provisions of pre-1978 U.S. bankruptcy law under which large public companies were supposed to file. Few did, because Chapter X required the appointment of a trustee in all cases. See *trustee.*

Chapter XI Provisions of pre-1978 U.S. bankruptcy law under which only smaller companies were supposed to file

charter The document issued by a state or country to create a corporation

circuit The geographical area served by a U.S. court of appeals. For example, the third circuit includes the states of Delaware, New Jersey, and Pennsylvania and the Virgin Islands.

claim Bankruptcy terminology for a debt owing by the debtor

clerk (of the court) The public official who maintains the records of a court

collateral Property that a debtor has contractually committed to satisfy a particular debt

company A corporation or corporate group

complex Chapter 11 cases Euphemism employed by the bankruptcy courts to refer to the big Chapter 11 cases they seek to attract

confirmation See *confirmation order.*

confirmation order A court order making a Chapter 11 plan binding on the parties to the case, including those who opposed the plan

consensual reorganization plan A reorganization plan is generally considered "consensual" if the debtor, the creditors' committee, and any other major participant in the case has agreed to it. See *reorganization plan.*

corporate group Two or more corporations in common ownership and control. For example, if a corporation owns and controls three subsidiaries, the four corporations together are a corporate group.

corruption Dysfunctional condition resulting from loss of integrity

court opinion An official explanation of a court's decision, written by the judge or judges

creditors' committee See *unsecured creditors' committee.*

critical vendor A supplier whose voluntary cooperation is said to be critical to the continued operation of the debtor's business

critical vendor order A court order often entered at the beginning of a bankruptcy case authorizing the debtor-in-possession to pay prepetition debts to critical vendors. See *critical vendor.*

debt restructuring A reduction in the amount that must be repaid on a debt, an extension of the debtor's time in which to pay, an exchange of the debt for stock, or some combination of the three

debtor (1) Person or company that owes a debt. (2) Person or company that is the subject of a bankruptcy case.

debtor-in-possession (DIP) Upon the filing of a bankruptcy case, the debtor becomes a debtor-in-possession and continues to operate the business unless the court orders the appointment of a trustee.

Delaware bankruptcy court The United States Bankruptcy Court for the District of Delaware

DIP See *debtor-in-possession.*

DIP lender A bank or financial institution that lends money to a debtor-in-possession. See *debtor-in-possession.*

disclosure statement A document filed in a bankruptcy case in which the debtor provides creditors with the information they need to make informed decisions in connection with voting on a Chapter 11 plan

district The geographical area served by a district court or bankruptcy court

district court Ordinarily, the U.S. district court is a trial court. In bankruptcy cases, however, the district court often functions as an appeals court.

division The portion of a district served by a panel of district court or bankruptcy court judges. See *district, district court, panel of judges.*

docket (1) The list of cases pending before a court. (2) A list of the documents in the court's file for a particular case.

domicile A person's permanent home

draw See *random draw.*

efficient In economics, wealth maximizing for society as a whole

estate The property owned by a bankrupt company

EU regulation European Union Regulation on Insolvency, adopted in 2000

examiner An individual appointed by the United States Trustee to conduct an investigation during the pendency of a Chapter 11 case

exclusivity The debtor's exclusive right to file a Chapter 11 plan during the first 120 days of a Chapter 11 case or such extensions of that period as the court may allow

extraterritorial law A law intended to apply to persons or events outside the borders of the country enacting the law

feasibility The requirement in Bankruptcy Code § 1129(a)(11) that "confirmation of the plan is not likely to be followed by the liquidation, or the need for further financial reorganization, of the debtor . . ."

fee caps Top limits placed by a bankruptcy court or judge on the rates bankruptcy professionals can charge for their services

financial advisers Investment bankers or other professionals authorized by the bankruptcy court to give financial advice to a debtor or an official committee

first-day motions Requests to the court made by the debtor on the day the Chapter 11 case is filed (or shortly thereafter). Typical first-day motions seek approval to use secured creditors' cash collateral, to pay current wages and salaries or prepetition debts owing to critical vendors, and to employ specified bankruptcy professionals.

first-day orders Bankruptcy court orders made in response to first-day motions. See *first-day motions.*

forum shopping Choosing from alternatives the court in which a case will be filed

franchise tax A tax imposed on the privilege of carrying on a business

haven A state or country that increases its revenues or improves its economy by enacting laws protecting foreigners from the laws of the foreigners' own countries

headquarters The geographical location of a company's principal executive offices. Public companies must specify their principal executive offices in filings with the Securities and Exchange Commission.

holding company A corporation that owns a controlling stock interest in one or more corporations and does not itself conduct a business

home country A phrase commonly used in international bankruptcy to specify the country whose courts should have jurisdiction over the assets of a multinational debtor worldwide

homestead A residence that a bankrupt debtor is permitted to keep free of unsecured creditors' claims

incorporation The creation of a corporation by a state's or country's issuance of a charter. See *charter.*

injunction An order by a court that some specified person not do some specified act

insolvent Not solvent. See *solvent.*

integration A test employed in international bankruptcy to determine which country's courts should have jurisdiction. If the business of a foreign subsidiary is integrated into the business of the domestic parent or group, the domestic court has jurisdiction over the foreign subsidiary. See *extraterritorial law.*

internal affairs doctrine Law providing that courts adjudicating disputes regarding the internal affairs of a corporation should apply the law of the state or country of incorporation, not the law of the state or country where the events in litigation occurred. See *incorporation.*

involuntary bankruptcy A bankruptcy case filed by creditors

Judicial Conference of the United States A federal agency composed of federal judges that makes policy with regard to the administration of the U.S. courts

jurisdiction The power or right of a court to decide a particular dispute

large company A company that reported assets in excess of $220 million (in current dollars) before filing its bankruptcy case

liquidation (1) The sale of a company. (2) The dismantling of a company followed by the sale of its parts.

liquidators In some foreign countries, the official term for the persons appointed by the court to liquidate a bankrupt company

local rules Rules made by the judges of a district. These rules apply only to cases in the district.

main proceeding In international bankruptcy, a bankruptcy case in a court of the debtor's home country. In a main proceeding it is considered legitimate for the court to attempt to administer the debtor's worldwide assets.

managers The top executives and members of the board of directors of a company

motion A request to a court

multinational bankruptcy The bankruptcy of a multinational company

multinational company A corporation or corporate group that operates in more than one country

National Bankruptcy Review Commission An independent commission established pursuant to Public Law No. 103-394 (1994) to investigate and study issues relating to the Bankruptcy Code and prepare a report to the president, Congress, and the chief justice making recommendations for legislative or administrative action. The commission completed its work in 1997.

New York bankruptcy court The Manhattan division of the United States Bankruptcy Court for the Southern District of New York

official creditors' committee An unsecured creditors' committee appointed by the United States Trustee and whose professionals are entitled to payment from the debtor's estate. See *unsecured creditors' committee.*

omnibus bankruptcy bill The Bankruptcy Abuse Prevention and Consumer

Protection Act of 2003, the provisions of which have been enacted by both the House and Senate at various times over the past five years but have never become law

omnibus hearings   The practice of holding hearings biweekly or monthly on all pending matters in big bankruptcy cases. Regular scheduling is particularly convenient for out-of-town lawyers.

opinion   See *court opinion.*

panel of judges   Two or more judges assigned to hear cases in the same district or division. See *district, division, random draw.*

parallel proceedings   In international bankruptcy, cases of equal rank and dignity filed by or against the same debtor in different countries

parent corporation   A corporation that owns and controls a subsidiary corporation

petition   The document filed with a bankruptcy court to commence a bankruptcy case

plan   See *reorganization plan.*

plan failure   A category of bankruptcy outcomes created by the author and Joseph W. Doherty in the course of their research. The outcomes in this category are the bankruptcies or distressed mergers of companies that emerged from bankruptcy reorganization less than five years earlier. A *distress merger* is a merger by a previously bankrupt company that has not reported an annual profit since emerging from bankruptcy.

postpetition   After the filing of the petition. See *petition.*

prenegotiated bankruptcy   A bankruptcy case that is not commenced until after the debtor has reached at least a tentative agreement with one or more major creditors on the terms of the plan

prepack   A prepackaged bankruptcy case. See *prepackaged bankruptcy.*

prepackaged bankruptcy   A bankruptcy case that is not commenced until after the debtor has proposed a plan to its creditors and the creditors have accepted the plan by the majorities required for confirmation. See *confirmation order.*

prepetition   Before the filing of the petition. See *petition.*

principal place of business   Legal term of art referring to a company's headquarters. See *headquarters.*

priority   The right of a creditor to be paid in full before creditors of lower priority are paid anything at all

professional fees   The fees of bankruptcy professionals. See *bankruptcy professionals.*

professionals   See *bankruptcy professionals.*

protocols   Agreements entered into between the bankruptcy courts of countries where cases are pending against the same debtor, in order to coordinate the courts' conduct of the cases

public company   A company whose stock or bonds are so widely traded that the company is required to file annual reports with the Securities and Exchange Commission

random draw Process by which the clerk of the court randomly assigns a bankruptcy case to a particular bankruptcy judge in a district or division where the panel of judges consists of more than one judge. See *district, division, panel of judges.*

recognition Acceptance by a court of the legitimacy of a foreign bankruptcy proceeding

reference See *automatic reference.*

refiling The filing of a bankruptcy case by or against a company that has already been through bankruptcy reorganization. See *bankruptcy reorganization.*

refiling rate The percentage of companies emerging from bankruptcy that file another bankruptcy. See *refiling.*

reorganization See *bankruptcy reorganization.*

reorganization plan A document filed in a bankruptcy case that provides the terms of a debt restructuring

restructure See *debt restructuring.*

retention bonuses Bonuses paid to executives or other employees of a bankrupt company to increase the chances they will remain in the company's employ for some period of time

retention loans Loans made to executives or other employees of a bankrupt company with the intention on the part of the company to forgive repayment if the executive or employee remains in the company's employ for some period of time

schedules Lists of all assets and debts that each bankrupt company is required to file with the bankruptcy court

secured creditor A creditor who is the beneficiary of a debtor's contractual commitment to satisfy a particular debt from particular property. A mortgage holder is an example of a secured creditor.

shop in The choice of a company with headquarters in some other district or division to file its bankruptcy case in this district or division

shop out The choice of a company with headquarters in this district or division to file its bankruptcy case in some other district or division

solvent (1) Having assets in excess of debts. (2) Being able to pay one's debts as they become due.

stakeholders All persons whose interests are at risk in a company, including not just creditors and shareholders but also employees, taxing authorities, communities, affiliated companies, and others

statistically significant Unlikely to have occurred by chance

stay See *automatic stay.*

subsidiary A corporation that is owned or controlled by another corporation. See *parent corporation.*

tainted managers The managers who were in charge of the company during the period of onset of financial distress

territoriality In international bankruptcy, the philosophy that each country should administer the assets of a multinational debtor that are within its borders

toxic judges   Derogatory term used to refer to judges who are unacceptable to case placers. See *case placers.*

trustee   A person appointed by the region's United States Trustee to administer the property of a bankrupt in Chapter 7 or Chapter 11. See also *Chapter 11 trustee; United States Trustee.*

turnaround managers   Managers hired after the company is in financial distress, particularly if the managers do not intend to remain with the company after bankruptcy

UNCITRAL Model Law on Cross-Border Insolvency   A law drafted and promulgated by the United Nations Commission on International Trade Law for adoption by countries. Where adopted, the law controls a country's response to bankruptcies involving foreign parties.

United States trustee   An agency of the U.S. government, located in the Department of Justice. The U.S. trustee is authorized by law to participate in certain aspects of Chapter 11 cases, including the appointment of trustees and examiners, the approval of plans and disclosure statements, and the control of professional fees.

universalism   In international bankruptcy, the philosophy that a single court should administer the assets of a multinational debtor worldwide

unofficial creditors' committee   An unsecured creditors' committee that is not an official creditors' committee. See *official creditors' committee, unsecured creditors' committee.*

unsecured creditor   A creditor that is not a secured creditor. See *secured creditor.*

unsecured creditors' committee   A committee, usually consisting of the debtor's largest unsecured creditors, formed to represent the unsecured creditors or some subgroup of unsecured creditors in connection with a Chapter 11 case

venue   The geographical location where a bankruptcy case proceeds

venue hook   A subsidiary with links to a bankruptcy court that qualify the subsidiary to file there, which filing will in turn qualify all members of the corporate group to file there. See *corporate group, parent corporation, subsidiary.*

Index